LABOUR LAW AND THE PERSON

Bristol Studies in Law and Social Justice

Series Editors: **Alan Bogg**, University of Bristol, and **Virginia Mantouvalou**, University College London

---

This series explores the role of law in securing social justice in society and the economy. The focus is on 'social justice' as a normative ideal, and the law as a critical tool in influencing (for good or for ill) the social structures that shape people's lives.

Scan the code below to discover new and forthcoming titles in the series, or visit:

bristoluniversitypress.co.uk/
bristol-studies-in-law-and-social-justice

LABOUR LAW AND THE PERSON

An Agenda for Social Justice

Lisa Rodgers

BRISTOL
UNIVERSITY
PRESS

First published in Great Britain in 2024 by

Bristol University Press
University of Bristol
1–9 Old Park Hill
Bristol
BS2 8BB
UK
t: +44 (0)117 374 6645
e: bup-info@bristol.ac.uk

Details of international sales and distribution partners are available at bristoluniversitypress.co.uk

British Library Cataloguing in Publication Data
A catalogue record for this book is available from the British Library

ISBN 978-1-5292-2316-3 hardcover
ISBN 978-1-5292-2318-7 ePub
ISBN 978-1-5292-2319-4 ePdf

Cover design: Blu inc
Front cover image: Stocksy/Colin Anderson
Bristol University Press uses environmentally responsible print partners.
Printed and bound by CPI Group (UK) Ltd, Croydon, CR0 4YY

FSC
www.fsc.org
MIX
Paper | Supporting responsible forestry
FSC® C013604

Contents

Detailed Contents

Series Editor Preface

Alan Bogg and Virginia Mantouvalou

Bristol Studies in Law and Social Justice explores the role of law in securing social justice in society and the economy. The focus is on 'social justice' as a normative ideal, and the law as a critical tool in influencing (for good or for ill) the social structures that shape people's lives. This international series is designed to be inclusive of a wide range of methodologies and disciplinary approaches. Contributions examine these issues from multiple legal perspectives, including constitutional law, discrimination law, human rights, contract law, criminal law, migration law, labour law, social welfare law, property law, international and supranational law. The Series has broad jurisdictional coverage, including single-country, comparative, international and regional legal orders, and encourages a critical and interdisciplinary approach to legal analysis.

Table of Cases and Statutes

Table of cases (UK)

Autoclenz v Belcher [2011] UKSC 41
Best v Embark on Raw Case No: 3202006/2020
Burke v Turning Point Scotland Case No: 4112457/2021
Dimitrova and others v Barchester Healthcare Case Nos: 1803315/2021, 1803339/2021, 2601442/2021 3207353/2021, and 3205334/2021
Gibson v Lothian Leisure Case No: 4105009/2020
Iceland Frozen Foods Ltd v Jones [1983] UKEAT 62_82_2907
IWGB v Deliveroo T/A Deliveroo, TUR1/985 (2016) (CAC)
IWGB v CAC and others [2021] EWCA Civ 952
IWGB v CAC and others [2023] SC 43
Kostal v Dunkley [2019] EWCA Civ 1009
Kostal v Dunkley [2021] UKSC 47
Kubilius v Kent Foods Case No: 3201960/2020
McGavin Toastmaster Ltd v Ainscough [1976] 1 SCR 718
Pimlico Plumbers v Smith [2018] UKSC 29
Quashie v Stringfellows Restaurants [2013] IRLR 99
R (The IWGB) v Central Arbitration Committee [2018] EWHC 3342
Rodgers v Leeds Laser Cutting [2022] EWCA Civ 1659
Royal Mencap Society v Tomlinson-Blake and Shannon v Rampersad and Another (T/A Clifton House Residential Home)
Shields v Alliance Healthcare Management Services Case Nos: 4110642/2021 and 4101741/2022
SSHD v Cox [2023] EWCA Civ 551
St Ives Plymouth Ltd v Haggerty UKEAT/0107/08
Tilson v Alstom Transport [2011] IRLR 169
Uber BV v Aslam [2021] UKSC 5
Wierowska v HC-One Oval Case No: 1403077/2021
Wilson and Palmer v United Kingdom [2002] ECHR 552
Windle v Secretary of State for Justice [2016] EWCA Civ 459, para [23]
X v Y Case No: 2413947/2020

Table of cases (outside UK)

Demir v Turkey (2009) 48 EHRR 54
Joined cases C-151/04 and C-152/04 *Durre*
Case C-268/99 *Jany and Others* [2001] ECR I-8615
Sindicatul 'Pastorul Cel Bun' v Romania app. no. 330/09 [2014] IRLR 49, ('the *Good Shepherd* case')

Table of statutes

Employment Act 1996
Equality Act 2010
Health and Safety at Work Act 1974
The Strikes (Minimum Service Levels) Act 2023

Table of statutory instruments

Control of Substances Hazardous to Health Regulations, SI 1994/3246
Control of Substances Hazardous to Health (COSHH) Regulations, SI 2002/2677
Health and Safety (Consultation with Employees) Regulations, SI 1996 No 1513
Health and Safety (Display Screen Equipment) Regulations, SI 1992/2792
Management of Health and Safety at Work Regulations, SI 1999/3242
Manual Handling Operations Regulations, SI 1992/2793
Personal Protective Equipment at Work Regulations, SI 1992/2966
Personal Protective Equipment at Work (Amendment) Regulations, SI 2022/8
Provision and Use of Work Equipment Regulations, SI 1992/2932
Safety Representatives and Safety Committee Regulations, SI 1977/500
Workplace (Health, Safety and Welfare) Regulations, SI 1992/3004
Working Time and Holiday Pay Bill (unpublished)
Working Time (Limitation) Bill (HC Bill 46)

EU law

Health and Safety Framework Directive 89/391

Acknowledgements

I would like to thank Professor Bernard Ryan for discussions which led to the book idea and professors Alan Bogg and Virginia Mantouvalou for their enthusiasm for this project and their support during its development. I would also like to thank professors Paul Almond, Eugenia Caracciolo di Torella, Stephen Wood, and Pascale Lorber for their encouragement throughout the writing process and Professor Ruth Dukes for invaluable feedback on an earlier draft of the book. I am also grateful to the University of Leicester for awarding me study leave which enabled me to complete the book. For everything else I would like to thank my friends and my family: mum, dad, Alice, Ian, Laura, and Arthur.

1

Introduction

1. Labour law and social justice: the problematic

There is a paradox facing labour law when it comes to social justice. On the one hand, many theories of labour law share the aims of social justice; namely, the dismantling of oppression and undue privilege and seeking to achieve a fairer distribution of resources and income (for workers). On the other hand, labour law has struggled to achieve social justice for workers. While there is a strong belief in the value of social justice for workers and embedding those values in labour law, the failures of labour law to reach individuals in need, to tackle inequalities,[1] and to achieve a fairer distribution of income[2] mean that social justice is often overtaken by other aims or labour law is abandoned altogether as a means of achieving social justice. Indeed, the frustrations in the relationship between labour law and social justice have led scholars to suggest that justice for workers can only be achieved through the enactment of political and social processes outside of the law, with the law only a secondary or supplementary part of that process.[3] Although the reason for this position is clear, the result is a downgrading of the status of social justice and ultimately a weakening of the labour law response. For social justice is worth fighting for: without the social justice instinct we throw ourselves more completely on the sword of the 'spontaneous order' of the market and existing unequal power relationships. The question is how to revive the social justice instinct and make it relevant for labour law.

In this book, I seek to understand and promote the social justice instinct of labour law. I argue that there are elements of labour law which make

1 International Labour Organization (ILO), 'ILO Centenary Declaration for the Future of Work' (21 June 2019), 2. Available at: www.ilo.org/wcmsp5/groups/public/@ed_norm/@relconf/documents/meetingdocument/wcms_711674.pdf

2 'ILO Centenary Declaration for the Future of Work', 3.

3 O. Kahn-Freund, *Labour and the Law* (London: Stevens 1983), 18.

it well placed to further social justice. It holds within it the promise of social justice. This promise is formulated at the very heart of labour law, as it concerns the way in which personhood is constructed which *potentially* sets it apart from other areas of law. In contrast to civil law, which considers personhood as an abstraction, labour law recognizes the reality and relationality of personhood. Of course, at first blush, this formulation may seem to be only of theoretical importance and a far cry from achieving greater equality or reducing oppression in practice. However, I seek to argue in this book that this consideration is of fundamental importance in the way in which law is constructed and the impetus that the law has for social justice.

Through the book I will explore the importance of relationality at the heart of (labour) law. I will argue that this relationality:

- sets up the impetus for social justice;
- allows for contextualization of worker relationships;
- allows for worker vulnerability to be considered in tandem with worker agency; and
- allows us to reflect on both the positive and negative effects of the law as an institution.

This is not to say that the potential of relationality at the heart of labour law is always recognized or activated. Although in some ways different from civil law, labour law has developed within the civil law frame and hence is often tied to its formulations. For example, labour law remains tied to private law through the 'contract of employment', which means that contract law remains a central and seminal influence. As a result, labour law presupposes the order of persons of civil law: it does not dissolve it, but only reshapes certain of its social effects.[4] This makes the promotion of social justice difficult and partial and undermines its effectiveness. Furthermore, labour law exists in a sometimes hostile political environment under which law and policies attempt to specifically deny the relationality of workers, or the importance of agency in achieving worker goals. So, the argument is not that social justice is always achieved for workers through labour law. Rather the argument is that a greater understanding of personhood for labour law sets up the impetus for social justice and aligns it well with other theories which challenge the liberal model of justice and some of its outcomes.

4 H. Sinzheimer, 'Das Problem des Menschen im Recht' (1933) in H. Sinzheimer, *Arbeitsrecht und Rechtssoziologie: gesammelte Aufsätze und Reden* (Frankfurt: Europaische Verlagsanstalt 1976), 61.

2. Social justice, critical theory, and labour law

Social justice is a very broad concept which is approached from a myriad of different perspectives and means different things to different people. Indeed, in the broadest sense, social justice principles can be seen as underlying any scheme of political and social organization from liberalism to conservatism to radical socialism.[5] In other words, social justice is simply a 'set of principles from which we may work out an ideally just distribution of rights and privileges, burdens and pains, which can be deployed to assess a society's institutions as a whole'.[6] This inevitably leads to quite different visions of the nature of social justice to the extent that those visions can stand in conflict with each other.

For example, the split between 'libertarian' and 'liberal' notions of social justice which had emerged by the mid-20th century revealed quite different stances on the nature of freedom and the responsibilities of the state in promoting social justice. While libertarians embraced a vision of social justice as 'negative liberty', emphasizing the desirability of a minimalist state, liberal writers favoured the promotion of 'positive liberty' which envisaged a role for the state not only in the protection of individual rights but also a fair(er) distribution of society's benefits and burdens to allow greater participation of all. Of central influence has been Rawls' conception of justice as fairness that provides a set of principles which allows for a level of redistribution while at the same time steering clear of strict egalitarianism.[7] For example, his famous second principle, the 'difference principle', stated that social and economic inequalities are to be arranged so that they are both (a) reasonably expected to be to everyone's advantage and (b) attached to positions and offices open to all. This principle allows for social inequalities to exist, but only within limits; namely, that they result in compensating benefits for everyone and in particular the least advantaged members of society.

It is perhaps obvious that the relationship between law and social justice is a point of negotiation in any society. On one level, social justice is a reflection of that compromise. However, that negotiation is fiercely contested and operates against a background of scarce resources and competing claims. Thus, while social justice theory can equate solely to the *description* of the distribution of benefits and burdens in particular political, economic, and social systems, it is fair to say that the prevailing concern of modern theories of social justice is not just to understand and describe the distribution of benefits and burdens of a political and social framework but also to attempt

---

5 M. Reitsch, *The Routledge International Handbook of Social Justice* (Oxford: Routledge 2014).

6 D. Johnson, *A Brief History of Justice* (Chichester: Wiley-Blackwell 2011), 174.

7 J. Rawls, *A Theory of Justice* (Oxford: Oxford University Press 1971).

to evaluate and reform the social world.[8] Social justice theories evaluate the pattern of distribution according to how far that pattern of distribution is either just, or instead responds to arbitrary factors such as the market, class divisions, or other bureaucratic conditions.[9] Hence, social justice-orientated scholarship tends to be critical of existing social/political/economic/legal institutions and the ways in which those institutions undermine social justice. As a result, this scholarship often draws from *critical theories* that view society as a system of oppression and inequality which is harmful to individuals or groups.[10] Those institutional arrangements must be challenged to reach a set of moral imperatives: fairness, equality, human flourishing, human dignity, and so on.[11] A great wealth of critical theories abound, reflecting the perceived sources and/or experiences of social inequality and oppression, including feminism, critical race theory, queer theory, Marxism, post-structuralism, and neo-republicanism.

Interestingly, although these critical theories might have much in common, they are often adopted singularly and in different academic circles. Certainly, Marxist thought is not often considered alongside other critical theories, because although Marx offers a deep mine of general conceptual resources, he is understood to fail 'to reckon systematically with gender, ecology, and political power as structuring principles and axes of inequality in capitalist societies – let alone as stakes and premises of social struggle'.[12] Indeed, the post-structuralist movement of the 1960s was concerned with the rejection of the 'grand theory' of Marxism and the conviction of the importance of the construction of different versions of the self and identity in human development, such that economic and social outcomes cannot be predicted in advance.[13] This post-structuralist movement has been very influential in the development of certain strands of feminist thought.[14]

---

8 B. Carniol, *Social Services and Social Justice in Canada* (Toronto: Between the Lines 2010), 36 states: 'working for social justice is a continuing unending process, not just an immediate goal or a once and for all event. Social justice calls for the dismantling of all oppressions and undue privileges. But social justice is about more than just dismantling justice. It is about constructing equitable personal/political/economic/social realities based on values such as caring, authentic democracy, and fairness. This process is sometimes called social transformation.'

9 B. Campbell, 'Social Justice and Sociological Theory' (2021) 58 *Society* 355.

10 O. Sensoy and R. DiAngelo, *Is Everyone Really Equal? An Introduction to Key Concepts in Social Justice Education* (New York: Teachers College Press 2017).

11 Johnson (n 6), 174.

12 N. Fraser, 'Behind Marx's Hidden Abode: For an Expanded Conception of Capitalism' in P. Deutscher and C. Lafont (eds) *Critical Theory in Critical Times: Transforming the Global Political and Social Order* (New York: Columbia University Press 2017).

13 N. Fraser, *Fortunes of Feminism* (London: Verso 2013), 146.

14 P. Dews, *Logics of Disintegration: Poststructuralist Thought and the Claims of Critical Theory* (London: Verso 1987).

Over time, there have been attempts to merge certain critical theories and perspectives. Historically, the 'critical legal studies' movement which emerged in the 1970s was constituted by a diverse group of legal scholars and aimed to critique the neutrality and formality of liberal law, arguing that liberal law could not be separated from politics and social power howsoever constituted. The argument proceeded that differences in power precluded legal neutrality, constrained law's potential as a reforming force, and shaped the construction of the common good in favour of the interests of dominant groups. This movement was sympathetic to the claims of Marxism but was not limited to the Marxist understanding of the constitution of power in capitalist societies. Rather it was accepted that the sources of power could be various, but that the ways that these power relations limit law making and preclude a genuinely common good are the same. In particular, the construction of legal subjects as formally equal autonomous individuals masked class, race, and gender inequalities that constrained freedom and autonomy.[15]

However, the critical legal studies umbrella did not hold the critical theorists together for long. Over time the critical legal studies movement abandoned Marxist theorizing of law. The central conviction that law was inherently political and therefore indeterminate ultimately led some scholars to suggest that Marxist theory was too reductionist to be used as an explanatory tool. The clear link between the material (economic) base and the law required on the Marxist scheme could not be determined, as every legal decision was entirely politically contingent, and the outcome could not be predicted in advance. Therefore, there could be no Marxist sociology of law.[16] Feminist legal scholarship and critical race scholarship also gained momentum as movements in their own right, following interest-based paths to legal reform.[17] From this position, critical theories tended to chart different paths, although the move towards the theorization of intersectionality was an opportunity for critical theorists to contribute to a more generalized understanding of individual and group oppression.[18]

---

15 D. Kairys, 'Law and Politics' (1984) 52 *George Washington Law Review* 243, 244. See also the contributions in D. Kairys (ed) *The Politics of Law: A Progressive Critique* (New York: Pantheon Books 1982).

16 M. Tushnet, 'Marxism as Metaphor' (1983) 68 *Cornell Law Review* 281, 288.

17 C. MacKinnon, 'Francis Biddle's Sister: Pornography, Civil Rights, and Speech' and 'The Sexual Politics of the First Amendment' in *Feminism Unmodified* (Cambridge, MA: Harvard University Press 1987).

18 A. Phoenix and P. Pattynama, 'Intersectionality' (2006) 13 *European Journal of Women's Studies* 187; L. McDowell, 'Thinking Through Work: complex inequalities, constructions of difference and trans-national migrants' (2008) 32 *Progress in Human Geography* 491.

The separation of these critical theories has been recognized as a severe limitation on their ability to support social justice. Nancy Fraser has argued that the schism that developed between feminism and Marxism following the political activism of the 1970s was problematic for the movement. While gender struggles were once focused on labour and violence, they became increasingly focused on identity and representation. The result was to 'subordinate social struggles to cultural struggles, the politics of redistribution to the politics of recognition'.[19] She sees this as problematic because although there is value in expanding the remit of gender justice beyond reductive economism, there has been a consequential loss in terms of the power of theories of gender justice to argue for redistributive equality. This, she argues, has meant that under the assault of neo-liberalism, feminist theories have lost their force.[20] Even more disturbingly, she argues that the cultural turn in feminism has colluded with and provided a 'key ingredient of the new spirit of neoliberalism'.[21] This she explains in the co-option by the neo-liberal movement of the rejection of the family wage which 'now supplies a good part of the romance that invests flexible capitalism with a higher meaning and a moral point',[22] and the critique of state paternalism and welfarism. She also points to the ambivalence of the globalizing trend of cultural feminism. Although this does expand the scope of justice beyond the state, this movement also serves neo-liberalism, 'dovetailing in some respects with the administrative needs of a new form of capitalism'.[23] She suggests that to understand and react to these trends, there is a need to revisit Marxist concepts around capitalism, crisis, and social order. This suggestion has also been made in terms of critical race theory; capitalism and Marxist theory provide crucial insights into the struggles for racial justice.[24]

In labour law, both Marxism and feminism have formed important critical perspectives for understanding labour law's potential for social justice. Marxist theory was very influential in the work of both Otto Kahn-Freund and Hugo Sinzheimer, widely considered the 'founding fathers' of modern labour law. It formed the backdrop of their understanding of the context of labour law, and the systemic nature of the challenges faced by labour. Marxist theory continues to form the implicit starting point for many theorists thinking about the purpose and goals of labour law.[25] It has also been adopted more

---

19 Fraser (n 13), 161.

20 Fraser (n 13), 161.

21 Fraser (n 13), 220.

22 Fraser (n 13), 220.

23 Fraser (n 13), 223.

24 T. Anthony, 'Marx and Anticolonialism' in F. Gordon (ed) *Leading Works in Law and Social Justice* (Oxford: Routledge 2020), 90.

25 R. Dukes, 'Constitutionalising Employment Relations: Sinzheimer, Kahn-Freund and the Role of Labour Law' (2005) 35 (3) *Journal of Law and Society* 341, 345.

explicitly to reveal the limitations of the law in the achievement of worker goals. Zoe Adams' recent work on the 'juridical form' sets out to remind labour lawyers of the structural imperative of capitalism and its influence on the development of labour law. It reminds us of the socially embedded nature of labour law and its service in the functioning of capital.[26] Ashiagabor relies on Marxist theorizing to show how colonialism and the experience of racial exploitation are bound up with global mechanisms of capitalism, albeit exposing the limitations of this kind of analysis.[27]

Feminist theory has also been influential in certain areas of labour law theory, particularly anti-discrimination law. In this field, feminist authors have outlined the inability of 'formal' equality to resist or upset persistent forms of subordination or address wider social or economic inequalities.[28] Feminist authors have identified the arbitrary and under-inclusive nature of equality law based on a set of static and historically defined 'protected characteristics'[29] which is reinforced by the individualistic enforcement mechanisms upon which equality law largely relies.[30] Feminist legal scholars in labour law have long argued for a more substantive approach to equality in order to achieve justice for workers.[31] They argue that the principle of equal treatment under the formal equality approach should be replaced by a focus on equality of opportunities or outcomes and policies which aim to disrupt the existing distribution of resources, assets, and opportunities in society.[32] It is argued that without this kind of substantive approach, equality law will have very little impact on equality in practice, particularly in light of the reliance on empowered individuals to bring employment equality claims.[33]

This book supports the conviction of the importance of critical theory to labour law and the value of exploring connections between critical theories in the pursuit of social justice. It sets out to reflect on both Marxist and feminist contributions to labour law, but also to drive the social justice instinct in

---

26 Z. Adams, 'Labour Law, Capitalism and the Juridical Form: Taking a Critical Approach to Questions of Labour Law Reform' (2021) 50 (3) *Industrial Law Journal* 434, 444.

27 D. Ashiagabor, 'Race and Colonialism in the Construction of Labour Markets and Precarity' (2021) 50 (4) *Industrial Law Journal* 506.

28 S. Fredman, 'Substantive Equality Revisited' (2016) 14 *International Journal of Constitutional Law* 712, 721.

29 C. MacKinnon, 'Substantive Equality Revisited: A Reply to Sandra Fredman' (2016) 14 *International Journal of Constitutional Law* 739, 741; L. Vickers, *Religious Freedom, Religious Discrimination and the Workplace* (Oxford and Portland, Oregon: Hart 2016).

30 M. Ventegodt Liisberg, *Disability and Employment: A Contemporary Disability Human Rights Approach Applied to Danish, Swedish and EU Law and Policy* (Mortsel: Intersentia 2011), 52.

31 A. McColgan, *Discrimination Law: Text, Cases and Materials* (Oxford: Hart 2005), 14.

32 L. Vickers, 'Promoting Equality or Fostering Resentment? The Public Sector Equality Duty and Religion and Belief' (2011) 31 (1) *Legal Studies* 135, 152.

33 Vickers (n 32), 167.

those critical theories forward. This involves emphasizing an aspect of those theoretical perspectives which has hitherto not been widely considered as part of theorizing about labour law; namely, the relationship between the (legal) person and social justice. The next section sets out the traditional narrative of labour law and its (theoretical) position on the 'person' of labour law. Section 4 outlines the problems with this narrative from the point of view of social justice. Section 5 discusses the need to reflect more fully on the contradictions in this narrative from the point of view of thinking about labour law and personhood. The final section outlines the way in which the book takes forward the question of social justice, personhood, and the law.

3. The traditional labour law narrative

In the previous section we mentioned labour law's traditional narrative of social justice. This narrative relies on ethical foundations. The argument is that there is an inequality of bargaining power between employers and employees as a result of their insertion into the capitalist mode of production. This 'commodifies' labour and hence makes humans in the labour process 'objects' rather than 'subjects'. The dehumanization of workers in the labour process is an ethical dilemma; workers rely on the capitalist system and their employers, but that system at the same time degrades and destroys them. Hence the role of labour law is to step in to equalize bargaining power and hence restore that dignity to workers which has been lost due to the systematic exploitation involved in capitalist production. The restoration of 'dignity' to workers satisfies the ethical dilemma involved in capitalist exploitation. The 'equalization of bargaining power' serves the purpose of achieving 'social justice' for workers; a more equal workforce is a more equal society. In this section, I set out this traditional narrative in more detail and the reasons for its success and endurance. In Section 4, I outline the fundamental problems with the narrative, both theoretically and practically and why we need an alternative theory of social justice for labour law.

The idea that labour is not a commodity is a 'basic instinct' of labour law which stands alongside the idea of an 'inequality of bargaining power' between employers and employees under the capitalist system of production.[34] The argument is that labour has a human quality and so should not be reduced to merely a 'good' to be traded on the market and exploited for profit. This idea is an extremely important part of the labour law narrative, as it allows labour law to set itself apart from economic accounts which appear to disregard the separateness of labour and hence the need for

[34] F. Hendrickx, 'Foundations and Functions of Contemporary Labour Law' (2012) 3 (2) *European Labour Law Journal* 108, 110.

labour law at all.[35] On these accounts, if labour law is a commodity, it is simply an economic abstraction and so can be bought and sold according to the rules of commerce. As long as these commercial, contractual rules are engaged, employers are 'free' to exploit employees to maximize their economic advantage and ensure the maximization of their profit. However, fundamental to the dominant narrative of labour law is the understanding that this reductive view of labour is unacceptable. It is unacceptable from the point of view of empirical reality, and it is unacceptable from the point of view of morality. Labour in reality is much more complex than other types of commodity. Labour embodies 'the human agent, his human needs, human nature and human feelings'.[36] It is this 'human' element of labour which set up the moral imperative within labour law. Labour has a non-market dimension which rests in the person. That person is worthy of respect, of dignity. Labour law is a necessary 'step to the realisation of human dignity for a person in relation to his labour'.[37]

It is generally accepted that the moral connection at work in the 'labour is not a commodity' narrative rests on Kantian foundations.[38] Kant's work is explicitly referenced by Hugo Sinzheimer, one of the founding fathers of labour law, when he talked about the threat to autonomy and dignity which results from the commodification of labour. Following Kant, he recognized that a fundamental part of what it means to be human is the possession of individual purpose and direction, which is independent of the direction of another.[39] Individual autonomy is critical to humanity, but that autonomy is compromised by the capitalist system. The capitalist system attempts to reduce workers to things which have a price: they serve the ends of others and can be replaced at any time with equivalent value. However, workers are, in fact, elements of 'dignity', 'spiritual beings' who cannot be reduced to commodities bearing a 'price' and who are 'not designed to serve the ends of others'.[40] Hence labour law must step in to address the moral problem of the treatment of individuals under the capitalist mode of production.

The Kantian foundations of labour law are viewed as extremely important, because they attach labour law to certain core legal principles and aims.[41]

---

35 Hendrickx (n 34), 112.

36 J.K. Ingram, 'Work and the Workman: An Address to the Trades Union Congress' (1880–1) *Journal of the Statistical and Social Inquiry Society of Ireland* 106, 109.

37 K. Hendrickx (n 34), 114.

38 R. Dukes (n 25), 345.

39 Sinzheimer specifically references Kant in his work. See H. Sinzheimer, 'Grundzüge des Arbeitsrechts' (1927) in H. Sinzheimer, *Arbeitsrecht und Rechtssoziologie: gesammelte Aufsätze und Reden* (Band 1) (Frankfurt: Europaische Verlagsanstalt 1976), 8.

40 Sinzheimer (n 39), 8.

41 For example, the 1945 UN Charter of Human Rights and the 1948 Universal Declaration of Human Rights.

Labour law can use and adapt the overarching moral principles of liberal law (for example, 'dignity') to explain its own action and create its own legitimacy.[42] It is able to 'latch' on to other successful liberal discourses in order to explain its own action and increase its influence.[43] However, at the same time, it is recognized that the application of liberal discourses and law to the employment relationship is insufficient to address labour's problems. Sinzheimer explains this by exposing the limitations of the liberal law of contract when it comes to the employment relationship.[44] Certainly, the application of contractual regulation in the labour market was a civilizing moment because it meant a move away from defining workers as the 'property' of their employers, as occurred under feudal systems.[45] Workers were now recognized as more than 'things'; they had a legal personhood defined by a recognition of their innate freedom, autonomy, and rights. The problem was that contractual regulation was insufficient. Without any recognition of the social position of labour, contract law simply acted to reinforce and strengthen the inequalities at work in the capitalist system. Labour law was necessary to fill this gap: it allowed the application of social justice to employment relationships.[46] The role of labour law was to supplement private law and limit its application, so that the power of employers over employees was restricted.[47]

It is at this point that a Marxist analysis of the injuries to workers involved in the capitalist system of production becomes important. For example, Sinzheimer started his theory of 'dependent labour' from an explanation of the personal value of work prior to the onset of capitalist relationships of production.[48] He identified that in the original position, work and activity fulfilled a personal and social function for workers. Workers were able to exercise control over their work and use work to pursue their own autonomous ends. However, with the advent of capitalism, labour became dependent on others for work; workers were directed in their work activities by capitalist entrepreneurs solely interested in their own profit making. In

---

42 P. Gilabert, 'Dignity at Work' in H. Collins, G. Lester, and V. Mantouvalou (eds) *Philosophies of Labour Law* (Oxford: Oxford University Press 2018).

43 V. Mantouvalou, 'Labour Rights in the European Convention on Human Rights: An Intellectual Justification for an Integrated Approach to Interpretation' (2013) 13 (3) *Human Rights Law Review* 529.

44 For a detailed analysis of this exposition, see R. Dukes, *The Labour Constitution: The Enduring Idea of Labour Law* (Oxford: Oxford University Press 2014), 14–18.

45 H. Sinzheimer, 'Demokratisierung des Arbeitsverhältnisses' (1928) in H. Sinzheimer, *Arbeitsrecht und Rechtssoziologie: gesammelte Aufsätze und Reden* (Frankfurt: Europaische Verlagsanstalt 1976), 115.

46 Sinzheimer (n 45), 124.

47 R. Dukes (n 25), 17.

48 H. Sinzheimer (n 39), 8–10.

Marxist terms, workers were 'alienated' both from the process of working and the fruits of their work, and hence the essential tie between personal autonomy and work became lost.[49] Capital became the 'material basis' of human life, but was external to workers and ultimately outside of their control.[50] This process was exploitative because the externalization of worker value meant that workers themselves were objectified. They lost a sense of their value going beyond the objectification of the interests of capital. Hence the exploitation that workers experienced through the capitalist system went beyond a threat to physical integrity: this exploitation was a threat to humanity in the deepest Kantian sense.[51] The insertion of workers into a capitalist system of production meant that they were separated from their own 'spiritual' existence because of the loss of autonomy they faced. This meant that not only their physical integrity but also their moral dignity was compromised.

This theorization has been supplemented by the specific injury involved in the 'subordination' of employees to employers under the capitalist mode of production.[52] This was the narrative adopted by Otto Kahn-Freund, Sinzheimer's one-time pupil, who brought many of Sinzheimer's ideas to play in the context of the UK system of labour law. Kahn-Freund was particularly concerned that there was very little 'freedom' at work in the employment relationship as a result of subordination.[53] As workers who entered into a work relationship suffered from an imbalance of bargaining power stemming from the privileged position of employers under the capitalist system, they had in reality almost no possibility to negotiate terms to their own advantage.[54] Instead, employees had to accept the terms laid down by employers in order to ensure the fulfilment of their subsistence needs. The purpose of labour law was to step in to provide a 'countervailing force to counteract the inequality of bargaining power' between employers and workers.[55] Through policies which recognized the social position of workers, labour law could serve to make the employment relationship more equal and temper the employer's power of command over the employee.[56]

49 K. Marx, 'Economic and Philosophic Manuscripts of 1844' in D. McLellan (ed) *Karl Marx: Selected Writings* (Oxford: Oxford University Press 2000), 85.

50 K. Marx, *Das Kapital: A Critique of Political Economy* (Seattle: Pacifica Publishing Studio 2010), 84.

51 E. Rosenstock, E. May, and M. Grünberg, *Werkstattaussiedlung: Untersuchungen über den Lebensraum des Industriearbeiters* (Berlin: Springer Verlag 2013), 17.

52 G. Davidov, 'Subordination vs Domination: Exploring the Differences' (2017) 33 (3) *International Journal of Comparative Labour Law and Industrial Relations* 365, 371.

53 Kahn-Freund (n 3), 25.

54 Kahn-Freund (n 3), 17.

55 Kahn-Freund (n 3), 18.

56 Kahn-Freund (n 3), 14.

This process of equalization would allow workers more power, and hence allow them space to give expression to their own needs, wants, and values. It would release the personal autonomy and dignity of workers and allow humanity to flourish.

There are a number of reasons why the traditional narrative has been so successful and enduring. First, this narrative is a call to arms. It identifies a moral injustice which needs correction, and hence can inspire outrage and action. Second, the scope of labour law is well defined. Labour law protects 'dependent labour': those workers who are under the control of others. Those workers constitute a site of injustice which is not of their making; this injustice is determined by the operation of capitalism and the operation of property rights under liberal democratic law. Spheres outside the operation of property and relationships of capital are outside the purview of labour rights. Third, and this is a crucial point, labour law stands in opposition to 'private law' or the law of property rights. Labour law is an element of social law which fills some of the blind spots of private law, and particularly the 'fiction' of the contract of employment. Under that private law, workers are treated as objects at the disposal of the property owner, rather than as a legal subject with rights and legal capacity.[57] Labour law imbues those individuals with legal status, and this in turn allows them to achieve their own self-directed (autonomous) goals.

4. Failings of labour law's foundational narrative

It is suggested here that, despite the enduring nature of labour law's foundational narrative, there are big problems with it from both a theoretical and practical point of view. The narrative suggests, on the one hand, that labour law can do too much – end social injustice. In fact, it is clear that labour law does not always or routinely have this effect. Many labour lawyers have recognized that the power of the law to influence the relationship between employers and employees in a deep or systemic way is limited. In practice, statutory intervention 'can do something, but cannot do much' to modify the power relation between labour and management.[58] The effect of the common law is even more limited in that it deals with the 'marginal, the exceptional, the abnormal' and so cannot deal with the protection of workers in general.[59] Moreover, labour law can actually serve to increase

57 R. Dukes (n 44), 16.

58 Kahn-Freund (n 3), 19.

59 O. Kahn-Freund, 'Hugo Sinzheimer 1875–1945' in R. Lewis and J. Clark (eds) *Labour Law and Politics in the Weimar Republic* (Oxford: Basil Blackwell 1981), 53.

inequalities and widen social injustice.[60] In this section I want to concentrate on a set of further concerns with the ethical narrative; namely, the way in which it presents the interaction between labour law and the person.

Under the traditional narrative, the two normative ideals of labour are not a commodity and inequalities of bargaining power are 'glued … to one another'.[61] Labour law steps in to halt or modify the 'wheels of commerce' to ensure equality between employers and employees, and the restoration of individual 'dignity' or humanity' which is otherwise compromised by the operation of the capitalist system. This is the core of the traditional narrative and its ethical promise. However, it is the argument here that this narrative presents several difficulties when it comes to thinking about the relationship between humanity, work, and the law, and leaves open more questions than it solves. For a start, it tends to present the labour process as an always-negative experience. Entry into the labour process is exploitative and bad for autonomy and expression. However, this negative experience is not reflective of the positive contribution that work can make to personal development and to the evolution of a sense of self.[62] For many workers, work is a source of autonomy rather than a destroyer of it.[63] Second, this labour law narrative reflects a static and one-dimensional view of human nature which tends to undermine the recognition of the complexity of worker experience.[64] Third, this narrative suggests that workers do not have agency in respect of themselves: their experience of dignity is reliant on the operation of external action by lawmakers. This can be experienced as disempowerment,[65] leading some authors to reject labour law as an ethical narrative at all:

> The temptation for labour law scholars is to focus their energies on developing an ideal theory of labour rights or social justice. But any theory is sterile unless we first try to understand why real employers, workers, politicians, and judges act as they do in practice. Labour law is

[60] H. Glasbeek, 'Coerced and Unfree in the Private Sector' (2018) 26 (2) *Critical Criminology* 579, 586; E. Rose, 'Reinterpreting Law's Silence: Examining the Interactions between Legal Doctrine and the Rise of Immaterial Labour' (2020) 47 (2) *Journal of Law and Society* 588, 601; V. Mantouvalou, *Structural Injustice and Workers Rights* (Oxford: Oxford University Press 2023).

[61] B. Langille, 'Labour Law's Theory of Justice' in G. Davidov and B. Langille (eds) *The Idea of Labour Law* (Oxford: Oxford University Press 2011), 105.

[62] K. Legge, 'Ethics and Work' in M. Korczynski et al (eds) *Social Theory at Work* (Oxford: Oxford University Press 2006), 311.

[63] Legge (n 62), 312.

[64] J. Nedelsky, 'Reconceiving Autonomy' (1989) 1 (1) *Yale Journal of Law and Feminism* 7, 12.

[65] L. McNay, *Foucault and Feminism: Power, Gender and the Self* (Cambridge: Polity Press 1992).

> not an exercise in applied ethics. It is the outcome of struggles between different social actors and ideologies, of power relationships. Labour laws are used by people to pursue their own goals, and sometimes they need rights such as to a minimum wage or to freedom of association simply in order to survive.[66]

It turns out that labour law's narrative is rather paradoxical. On the one hand, labour law is presented as a scheme of 'social' law, acting as a corrective to exploitative labour market practices. Social law is viewed as a corrective to liberal private law where that produces market injustice. However, liberal private law always remains the bedrock of this social law and ultimately its end goal because liberal private law is the law of market justice rather than market failure. In 'well-functioning' labour markets then, social law as a corrective is not required, or is only required in a marginal sporadic way to correct aberrant behaviour on the part of employers or workers. Labour wants nothing more of the law than it should 'leave them alone'.[67]

It is argued in this book that fundamental to this problematic is the acceptance in labour law of an understanding of personhood which simply reflects that of private law. By adopting this view of personhood, labour law is never able to escape its clutches. The adoption of the Kantian vision of humanity at the heart of labour law shows that it does not challenge the foundations of liberal law at all. Indeed, at the same time that the contract of employment is rejected, it still forms the bedrock for the majority of labour rights. At the same time that inequality of bargaining power is recognized between employer and employee, labour law respects and deepens the managerial prerogative through schemes such as unfair dismissal law and the acceptance of implied terms.[68] By adopting the liberal legal subject, labour law holds within it the real prospect of its own annihilation.

Here we reach the central theme and problematic of this book. Labour law as social law does not challenge the foundational assumptions of liberal law, and so does not in fact represent a corrective to it. Of central concern is the assumption of the liberal subject of law: as rational, autonomous independent (and male). Although this assumption appears on the face of it to be of marginal significance, the argument pursued here is that this is absolutely central to the failures of liberal labour law to achieve justice for workers. This is the foundation upon which the structure of liberal law is

[66] B. Hepple, 'Factors Influencing the Making and Transformation of Labour Law in Europe' in G. Davidov and B. Langille (eds) *The Idea of Labour Law* (Oxford: Oxford University Press 2011), 30.

[67] This is a corruption of the statement by Lord Wedderburn in L. Wedderburn, *Worker and the Law* (Middlesex: Penguin 1986), 1.

[68] Glasbeek (n 60), 586.

based, and it is a central reason for its failure to properly engage with the narratives and criticisms of social justice. This is the reason why the social and the legal can be considered as separate fields of enquiry, and why social critiques of justice have only reached a certain level of traction. It is also the reason why the discourse of human rights has gained such a following in labour law despite having only marginal influence on most working lives. This will be discussed further in Section 6.

5. The importance of the personhood reflection

In labour law theory, the work of Sinzheimer and Kahn-Freund has been used to reinforce the assumed coincidence between 'labour law is not a commodity' and 'inequality of bargaining power' as the foundational narrative of labour law. Certainly, both authors were interested in the interaction between labour, law, and the person and understood the importance of recognizing the systemic problems of capitalist exploitation. However, I would like to suggest that both authors were sceptical of the ability of labour law to 'decommodify' labour or achieve equality of bargaining power between employers and employees. Indeed, Kahn-Freund saw the problems of inequality of bargaining power as a social problem which could only be resolved through social means – outside of the law.[69] Sinzheimer recognized the need to think about the social context of labour and the impact of that social context on the 'humanity' of workers and the experience of work. He did make the connection between capitalist exploitation and the experience of humanity.

However, it is the argument in this book, that Sinzheimer's characterization of 'dependent' work and the experience of objectification or commodification of labour experienced under capitalism should be viewed in the context of his wider reflections about the relationship between labour, law, and the person. Although he mentioned Kant in his work, his conceptualization of personhood was not limited to Kantian understandings. He was convinced by the importance of empirical experience to the labour law subject; indeed it was this empirical view of the person which represented the opportunity to move beyond private law in the regulation of labour.[70] His reliance on Marx showed that he was not committed to a transhistorical view of human nature in the Kantian sense.[71] He was interested in legal and social

[69] Kahn-Freund (n 3), 35.

[70] Sinzheimer (n 39), 61.

[71] H. Sinzheimer, 'Der Mensch im Arbeitsrecht' (1930) in H. Sinzheimer, *Arbeitsrecht und Rechtssoziologie: gesammelte Aufsätze und Reden* (Frankfurt: Europaische Verlagsanstalt 1976), 50; K. Struhl, 'Marx and Human Nature: The Historical, the Trans-historical, and Human Flourishing' (2016) 80 (1) *Science and Society* 78.

evolution and the impact of that evolution on the experience of 'humanity' for workers. The law was important in not only responding to humanity but also in forming it:

> Acting not to replace private law, but to supplement it and to limit its application, labour law recognized the social condition of the worker and restricted the exercise of the social power inherent in private property. Through protective labour laws, social insurance, and codetermination laws, labour law gave expression to the social existence of the worker. Just as law had been used in bourgeois society to elevate the worker from thing to legal person, so it was used now to elevate him from legal person to human being.[72]

Certainly, in labour law, Sinzheimer saw progress from civil law.[73] The conceptualization of dependent beings at the heart of labour law embedded a recognition of social position. If the person was recognized as a 'class being' as part of labour law, this was an internal recognition of the very real inequalities (of bargaining power) that exist between workers and employers. This internal recognition of social inequality was missing in the abstract and 'neutral' view of the person which was at the heart of civil law. As a result of this shift in the view of the person from civil to labour law, labour held within it the possibility of social transformation. The recognition of the reality of the social position of workers in the law meant that labour law could act to change it. However, for Sinzheimer, although labour law could elevate the position of workers, this was not the end of the story in the relationship between labour law and the person. For Sinzheimer, 'freedom' for workers could not occur just through the operation of (individual) labour law as we might understand it. Freedom for workers required an imagination of a new 'economic constitution' in which the relationality of workers could be fully recognized. This required reflection on the benefits of the conception of the (legal) person as a 'communal' being: a person with a real stake in the law and the economy. Without this change in the conceptualization of the person, the same mistakes in the law would continue to repeat themselves.

The problem for labour lawyers is that when we consider Sinzheimer's work in its totality, we are seemingly left with a set of contradictions when it comes to the theorization of labour law. On the one hand, Sinzheimer tells us that the theorization of personhood and labour law is critical to understanding its potential. On the other hand, labour law's potential is constantly undermined by its view of the person. Furthermore, Sinzheimer appeared committed to two opposing views on personhood and the law: the

72 R. Dukes (n 44), 17.

73 Sinzheimer (n 71) 50 ff and the detailed discussion of his ideas in Chapter 2.

Kantian view of the person and the Marxist view of the person. We see above that Sinzheimer recognized the threat to the 'person' on the Kantian view of the insertion of workers into the capitalist mode of production. This insertion was a threat to the 'autonomy' and (hence) 'dignity' of human beings. Labour law steps in to try to restore this autonomy. However, this correction is only possible through adopting a conception of the person which is not Kantian but is based on the (Marxist) recognition of the centrality of empirical experience and social position to our understanding of humanity. This appears contradictory, because two opposing views of the person must be accepted at once. Sinzheimer recognizes this contradiction in so far as he points out that the reconceptualization of the person which occurs through labour law is constantly and consistently threatened by the sceptre of civil law (which adopts a different view of the person). As long as labour law continues to operate alongside civil law, the inequalities which exist in the person of labour law will be at once accepted but also denied. Its potential, without more, will never be achieved.

Hence, although Sinzheimer sets out the contradictions and the problematic of personhood at the heart of labour law, he does not clearly suggest how that contradiction can be resolved in the absence of constitutional change. The aim of this book is to take up the mantle on this issue. In investigating Sinzheimer's position further, Chapter 2 investigates the possibility for the resolution of this conflict through the association of individual labour law with the Kantian position, and collective labour law with the more Marxist one. Chapter 3 reaches outside of labour law to incorporate a feminist perspective on law and the person, and integrate that into labour law. This has two aims. The first is to bring the analysis of personhood and labour law centre stage. It is the conviction expressed in this book that many of the problems that labour law experiences boil down to the conceptualization of the person at the heart of labour law. In that sense it agrees with Sinzheimer's position. The second aim is to try to find a satisfactory reconciliation of some of the contradictions expressed by Sinzheimer in his analysis. The argument pursued is that we need to reconsider and reconceptualize personhood in labour law in order for labour law to achieve social justice and that we can do this through changes to labour law itself. We need to embrace the relational subject of law and integrate that into labour law's interpretive matrix. In that way we can improve the social justice outcomes of labour law for workers.

6. Reimagining personhood: the relational subject of law

Feminist theorists have long been critical of the characterization of the 'person' at the heart of liberal law. This criticism aligns with Sinzheimer's critique of the 'person' of civil law. The argument goes that the 'liberal legal subject' has pursued us since the Enlightenment and informs our economic, legal, and political principles (including labour law).[74] It represents a conception of the individual as a rights holder, separate from but potentially in competition with other rights holders.[75] Rights holders are autonomous human beings, protected in their individuality from encroachment from others and from the state. These universal subjects of law are understood to exhibit self-sufficiency and personal responsibility, having the capacity to manipulate and manage their independently acquired and overlapping resources.[76] Crucially the universal liberal subject is rational and makes decisions based on reason unencumbered by distractions such as emotions, feelings, care, and so on.[77] This rationality is understood in a narrow economic sense, with individuals seeking to maximize utility by taking the most efficient means to given ends.[78] The implication of this rationality is that these individuals are persons in the highest or most absolute sense. These individuals are moral persons, because they make decisions through rational choice and are imbued with 'a conception of their good and capable of a sense of justice'.[79] Thus the liberal conception of the person is at once stripped of humanity (a person is human in only a limited economic sense), while at the same time achieving the full status required to have access to rights.[80]

Feminists object to the liberal legal subject not (just) because it is 'neutral' or 'abstract' (as Sinzheimer suggests), but because it is inherently gendered and racialized.[81] At the heart of our law is 'economic man' – 'a rational self-regarding Hercules'. For feminist writers, that version of human nature is a stripped-back and unrepresentative version of what it actually means to be human. This is problematic for law, and it is problematic for social justice. If the economic man does encapsulate the true meaning of what it means to be human then we have at the heart of our law a conception of the person

---

74 The inclusion of labour law is implicit rather than explicit here.

75 M. Fineman, *The Autonomy Myth: A Theory of Dependency* (New York: The New Press 2004), 19.

76 M. Fineman, 'The Vulnerable Subject: Anchoring Equality in the Human Condition' (2008) 20 (1) *Yale Journal of Law and Feminism* 1, 10.

77 R.L. West, 'Economic Man and Literary Woman: One Contrast' (1988) 39 *Mercer Law Review* 867, 870.

78 J. Rawls, *A Theory of Justice* (Oxford: Oxford University Press 1976), 17.

79 Rawls (n 77), 17.

80 T. Finegan, 'Conceptual Foundation of the Universal Declaration of Human Rights: Human Rights, Human Dignity and Personhood' (2012) 37 *Australian Journal of Legal Philosophy* 182–218, 209.

81 For feminism: see M. Fineman, *The Autonomy Myth* (n 74). For queer theory, see D. Otto (ed) *Queering International Law* (Abingdon: Routledge 2018). For environmental reflections, see A. Grear, 'Deconstructing Anthropos: A Critical Legal Reflection on "anthropocentric" law and Anthropocene humanity' (2015) 26 *Law and Critique* 52.

who is an 'empathetic, other-regarding weakling': he 'knows everything there is to know about his subjective life, but nothing whatsoever about the subjective life of others'.[82] In that case, there is no role for other-regarding social justice policies which aim towards either recognition or redistribution (or both). Justice is served merely by supporting the interest of the economic man in the 'good life'.

Thankfully, there are other versions of humanity and human nature that we can explore, and which will be explored throughout this book. An extremely influential perspective in this regard has been provided by vulnerability theory, which suggests the replacement of the liberal legal subject with the 'vulnerable subject' (discussed further in Chapter 3). It is argued that the 'vulnerable subject' better represents the human condition because it recognizes our ontological, relational, and institutional vulnerability to harm and the contingency and temporality of human action. This has profound implications for the construction of law; it requires a state which is responsive to vulnerability in all its forms. The implications of this theory for this project will be discussed in Chapter 3, but although it provides interesting insights this perspective has been criticized for a negative view of humanity which leads to paternalistic intervention. For our purposes too, its usefulness is limited by its failure to differentiate human 'vulnerability' from non-human forms. This means that corporate 'vulnerability' is placed on the same plane as human suffering and an attempt is made to balance the two. This is insufficiently sensitive to critical theories which recognize the problematic of the economic and political domination of capital and capitalism.[83] Rather, this book suggests that instead of replacing the liberal subject with the vulnerable subject, the project should be to engage instead with relationality in a more positive sense.

It is argued here that a *relational* subject of law sets up and delivers the imperative of social justice. This draws on feminist literature which suggests that relationality constitutes the reality of human nature and its moral compass.[84] For example, West suggests that the 'Literary Woman' better describes human nature than the 'Economic Man'. This literary woman is not a rationalist, for she is 'multi-motivational' and 'does not know herself as well as she might'.[85] However, the literary woman is capable of knowing and empathizing with the joys and sorrows of others, and this skill is crucial

---

[82] West (n 76), 870.

[83] L. Rodgers, 'The Potential and Limitations of a Vulnerability Approach for Labour Law' in D. Bedford and J. Herring (eds) *Embracing Vulnerability: The Challenges and Implications for Law* (Oxford: Routledge 2020).

[84] J. Nedelsky, *Law's Relations: A Relational Theory of Self, Autonomy and Law* (Oxford: Oxford University Press 2011), 19.

[85] West (n 76), 870.

to both humanity and justice. Reaching out to each other and understanding each other are what make a community and 'without it, we would not crave, much less attain, justice'.[86] This relational subject has profound implications for law. It suggests that law should have a role in supporting and facilitating relationality. It also suggests that the moral direction or compass of the law changes. Moral outcomes such as fairness, equality, freedom, and autonomy must also be imbued with relationality. This is relationality *between* moral outcomes as well as within them. Thus 'autonomy', 'freedom', and 'equality' are not separate goals: relational autonomy also suggests freedom and equality in a relational sense. The aim of law 'at its best' is to 'bring about an empathetic and loving community'.[87]

This book explores the implications of the adoption of this scheme for labour law. Fundamentally, the relational analysis implies that the traditional narrative of labour law needs to be reimagined. 'Inequality of bargaining power' and 'commodification' should not be seen as system failures to be corrected by labour law. Rather, these concepts should be seen as normative proxies for the proposition that it is our relationships which make us who we are. The identification of commodification and inequality of bargaining power is a recognition of the relational nature of our existence brought to bear on our experience of work. The embedding of these relationships in the capitalist system both reinforces and contradicts them. Some of these relationships are constructive, and some destructive, but all are constitutive in the sense that they have a role in the construction of our 'selves' at work and beyond. When we make labour law, we recognize this set of propositions. This is what sets labour law apart from private law and represents our future.

7. Structure of the book

The first part of the book outlines the context of the book, both theoretically and practically. Chapter 2 discusses the relationship between personhood and the law. Chapter 3 explores the alternative visions of personhood in feminist analysis and sets out the potential of the 'relational subject' for labour law. The second part of the book applies the relational analysis in detail to the theoretical and practical schemes of labour law. Chapter 4 analyses the potential of the relational subject for individual labour law, and Chapter 5 discusses whether collective labour law could benefit from this analysis. Chapters 6 and 7 apply the relationality analysis to recent developments or 'crises' in labour markets. Chapter 6 looks at the relationship between the 'self' and work during the COVID-19 pandemic and how far the application

86 West (n 76), 870.

87 West (n 76), 877.

of health and safety law in the workplace implies a relational analysis of self. Chapter 7 investigates the increasing incursion of AI into our experience of work, and the implications for worker experience. This chapter suggests that a relationality agenda, which is sensitive to both human embodiment and embeddedness, is essential for ensuring that digitalization does not restrict freedom and autonomy (in a relational sense).

2

Labour Law and the Concept of Personhood

1. Introduction

It is the argument in this book that the conceptualization of personhood and how that has become incorporated into (labour law) rights and protections is essential to understanding the effectiveness of labour law in achieving and promoting social justice. Hugo Sinzheimer, one of the 'founding fathers' of labour law, was centrally interested in legal personhood. He argued that this endeavour was critical if scholars wanted to move beyond 'stating facts or norms' to also 'grasp their significance, at their ultimate point of reference'.[1] For Sinzheimer, this significance was both theoretical and practical. He saw something distinctive in the way in which personhood was understood (or should be understood) in the context of labour law. This set it apart from other theorizations of personhood in 'civil' law.[2] He suggested that an understanding of the relationship between humanity and labour law was central also to its goals; namely, how to ensure that the peculiar nature of labour is respected, even where it is traded as a commodity and subjected to managerial control.[3] This conceptualization of the relationship between legal personhood and labour law is central to the project in this book.

The aim of this chapter is to explore the different ways in which personhood can be conceptualized in law generally and how far those

1 H. Sinzheimer, 'Der Mench in Arbeitsrecht' (1930) in H. Sinzheimer, *Arbeitsrecht und Rechtssoziologie: gesammelte Aufsätze und Reden* (2 vols) (Frankfurt: Europaische Verlagsanstalt 1976), 50–2. Translation by R. Knecht.

2 We can understand this as 'private law'.

3 R. Dukes and W. Streek, *Democracy at Work: Contract, Status and Industrial Justice* (Cambridge: Polity Press 2022), 36.

conceptualizations could and have infiltrated labour law. The chapter starts with an investigation of legal personhood and the law and the distinction between naturalist and legalistic approaches to legal subjectivity. Rationalist, religionist, and naturalist positions are explored in terms of how far they have been incorporated into labour law theory and the implications of their adoption for labour law. The next chapter will further this discussion by seeking to explore the possibilities and values of adopting a more naturalistic or relational approach to labour law.

2. Legal personhood and the law

It is argued here that the connection between labour law and humanity gives it moral force and sets up its imperative for social justice.[4] As such the way in which the notion of 'humanity' is conceptualized and incorporated into the law is important. However, it turns out that this issue is extremely complex. The notion of 'humanity' or the human subject is incorporated into the law through legal personhood. This legal 'person' must fulfil the twin aims of being sufficiently universal and neutral to allow for legal incorporation, while at the same time representing the 'essence' of what it means to be human. In liberal law, this compromise is reached in a way which tends to favour the first rather than the second outcome. The 'essence' of what it means to be human in the designation of the 'legal person' must reach such stringent neutrality criteria, that it ends up hardly being a representation of humanity at all. When applied in the field of labour rights, this leads to a number of undesirable or irresolvable tensions which stand in the way of justice for workers.

The distinction between positivistic/legalistic and naturalistic/realistic approaches to legal personhood is fundamental and foundational to understandings of the operation of legal personhood and the attachment of persons to rights.[5] Legalistic approaches understand the 'legal person' as a strictly formal or neutral legal device for enabling a being or entity to act in law, to acquire what is known as 'legal personality': the ability to bear rights and duties.[6] According to the legalist approach to legal personhood, the 'person' of the law does not bear any relationship to the metaphysical, ontological human being. Personhood is not defined according to some idea of what constitutes 'humanity' or a 'true' human being. Rather, personhood is a 'piece of pure legal artifice, a clever device of law, law's basic unit of

---

4 See the discussion of this issue in the previous chapter.

5 N. Naffine, *Law's Meaning of Life: Philosophy, Religion, Darwin and the Legal Person* (Oxford: Hart 2009).

6 Naffine (n 5), 21.

analysis'.[7] It is created by the law and serves a set of purely internal legal purposes.[8] It sets the basic unit or reference point of the law which is necessary to ensure its legal coherence:

> Just as the concept 'one' in arithmetic is essential to the logical system developed and yet is not one something (e.g., apple or orange, etc.), so a legal system … must be provided with a basic unit before legal relationships can be devised which will serve the primary purpose of organizing the social facts. The legal person is the unit or entity adopted.[9]

The legal 'person' on this tradition is essentially empty: it is not imbued with any pre-conditioned characteristics, social or otherwise. While it is possible that physical persons can fall within the reach of the definition of the legal person, the starting point is the body of legal norms which determine rights-bearing capacity. Thus, the connection between the human subject and the legal person is extremely tangential. New 'legal persons' can be stipulated and defined into existence at any time, as long as this creation does not threaten legal coherence. This means that the concept of the legal person is almost infinitely flexible and has extremely large capacity for inclusion of different kinds of subjects: humans, non-humans, groups, companies, governments, and so on. It follows that there are very few restrictions on what or who can be counted as a 'person' as a matter of law. Anything or anyone can count as a legal person, provided that the assignment of legal personhood is compatible with the purposes of any particular law.[10]

The legalist position can be contrasted with that adopted by realists. Realists believe that the legal person is (or should be) the expression of some important defining features of 'real' human nature. This implies that it is necessary to reach beyond the law to find the essential characteristics of humanity which the law can then adopt in the constitution of the legal person. The law's success is to be judged by the faithful rendering of the 'truth' of human nature. However, the definition of the 'truth' of human nature varies as well as the strength of attachment to the naturalist position. For example, it is possible to divide realists' conceptions of legal personhood according to the level of their attachment to the correspondence between

---

7 A. Grear, *Redirecting Human Rights: Facing the Challenge of Corporate Humanity* (London: Palgrave Macmillan 2010), 50.

8 Naffine (n 5), 27.

9 D. Derham, 'Theories of Legal Personality' in L.C. Webb (ed) *Legal Personality and Political Pluralism* (New York: Cambridge University Press 1958), 5.

10 Naffine (n 5), 27.

'natural' persons and legal personhood. Kurki makes a distinction between 'moderate' realists on the one hand and 'strong' realists on the other. Moderate realists would assert that all persons should be legal persons (but legal personhood could extend beyond 'persons' howsoever defined). Strong realists, such as Finnis, would argue that *only* persons should be legal persons. Entities which do not display the characteristics of natural personhood should not be persons in a legal sense.[11] It is also possible to divide realists according to their characterization of personhood. Naffine identifies three different theoretical constructions of personhood: rationalist, religionist, and naturalist. These theoretical constructions are selected on the basis that they represent the dominant schools of existential thought in law and exert the greatest influence.[12] They are not presented as mutually exclusive conceptualizations, and they can often exist alongside each other 'without too much animosity or open disagreement'. However, at times, there is profound disagreement about the 'proper' value of legal personhood: there is 'open warfare'.[13] Furthermore, it is important in the context of this book, that it is recognized that rationalist, religionist, and naturalist positions do not represent all of the possibilities for thinking about human nature and its connection to personhood. Another possibility is 'relationality', which is important for labour law, but which has not infiltrated legal thinking very far. Alternative conceptualizations will be explored later in this book, but for now, it is important to outline the dominant modes of thinking about personhood in the law.

Each of the realist modes of thinking characterize the 'legal person' in different ways. Rationalists argue that the true legal person is the rational human being; legal rights derive from the human ability to reason. That rationality is closely connected to the notion of autonomy. The autonomy of persons, the ability to pursue their own self-directed goals, arises because of the capacity of humans for rational thought. There is the tendency within this scheme to separate 'passive' and active subjects of the law. While 'passive' subjects of the law can achieve legal protection, they do not achieve full legal personhood. That is reserved for those subjects who can demonstrate rationality, autonomy, and independence. There are other realist conceptions of the person. The religionist conception of the person relies on human 'sanctity'. All human life is sacred because it is created by God. The mere presence of human life therefore dictates the assignment of rights. Naturalist conceptions of the person are more focused on the corporeal aspects of human existence. Human beings are natural beings with capacity for

[11] V.A.J. Kurki, *A Theory of Legal Personhood* (Oxford: Oxford University Press 2019), 22.
[12] Naffine (n 5), 21.
[13] Naffine (n 5), 21.

pleasure and pain, and conception of the corporeal person should inform the construction of legal personhood.

For Naffine, all the ways of seeing and explaining legal personhood constitute belief systems for which it is possible to identify a set of disciplinary connections and 'creation stories'.[14] These stories are contested, and some creation stories have had more influence than others on the development of our law. Broadly speaking, rationalist realist thinkers tend to represent the humanist or Enlightenment idea of man which is inspired by modern Western political and philosophical tradition. The authoritative discipline is moral and political philosophy. The 'creation story' associated with rationalism is that of the Social Contract and the emergence of the contractual individual and its roots can be traced to the writings of Locke and Immanuel Kant. The rationalist idea of personhood has been extremely influential in the development of law and legal thought. By contrast, the sanctity of human life story of personhood derives from Christian theology and has been influential in the development of human rights law. It is also present in medical law decisions. Naturalist accounts of personhood tend to privilege biological understandings of the person and focus on sentience. This account has arguably the greatest connection to the critical accounts of labour law, although for various reasons has been the least influential in terms of the development of legal rights.

The next section discusses these creation stories as far as they are relevant to employment or labour law. The first creation story is that of rationalism and classical contract law. This is important given the centrality of the contract of employment to the instigation of employment rights. The second creation story is that connected to religionist understandings of the sanctity of life, which has emerged at various points in the debates around the need for or value of labour law protection. This is particularly interesting in the context of the increased reference to human rights law in employment matters and debates around the conceptual conversion between labour and human rights. However, neither of these accounts fully capture labour law's understanding of the person, and both are criticized by labour law theorists. The alternatives and applications proposed by labour lawyers are presented in the final part of the chapter.

3. Rationalism and civil law: tensions and effects for labour law

The rationalist view of personhood is informed by the moral and political philosophy of the Enlightenment and finds its expression in the theory of the Social Contract and classical contract law. This 'creation' story has been extremely successful and enduring because it speaks to a set of values which

[14] Naffine (n 5), 28.

represent a version of social justice, while at the same time engaging with the necessity for the neutrality and impartiality of the law. Classical social contract theory, and the broader argument that all social relations should take a contractual form, stem from a revolutionary claim.[15] That claim is that all individuals are free and equal to one another. This doctrine of natural individual freedom and equality swept away the grounds through which the subordination of some individuals or categories of people had previously been justified. Subordination of one individual to another could no longer be justified on the basis of God's will, custom, or tradition, or arguments that some individuals were naturally more powerful or deserving than others as a result of their superior 'status' generated by birth or inheritance. Legally and conceptually, individual ambitions and possibilities were no longer to be limited by the accident of birth. All individuals were now free to use their talents as they saw fit. They could set up their own ventures or choose to exchange their skills and qualifications for wages in order to enable them to purchase what they wanted. Entry into any employment relationship was a matter of choice; individuals could choose where to work, who to work for, and on what conditions.[16]

Attached to this creation story is a particular view of personhood. To rationalists, the true legal person is the rational human being. Its subject is the 'man' of reason, a full-fledged contracting individual who interacts with others on the basis of rational decisions. It assumes a vision of personhood which is individualistic in the sense that autonomy and 'freedom' (to contract) is prized above all. The focus here is on human independence as the basis of rights and personality. Individual rationality and independence allow rational adults to assume moral and legal responsibility for their actions, and this is the basis for all social relations. It is this rationality and capacity of individuals to reason which permits them to enter into moral and legal community with others of a similar nature. Social justice lies in freedom and the pre-existing equality of all.

This is an attractive proposition for liberal law which aims for neutrality and impartiality. Indeed, in the application of the rationalist conception of the person, freedom and equality means that all 'externalities' are irrelevant. At base, the 'person' of private law is a juridical construction which is freed from external determinations and therefore autonomous. This freedom from externalities is represented in the construction of formalist accounts of contract law.[17] Those readings adopt the Kantian position of the concept of right as the 'reciprocal relation of choice'. In this conceptualization, legal rights (under private law) arise where the 'action of one of the two parties

15 C. Pateman, *The Sexual Contract* (Cambridge: Polity Press 1997), 36.

16 Pateman (n 14), 37.

17 E. Weinrib, *The Idea of Private Law* (Oxford: Oxford University Press 1995), 95.

can be united with the freedom of the other'.[18] This can only happen where irrelevant considerations of individual or collective motivation or need are completely removed from the equation. So, in the 'external relations' of binding promises between two parties in contract law, what matters is not the specific object that free choice is attempting to achieve but only that it is free choice that attempts to achieve it. Only the form of the choice as free, not its content, is worthy of consideration. In this world of contract law, then the concern is the abstract unbounded right-holder.

Labour lawyers have long recognized the paradoxical position of the contract of employment at the heart of employment (or labour) law. On the one hand contracts provide stability and certainty for employers and employees, and constitute a source of employment rights. Contracts are 'indispensable' to the ordering of employment relationships and the allocation of rights. On the other hand, contracts of employment are a 'conceptual screen' which conceal the realities of subordination between employers and employees.[19] According to the conceptual scheme, contracts are formed voluntarily between equals and thus represent a fair bargain between individuals. However, the reality is that choices are constrained by social conditions and social position.[20] As workers who enter into a work relationship suffer from an imbalance of bargaining power stemming from the privileged position of employers under the capitalist system, they have in reality almost no possibility to negotiate terms to their own advantage. Employees have to accept the terms laid down by employers in order to ensure the fulfilment of their subsistence needs. Inequality is also built into the contract. It is accepted that all employment relationships involve a power to command and a duty to obey. This is necessarily written into the contract of employment. Thus, employment law steps in to be a 'countervailing force to counteract the inequality of bargaining power which is inherent and must be inherent in the employment relationship'.[21] Labour law serves to make the employment relationship more equal and temper the employer's power of command over the employee.

However, the ability of labour law will necessarily be constrained by the acceptance of the premises of contract law. Kahn-Freund was particularly scathing about the ability of the common law to 'mitigate the disequilibrium inherent in the employment relation'.[22] He explained that the common

18 I. Kant, *The Metaphysics of Morals* (tr M. Gregor, Cambridge: Cambridge University Press 1991), 230.

19 H. Glasbeek, 'Coerced and Unfree in the Private Sector' (2018) 26 *Critical Criminology* 579, 581.

20 Kahn-Freund, *Labour and the Law* (London: Stevens 1983), 25.

21 Kahn-Freund (n 19), 18.

22 Kahn-Freund (n 19), 35.

law is set up to ignore any disequilibrium which results from normal social conditions (as distinct from 'abnormal personal conditions'), and in particular the realities of social constraint and economic power. This can be explained in a number of ways. It is possible to explain this phenomenon in terms of the operation of and integration of law into capitalist society which associates social justice with the aims and devices of the dominant group. This is essentially the set of insights which arise from a Marxist analysis of law. According to this position, not only do capitalists control the means of production, but they also control the 'ideologies' which surround the system of capitalist accumulation. They therefore have the power to create laws which serve to legitimate the system and thereby sustain practices of accumulation and exploitation. Of course, labour law does recognize to some extent the inequalities which arise as part of this system and serves to correct them. However, it can be argued that this correction is itself constitutive of capitalist relations.[23] This is because inherent in the system of capitalist relations is the tendency towards over-exploitation, which in the end is detrimental to capitalist accumulation. Essentially, the downward pressure on the value of labour power created by the capitalist system threatens the capacity of workers to produce in the longer term. Without mechanisms capable of counterbalancing these tendencies then social reproduction will be compromised to the extent that capital accumulation will be limited. So, labour law steps in to limit the social ills of over-exploitation and equalize the contractual conditions which have tipped too far in favour of the employer. Labour law does not challenge as such the unfair premises upon which law has been created, nor does it serve to address social inequality in general. Rather, labour law only serves to make the outcomes of those premises more palatable to workers and to ensure the support of the capitalist system in the longer term.[24]

Essentially the common law plays its role in the furtherance of this system. Contract law operates according to the premise of equality. Social justice is achieved because the parties are granted autonomy or freedom to follow market opportunities. An individual is free because he or she is bound only by 'general rules' of just conduct[25] which determine the 'formal character of the order of activities that will form itself, but not the specific advantages particular groups or individuals will derive from it'.[26] These general rules are provided by civil law. However, this system assumes equality of starting points

---

[23] Z. Adams, 'Labour Law, Capitalism and the Juridical Form: Taking a Critical Approach to Labour Law Reform' (2021) 50 (3) *Industrial Law Journal* 434.

[24] Adams (n 22), 434.

[25] F. Hayek, *Law, Legislation, and Liberty: A New Statement of the Liberal Principles of Justice and Political Economy* (London: Taylor and Francis 1982), 293.

[26] Hayek (n 24), 208.

in terms of resources and capabilities, and so on. In a situation of unequal starting points, the 'yawning chasm between legal equality and material inequality of contracting parties, especially in the work-for-wages sphere' means that a 'hands-off' contractual approach leads to highly visible anti-social outcomes.[27] Dealing with these inequalities by means of employment law mediated contract law only scratches the surface. The common law of contractual mediation operates against an assumed baseline of equality and deals with the 'pathological', the 'unforeseen', and the 'exceptional'; it does very little to constitute the employment relationship.

Hence, labour lawyers in the past have been sceptical of the ability of the law to really achieve social justice. Kahn-Freund argued that the inequality of bargaining power between employers and workers was essentially a social condition, and that condition depended on 'conditions largely outside the control of the law'.[28] In the determination of inequality, the law was 'secondary' both to the 'impact of the labour market' and also the 'spontaneous creation of social power on the part of workers to balance that of management'.[29] As a result, the extent to which workers were organized was crucial to the effectiveness of the law in the management of employment relationships.[30] Indeed, to Kahn-Freud, the law and legal norms could not be effective unless they were backed by 'social sanctions'; that is, 'by the counterveiling power of trade unions and of the organized workers asserted through consultation and negotiation with the employer, and ultimately, if this fails through withholding their labour'.[31]

Kahn-Freund saw advantages in the techniques of collective bargaining as opposed to legislative intervention, as this allowed for a greater dynamism in the establishment of rules, and better response to market conditions. Moreover, there was something special about collective bargaining which could not be captured by the law. He refers to the 'spirit of cooperation' which characterized British industrial relations after the Second World War which could not be 'engendered by the application of legal sanctions'. Furthermore, a 'mature' system of industrial relations can extend beyond the mere peace obligation, with investment in the relationships themselves. In this kind of situation, it can be that the law becomes unnecessary or can have a destabilizing effect on inter-group relationships, including between management and labour:

27 H. Glasbeek (n 18), 582.

28 O. Kahn-Freund (n 19), 18.

29 O. Kahn-Freund (n 19), 17.

30 R. Dukes, 'Constitutionalising Employment Relations: Sinzheimer, Kahn-Freund and the Role of Labour Law' (2008) 35 (3) *Journal of Law and Society* 341, 345.

31 Kahn-Freund (n 19), 17.

> Legal norms and sanctions are blunt instruments for the shaping of intergroup relations which have developed into a higher community. In many social and human spheres, the application of the law to intra-community affairs signifies the collapse of the community. This is true of labour relations no less than of international affairs, of commercial associations and of the family.[32]

4. Religionism and labour law: tensions and effects

In the early development of labour law, the religionist perspective on legal personhood is clearly evident. The proposal for a set of factory acts to limit the working hours of children in the early 1800s was made both on the basis of the physical injury involved in excessive working hours and on the basis of the moral and spiritual weaknesses of a system (of law) which allowed such injury to take place, particularly among the most 'helpless' in society. In the parliamentary debates on the development of the factory acts[33] it was argued that the treatment of children working in factories was an 'outrage against humanity': 'No case of hardship, no scenes of degradation, could be found to equal those which were endured in the mills and factories of this country.'[34] This treatment was 'demoralizing' for children because it meant that they had no opportunity for 'moral or mental' improvement. This treatment also offended the Christian values upon which the country was based[35] because it failed to recognize the intrinsic or divine value of all human life, especially among those who were unable to protect themselves. Children were essentially treated as machines by factory owners:

> They were regarded as machines of no value. The employer made his calculation as to how many hours his machines were to work to yield a certain profit; but, as to what the human machine would bear, he made no calculation; he did not calculate how long that would continue to exist, and these infants were condemned to general hard labour, through

32 O. Kahn-Freund, 'Intergroup Conflicts and Their Settlement' (1954) *The British Journal of Sociology* 193, 204.

33 A series of factory acts between 1819 and 1833 dealt with the working conditions of children. These Acts set a maximum 9-hour day and 48-hour week for the under-13s, a 12-hour day and 69-hour week for those between 13 and 18, and mandated the abolition of night work for all under 18s in textile mills. Women were the subject of the subsequent Mines Regulation of 1842, which barred them from underground working, and the Factories Act of 1944 extended the protections of the 18-hour day in the textile industry to women workers.

34 Mr Sadler, HC Deb 7 June 1832 vol 13 cc500-550, 501.

35 Sadler (n 33), 501.

> which they became crippled in their limbs, and incapable of future exertion, from their being exposed to all this at a period when nature would not bear it; and then, at a certain age, like the chimney-sweeps, they were turned out of employ, to be supported by the public, or to be exposed to all the evils consequent upon a state of moral depravity.[36]

In relation to the limitation of working hours for children, there was a high degree of consensus that such a limitation was 'consistent with humanity, mercy, and sound policy'.[37] Arguments made against the introduction of these factory acts did not challenge the religionist view directly. Rather they pointed either to the paucity or flaws in evidence regarding the negative treatment of workers, or the efforts of factory owners to treat children fairly in the absence of legislation. Some even pointed to the 'choice' of children to work longer hours in order to gain greater compensation in terms of time or money.[38] However, there was very little dispute about the need to protect children for moral and spiritual reasons.

By contrast, there was sustained objection to the extension of the limitation of working hours to adults. These objections were made primarily on rationalist grounds. It was argued that the extension of the limitation of working hours to adult males would be a threat to personal liberty and freedom of contract. Such limitations would be 'in violation of the principle that the adult labourer should be left free to make what contracts he thought fit, and to dispose of his labour to the best advantage'.[39] Indeed, the extensions put forward in the Factory Act 1895 were also rejected by important feminist figures, arguing that any special limitation of women's labour must militate against their employment and hence decrease their independence and personal freedom. This 'middle-class' argument was fiercely rejected by others, who felt that it represented 'ignorance of the economic position of the wage earner'.[40] Beatrice Webb, an important voice for social reform at the time, argued that '[f]ar from diminishing personal freedom, Factory legislation positively increases the individual liberty and economic independence of the workers subject to it'.[41] It was further argued that such a paternalist policy would ultimately work against the interests of labour. Such a policy would reduce the profits accruing to factory owners, and this would result in the depression of wages and a demand for labour

---

36 Sadler (n 33), 501.

37 Lord Molyneux, HC Deb 3 April 1833 vol 17 cc79-115, 83.

38 Mr Wynn, HC Dev 3 April 1833 vol 17 cc79-115, 96.

39 C. Torrens, HC Deb 18 July 1933 vol 19, 898–913, 901.

40 B. Webb, 'Women and the Factory Acts' (Fabian Tract No. 67), 15.

41 Webb (n 39), 16.

which was less than the supply. This policy would therefore result in unemployment for workers and a loss of competitive position for employers.[42]

5. Sanctity and human rights

There has been an increasing alignment of labour law and human rights in recent years. On the one hand, this has been a strategic decision, taken by labour organizations to further their own instrumental goals. Human rights rhetoric has been adopted by trade unions and other organizations when campaigning for improvements in working conditions.[43] The provisions relating to both individual and collective labour law in international human rights conventions and domestic instruments have been utilized with some success to protect individual and collective labour rights and to fill the gaps in labour law protection. On the other hand, there has been a more considered theoretical and philosophical reflection on whether human rights ideals could form the normative foundation for labour law.[44] One particular area of enquiry is the value for labour law of the 'naturalistic' conceptualizations of the person which inhere in the philosophical justifications for human rights law.

On the face of it, the naturalistic tradition sets up the moral imperative in human rights law. This connection is founded on the universality and inalienability of human rights.[45] The universality of human rights describes their equal possession by all members of the human family. All humans possess human rights unconditionally, equally, and at all times as a result of their humanity. The absolute connection between law, morality, and humanity also determines that human rights are universal in the sense that they are held against all others. They have such moral significance that they take precedence over other moral considerations, including other moral rights.[46] Not only that, no human being has any greater claim to human rights than any other; it is impossible to be 'more' or 'less' human. Human

---

42 Lord Molyneux, HC Deb 3 April 1833 vol 17 cc79-115, 84: 'He hoped, therefore, that the House would not, by acting on a false notion of humanity, proceed to pass an Act which would reduce the profits of the manufacturers one sixth.'

43 K. Kolben, 'Labor Rights as Human Rights' (2009) 50 *Virginia Journal of International Law* 449, 451.

44 J. Atkinson, 'Human Rights as Foundations for Labour Law' in H. Collins, G. Lester, and V. Mantouvalou (eds) *Philosophical Foundations of Labour law* (Oxford: Oxford University Press 2018), 124.

45 T. Finegan, 'Conceptual Foundations of the University Declaration of Human Rights: Human Rights, Human Dignity and Personhood' (2012) 37 *Australian Journal of Legal Philosophy* 182, 185.

46 T. Campbell, 'Human Rights: Moral or Legal' in D. Kinley, W. Sadurski, and K. Walton (eds) *Human Rights: Old Problems, New Possibilities* (Cheltenham; Edward Elgar 2014), 2.

rights are wedded to human beings because of their human status, and so they are not only universal, they are also inalienable. They cannot be taken away from any human being, especially not by those in power, particularly governments or judges. This makes human rights important in the promotion of social justice, because, morally, there is no distinction between the rights of the oppressor as opposed to the oppressed. Therefore, rights principles can be used in advocating for the interests of the oppressed and therefore the creation of a more equal society. Indeed, this moral compulsion can be seen as a driving force in the very establishment of the Universal Declaration of Human Rights (UDHR), in the wake of the experience of gross acts of inhumanity and genocide during the Second World War.[47]

This narrative is intimately connected to the idea that 'labour is not a commodity'. The argument is that labour has a human quality and so should not be reduced to merely a 'good' to be traded on the market and exploited for profit. This idea is an extremely important part of the labour law narrative, as it allows labour law to set itself apart from economic accounts which appear to disregard the separateness of labour and hence the need for labour law at all.[48] On these accounts, if labour is a commodity, it is simply an economic abstraction and so can be bought and sold according to the rules of commerce. As long as these commercial, contractual rules are engaged, employers are 'free' to exploit employees to maximize their economic advantage and ensure the maximization of their profit. However, fundamental to the dominant narrative of labour law is the understanding that this reductive view of labour is unacceptable. It is unacceptable from the point of view of empirical reality, and it is unacceptable from the point of view of morality. Labour in reality is much more complex than other types of commodity. Labour embodies 'the human agent, his human needs, human nature and human feelings'.[49] It is this 'human' element of labour which set up the moral imperative within labour law. Labour has a non-market dimension which rests in the person. That person is worthy of respect, of dignity. Labour law is a necessary 'step to the realisation of human dignity for a person in relation to his labour'.[50]

However, difficulties arise because of the need to essentialize the human 'subject' as part of this project and make the connection between that human

47 A. Grear, 'Challenging Corporate "Humanity": Legal Disembodiment, Embodiment and Human Rights' (2007) 7 (3) *Human Rights Law Review* 511.

48 B. Langille, 'Labour Law's Theory of Justice' in B. Langille and G. Davidov (eds) *The Idea of Labour Law* (Oxford: Oxford University Press 2011), 106.

49 J.K. Ingram, 'Work and the workman: an address to the Trades Union Congress' (1880–1) *Journal of the Statistical and Social Inquiry Society of Ireland* 106, 109.

50 K. Hendrickx, 'Foundations and Functions of Contemporary Labour Law' (2012) 3 (2) *European Labour Law Journal* 114.

subject and the allocation of rights. There have been different views about the central characteristics of 'humanity' which should inform human rights law. According to Naffine, the idea of the 'sacred' implicitly forms the basis of human rights law, for the idea is that human life is innately precious.[51] Human sanctity derives from our divine creation and is the reason for our inherent (and pre-legal) spiritual value. Indeed, Naffine points to the centrality of these views among the drafters of the UDHR, and particularly the leader of the Declaration's Drafting Committee, Eleanor Roosevelt, that: 'we are born free and equal in dignity and rights because there is a divine Creator, and there is a divine spark in men'.[52] In fact, many modern naturalist theorists of human rights distance themselves from this kind of religionism, but a number have retained the appeal to the connection between human status and moral rights.[53] For example, Tasioulas argues that a human right is a moral right generated by a universal human interest.[54] Those interests inhere in all of us simply in virtue of our humanity or human status.[55] Those interests are open ended, but must be of sufficient moral importance to generate duties on others, and it is on this basis that we should decide which rights constitute 'human' rights. However, there are problems with these approaches, not least in deciding the essential human attributes or interests which are sufficiently universal while also reflecting contextual and historical contingencies. Tasioulas suggests that his model is sufficiently flexible to accommodate these changing socio-historic conditions, but other authors suggest that a different model is required.

Griffin suggests instead a naturalistic theory of human rights based on 'personhood'.[56] In this he attempts to offer a more dynamic vision of human nature than the human status theories previously mentioned. He argues that the focus should be our distinctive capacity for normative agency; namely, the ability to pursue our own conception of the good life. This normative agency informs our moral (human) rights to autonomy and liberty, as individuals must be able to choose their own life path free from interference. It also assumes 'minimum provision' because it is only with a basic level of resources at our disposal that we have some chance of success at pursuing our

---

51 Naffine (n 5), 102.

52 E. Roosevelt, 'Making Human Rights Come Alive' in A. Black (ed) *What I hope to Leave Behind: The Essential Essays of Eleanor Roosevelt* (Brooklyn, NY: Carlson 1995), 559.

53 J. Atkinson (n 43), 125.

54 J. Tasioulas, 'On the foundations of Human Rights' in R. Cruft, S. Liao, and M. Renzo (eds) *Philosophical Foundations of Human Rights* (Oxford: Oxford University Press 2015), 51.

55 J. Tasioulas, 'On the Nature of Human Rights' in G. Ernst and J.-C. Heilinger (eds) *The Philosophy of Human Rights: Contemporary Controversies* (Berlin, Boston: De Gruyter 2011), 9.

56 J. Griffin, *On Human Rights* (Oxford: Oxford University Press 2008), 10.

own sense of the good life. The problem with this theorization in particular is that recourse to 'autonomy' and 'liberty' as the foundational cornerstone of personhood means that there is the potential for human rights theory to descend into the rationalism of the common law. The problems and issues this creates will be explored further in the next section. There is also the potential for conflict between Griffin's theory of personhood and the human dignity or sanctity theories explored previously. For example, Griffin's theory would seek to exclude those without the capacity for 'normative agency' from gaining access to human rights. This undermines the assertion of other naturalists that human rights should be universal and protect all by virtue of their humanity.

Furthermore, there are problems with all of these theories when it comes to deriving from them a normative foundation for labour law. The requirement of universality is problematic. For example, Atkinson outlines the problem with establishing a (human) right to 'decent working conditions' by reference to human status theories of human rights.[57] In order to do so, it must be shown that all humans have their universal interests furthered by the establishment of this right. This is difficult (if not impossible) because this furthers the interests only of those in work. This appears to introduce a conditionality to human rights which does not work on the naturalist scheme. Seen another way, it could be argued that the lack of universality of labour rights necessary means that the claims of labour rights are morally less compelling or stringent. If they only pertain to a certain group (workers) and to a certain aspect of life (work), then they are less important than other moral claims. These arguments can certainly be refuted, and certainly some labour rights do involve important moral considerations. For example, Mantouvalou argues that ill-treatment or abuse at work deserves protection under human rights law because it involves violation of dignity or human sanctity. It presents no less a compelling moral claim than the protection of freedom from torture or degrading treatment under Article 3 of the European Convention on Human Rights.[58] Privacy is also a cited as a human right of central importance which should be given protection in the context of work. The dismissal of individuals from work on the basis of private activities undermines dignity and should be accepted by naturalists as an interest worthy of protection.[59] However, it is difficult to argue that *all* labour rights are human rights or give rise to compelling universal moral claims. Take, for example, the right to paid

57 J. Atkinson (n 43), 133.

58 V. Mantouvalou, 'Are Labour Rights Human Rights' (2012) 3 (2) *European Labour Law Journal* 151–72, 164.

59 Mantouvalou (n 57), 165.

holiday. Certainly, there is the argument that failure to allow workers rest time violates a human right to physical safety, but this argument would not lead inevitably to annual leave guarantees to the extent they are protected as a matter of labour law.[60] As a result, some authors have suggested that labour rights should not be categorized as 'human' rights at all,[61] and we should explore other justifications for giving labour law rights priority. Others have suggested that while some labour rights should be considered human rights, other rights do not carry the moral compulsion of human rights and should carry the lesser status of 'labour standards'.[62]

6. Embodiment and materiality

It appears from the above discussion that there are limitations to the rationalist *and* the religionist accounts of personhood from the point of view of labour law. There are difficulties translating these views of personhood into an effective regime of rights for labour. The scheme of rationalism fails for labour law because it tends to protect only those rights which are 'freely' negotiated through the contract of employment (subject to some exceptions) and this fails to respect the social condition of workers. The religionist scheme also fails because it aims to protect a set of rights which derive from universal human interests. Although some labour rights could feasibly fit into this scheme, there are many labour rights which would not, or would require a strained interpretation in order to do so. It is argued in this section that these failures are inherent in the particular view of personhood adopted on *both* the rationalist and religionist scheme. Indeed, both of these views of personhood share a failing or flaw when it comes to the understanding of personhood and labour law rights.

The failing is that both rationalism and religionist views of human nature reject our corporeal, material nature. The influential ideas of the legal person as either a mature reasoner (rationalism) or a spiritual being tend to play down the person as a body. The person as a reasoner is only incidentally embodied and certainly is not defined by the body, for the legal focus is on the mind.[63] Indeed, the rational legal person is imagined with a rather well-controlled, able, and healthy body which provides no constraint on reason. This fits well with the dualist underpinnings of philosophical rationalism which adopts a Cartesian approach to mind and body. According to this approach the mind and body are separate and stand in a hierarchical relationship with each

---

60 H. Collins, 'Theories of Rights as Justifications for Labour Law' in G Davidov and B Langille, *The Idea of Labour Law* (Oxford: Oxford University Press 2011) 137

61 Collins (n 59), 137.

62 Mantouvalou (n 57), 162.

63 Naffine (n 5), 144.

other. The insistence of the supremacy of 'reason' over nature presupposes that the mind, as the internal aspect of the rational self, reigns supreme. It is the operation of the mind and its capacity for independent reason which gives us our essential natures and our inherent dignity. According to Kant, it is this capacity for reason which gives us access to the universal truth that man must treat other rational beings not as instruments of his own ends but as beings with their own ends, with their own goals, as moral agents:

> A rational being belongs to the kingdom of ends [is an end in itself] as a member when he legislates in it universal laws while also being himself subject to these laws. He belongs to it as sovereign when as legislator he is himself subject to the will of no other.[64]

Under this Kantian scheme, the body is of a different order to the mind. It is merely an external 'thing' or 'object' which is part of the baseness of nature. According to Kant, the body should be recognized but contained and subdued.[65] It should not be permitted to interfere with the cool exercise of reason. It is argued that this discourse of reason has come to underpin all forms of liberal law, such that liberal law pursues a 'discourse of disembodiment'.[66] Liberal legal justice is conceived of as neutral, abstract, and blind to concrete particularities. Central to its legitimacy is that legal justice is achieved through the recognition of formal equality between universal subjects, understood as rational, independent, autonomous beings. This can only be possible by the separation of 'will' from any particular form of embodiment. The result is that liberal law tends to distance itself from naturalism and seeks to exclude considerations of sociality, relationality, materiality: our species nature.

This is not to argue that human rights law or even contract law necessarily excludes considerations of materiality. Certainly, it is possible to see the emergence of modern human rights law as a direct recognition and response to the suffering of the human body. The driving force of the UDHR can be seen as a response to the 'catalogue of gross inhumanity and genocide' which was experienced during the course of the Second World War.[67] However, a number of scholars have argued that, at least over time, the corporeal beginnings of human rights law have been replaced by a focus on dignity, understood as (disembodied) reason. As a result, the humanist

64 I. Kant, *Grounding for the Metaphysics of Morals* (J.W. Ellington tr, Indianapolis: Hackett 1981), 40.

65 Naffine (n 5), 145.

66 A. Grear, *Redirecting Human rights: Facing the Challenge of Corporate Humanity* (London: Palgrave Macmillan 2010), 42.

67 Grear (n 65), 40.

subject undergirding human rights faces a deepening crisis of legitimacy.[68] The tendency towards disembodiment squeezes the material elements of the human subject, such that these become morphed into emptiness and abstraction. Thus, the paradigmatic naturalism of human rights is represented by abstractions. Biological features of the natural condition of being human become melded with metaphysical assumptions concerning 'natural persons', such as 'dignity', 'equality', and 'freedom'. At the same time, the abstraction process becomes material. Suddenly it is not the embodied human subject that is worthy of legal protection, but the empty abstraction of an individual represented by dignity, equality, and freedom. The naturalistic human subject becomes the positivistic legal person, and this is all that represents humanity as a matter of law.

According to this line of argument, the process of disembodiment of the legal subject of human rights has had various pernicious effects. It is has meant that the radical potential of human rights law has been disciplined and tamed over time. Indeed, the disembodied nature of legal subjectivity in human rights law has allowed it to be hijacked by non-human subjects such as corporations.[69] This 'corporation-driven paradigm of human rights' undermines the ability of human rights to protect the vulnerable as it 'insists upon the promotion and protection of the collective human rights of global capital in ways that "justify" corporate well-being and dignity, even when it entails gross and flagrant violation of human rights of actually existing human beings and communities'.[70] Furthermore, despite the proliferation of legally enforceable rights per se, the regime has been weakened by hyper-pragmatic modes of interpretation and enforcement (for example, through the doctrine of proportionality) which render rights meaningless for the vast majority of citizens.

7. The social and the corporeal: Sinzheimer and the class being

In Section 6, we analysed how the liberal legal subject fails to reflect 'humanity' or human nature because it fails to incorporate embodiment. In the name of universality and impartiality, human beings are stripped of their corporeal nature as a matter of law. In this section we consider further the failures of the liberal legal subject and legal subjectivity. We analyse the

---

68 A. Grear, 'Embracing Vulnerability: notes towards human rights for a more-than-human world' in D. Bedford and J. Herring (eds) *Embracing Vulnerability: The Challenges and Implications for Law* (Oxford: Routledge 2020), 157.

69 J. Slaughter, 'Hijacking Human Rights: neo-liberalism, the new historiography and the end of the Third World' (2018) 40 *Human Rights Quarterly* 735.

70 Baxi, *The Future of Human Rights* (Oxford: Oxford University Press 2002), 132.

claim that the liberal legal subject fails also to respect the social position or condition of working people; their 'sociality'. This criticism abounds in the communitarian critique of liberalism, which aims to highlight the inevitability of the social nature of liberalism and its subjects.[71] However, more interesting for our purposes is the work of Hugo Sinzheimer, who discussed the particular implications for labour law of the asocial view of legal subjectivity which abounds in civil law. He suggested that the very conception of labour law enables or assumes a view of the person which differs from this civil law subject. This view of the person is by nature socially situated and defined by empirical experience. This is important because it suggests that both sociality and materiality must be embedded in the subject of labour law for labour law to meet its ends. This sets the groundwork for the claim that the reality of human nature is 'relational' and that 'relationality' must be reflected in law. These claims will be considered further in the next chapter.

Sinzheimer adopted a humanistic view of the goals of law. He asserted that law is there to 'solve the problem of the existence of man' and 'allow man a human existence'.[72] According to Sinzheimer, civil or private law is unable to address this problem because the conception of the person at its heart is 'not real man, but a generic type'. It is an abstraction, related 'not to reality, but to the essence of man that lies outside of reality'.[73] The 'person' of private law is not concerned with actual situations or constraints on action. Indeed, under private law personal freedom has no material limits: all goods of the earth are equally available to all. Importantly, the person of private law is an entirely individualistic conception: it has no relational or collective limits. No person has any relationship with another and there is no subordination or subjugation at all. As private law does not recognize relationships it does not recognize inequalities, and thus has no concern with any progressive or political ideals (of which social justice would be one). Rather, according to this scheme, the role of the law is simply to validate the acts of free individuals as and when they occur.

Under the private law scheme, human existence takes form through 'property'. Property connects the freedom of abstract man to materiality; 'through property all moments of freedom are being realised'.[74] Property is

71 M. Waltzer, *Communitarian Critique of Liberalism* (1990) 18 *Political Theory* 6, 7; M. Sandel, *Liberalism and the Limits of Justice* (2nd edn, Cambridge: Cambridge University Press 1998), 11–13.

72 H. Sinzheimer, 'Das problem des Menschen im Recht' (1933) in H. Sinzheimer, *Arbeitsrecht und Rechtssoziologie: gesammelte Aufsätze und Reden* (Frankfurt: Europaische Verlagsanstalt 1976), 53.

73 Sinzheimer (n 71), 55.

74 Sinzheimer (n 71), 57.

the expression of personal freedom and independence under the regime of private law, and hence is held in the highest regard. Following Kant, property is understood to be the expression of personhood under civil law and hence determines citizenship. 'Man' becomes a citizen of the state when he expresses his freedom and independence through the acquisition of property. If this condition is lacking, if a person depends on another for his existence, then he cannot be a member of the political community of the state. Of course, this position is extremely problematic for labour. Workers are defined by their relationship with another. Under the civil law scheme, they disappear from view. Indeed, according to Kant, workers who are at the disposal of others have neither civil personality nor 'existence' under civil law. As they are not independent or 'free' their existence is 'merely inherent' and they are barely viewed as human at all.[75]

With the advent of labour law, Sinzheimer sees a change in the conceptualization of the legal person. According to Sinzheimer, labour law is based on a 'new view of man' which looks to the 'real situation' and 'social reality' of personhood.[76] This represents a 'complete turn' in legal thought; a move towards an abstract philosophy of law to a materialistic conceptualization of legal function. Sinzheimer's conceptualization of the legal person of labour law is heavily influenced by Marx.[77] It starts from the 'reality of man as a class being'.[78] As a class being, man is not 'free' but 'dependent' because he is inserted into the capitalist system supported by civil law. This dependency creates a host of restrictions, such that it is no longer possible to consider personhood in terms of freedom. These restrictions are material: an individual only has access to goods if the possessor of the means of production makes them available to him; collective: the conditions of life and working are determined by collective economic forces; and personal: due to his lack of means of production the worker is subjected to the direction of him who controls him.[79] Sinzheimer recognized that the material position of workers and their material needs are central to personhood. The social experience of workers which arises from their subordination to employers and their experience of membership of a subordinated social class should

75 Sinzheimer (n 71), 58.

76 Sinzheimer (n 71), 58.

77 H. Sinzheimer, *Grundzüge des Arbeitsrechts* (2nd edn, Jena 1927) citing K. Marx 'Estranged Labour' in *Economic and Philosophical Manuscripts* (1844). Marx argued that the essentiality of the labouring process to human beings both responded and evidenced their sociality and relationality. See K. Struhl, 'Marx and Human Nature: The Historical, the Trans-Historical, and Human Flourishing' (2016) 80 (1) *Science and Society* 78, 88; C. Byron, 'Marx's Theory of Human Nature' (2016) 80 (3) *Science and Society* 375, 376.

78 Sinzheimer (n 71), 59.

79 Sinzheimer (n 71), 59.

also be recognized as central to their being. This 'socialist' conceptualization of the person is precisely that which is recognized through labour law.[80]

For Sinzheimer, the recognition of the empirical reality of human existence at the heart of labour law had profound effects for its potential.[81] First, the law recognizes the importance of material need. Under the civil law, 'need' is a purely internal consideration for individuals and has no part in the realm of practical reason under which the law operates. For example, under contract law, the law's role is to validate agreements made through the external expression of free will; consideration of need would cloud this process and disrupt freedom. Second, empirical conditions set the *standard* of intervention, and this implies a major interventionist role for the state. Third, rights do not attach to individuals based on ownership and property. It is understood that 'property' and (contractual) ownership do not only constitute legal concepts but they also imply social power. That social power is reflected in the experience of workers. The law cannot remain neutral on questions of the social distribution of power, because to do so would mean that the experience of the reality of work would not be respected, and labour law recognizes that the experience of the reality of work is central to the humanity of workers. Indeed, the action of labour law is specifically to allow individuals to control areas of social life over which they do not have proprietary control. This implies a wide reach for labour law: medical care, sick pay, and disability benefits all fall within its purview. On Sinzheimer's view, if the person of the law is couched in real social experience, it follows that the law can have a transformative effect by changing social conditions. This 'opens up the way to interventions in the life process of humanity that used to be closed off by the reign of absolute principles'.[82] Labour law 'builds upon man's reality, not by merely accepting and legally recognising it, but by reshaping it'.[83]

Despite Sinzheimer's recognition of the normative and practical benefits of the instigation of labour law, he was also quick to identify that its potential had not been achieved. He sees this as a problem of politics, but also of the failure of labour law to properly release itself from the ties of civil law. He argues that the development of labour law has proceeded 'within the individualistic' frame of civil law, at the same time that it purports to reject its foundational premise.[84] He suggested that the individualism of labour law

80 I am very grateful to Prof R. Dukes for this suggestion.

81 H. Sinzheimer, 'Der Mensch im Arbeitsrechts' (1930) in H. Sinzheimer, *Arbeitsrecht und Rechtssoziologie: gesammelte Aufsätze und Reden* (Frankfurt: Europaische Verlagsanstalt 1976), 51.

82 Sinzheimer (n 71), 58.

83 Sinzheimer (n 71), 59.

84 Sinzheimer (n 71), 60.

(albeit based on the relational subject) necessarily tied it to the systems of civil law which it was never completely able to escape. Something more was required in order to effect social transformation which would really assist workers. As such, labour law was only part of the process of social reform which involved a body of norms that had still to be implemented in formal law.[85] Labour law was in the process of 'becoming' but had not yet been properly formulated.[86] Sinzheimer argued that in liberal democratic societies, the application of social law would have little effect without wider controls on the economic power. Without 'economic democracy' to support political democracy, the majority of workers would remain unfree and subject to the whims of those wielding all the economic power.[87]

Sinzheimer was fundamentally concerned with 'emancipation' or 'freedom' for workers.[88] That concept of freedom was a complex one, in that it involved not only individual freedom or emancipation from employer control but also the freedom to be involved in the collective regulation of the economy, which invoked the idea of the importance of collective or relational experience and workers acting collectively. As such it was not possible to separate the individual from the collective; individual autonomy was bound up with collective autonomy. In this way, Sinzheimer was able to find a resolution between the promotion of Kantian versions of personhood on the one hand, and a more 'relational' or 'socialist/Marxist' view of the person on the other. For Sinzheimer, the individual autonomy of workers was compromised by entry into the capitalist system. That capitalist system treated workers as means to an end rather than an end in themselves.[89] The end of labour law was to achieve 'emancipation' for workers such that they were able to assert their individual autonomy and, in that way, achieve freedom.[90] At the same time, emancipation was a collective *process* and a means to secure an improvement in terms and conditions for workers. Sinzheimer's vision was that the state would support these collective processes of emancipation through the creation of an 'economic constitution'. The economic constitution would be founded

---

85 H. Sinzheimer, 'Eine Theorie des Sozialen Rechts' in *Arbeitsreden und Rechtssoziologie: Gesammelte Aufsätze und Reden* (Frankfurt: Europaische Verlagsanstalt 1976) quoted in R. Dukes and W. Streek, *Democracy at Work* (Cambridge Polity Press 2022), 37.

86 R. Dukes and W. Streek, *Democracy at Work: Contract Status and Post-Industrial Justice* (Cambridge: Polity Press 2022), 36.

87 R. Dukes, *The Labour Constitution: The Enduring Idea of Labour Law* (Oxford: Oxford University Press 2014), 17.

88 Dukes (n 86), 31.

89 Sinzheimer specifically references Kant in his work. See H. Sinzheimer, *Grundzüge des Arbeitsrechts* (1927) in H. Sinzheimer, *Arbeitsrecht und Rechtssoziologie: gesammelte Aufsätze und Reden* (Band 1) (Frankfurt: Europaische Verlagsanstalt 1976), 8.

90 Sinzheimer (n 88), 8.

on the understanding that the economy was a public rather than a private matter and that it should be managed in the pursuit of collective ends. It would involve the establishment of a legal framework which would guarantee the right of workers to participate in the exercise of power, and would also provide a means to limit the power of the state and employers to control or manage their employees.[91] This would ensure both collective freedom or 'autonomy' in terms of the involvement of workers and workers groups in the management of the economy (and in the creation of 'autonomous law') but also ultimately individual emancipation and freedom for individuals to pursue their own life plans (through work).

However, this was not the end of the story for personhood. Sinzheimer argued that through the economic constitution, it was possible to envisage a situation in which personhood became defined not by individual need (individual autonomy) or class (collective autonomy), but by communal interest. This would lead to a different understanding of the worker/person as a 'communal being'.[92] This communal being would no longer be defined by dependence but by 'membership' of the constitution. The benefit of this situation would be that there would be a greater equality between economic actors; workers and employers were both members of the economic constitution without one having superior claims over the other. The connections between economic actors would become more important than the distinctions between them. This would bring a final resolution to the problems of inequality of bargaining power between workers and their employers. That said, while this resolved the problem of inequality, it did not appear to resolve the problem of personhood. Sinzheimer was conscious of the 'large danger' such a communal conception of the person would bring. This conception represented a threat to the 'creative power of free personality' and so must be undesirable.[93]

Ultimately, Sinzheimer's aim was to urge the academy to engage with the problematic of personhood and its relationship with (labour) law. A suitable conceptualization of the person of labour law would need to be expansive and involve elements of both individuality and collectivity:

> The concept of man that comes up from the idea of its development, gathers the features of all these legal orders without being absorbed by one of them. From economic law it adopts the idea of a direct connectedness of all economic forces in one whole. From labour law, it adopts the idea of secured spheres of life and work of individuals within

[91] Dukes (n 86), 32.
[92] Sinzheimer (n 71), 62.
[93] Sinzheimer (n 71), 66.

> this whole. From civil law, finally, it adopts the idea of independent individual spheres in which man belongs only to himself and to his spiritual powers.[94]

8. Conclusions: moving forward with (feminist views of) relationality

For Sinzheimer, the idea of the person and the relationship to the law was central to understanding the capacity of the law to improve people's lives. It provided a way in to criticize the regulation of employment law through civil law, and to understand the potential of labour law in shaping the experience of individuals at work. He argued that inherent in labour law was a view of the person which recognized the importance of material and social position and hence could act to change not just individual positions but society as a whole. Through labour law there was the possibility of achieving freedom for workers. Individual labour laws could address abuse in employment relationships by employers and ensure that workers were not treated merely as a means to an end, but also according to their inherent dignity. A legal framework sympathetic to collective bargaining and negotiation could also ensure positive freedom for workers and allow them to direct their working lives. As such he was convinced by the central importance of the integration of the individual and collective through law and the importance of industrial regulation for 'freedom': 'freedom' for workers would only be meaningful to workers if it concerned 'neither abstract freedom, nor political freedom, but freedom in the factories of our times that compress people more heavily and severely than ever before'.[95]

This argument is an important dimension in the call for the autonomy of labour law. Labour law cannot be viewed simply as a 'corrective' in the equality of contracts if the view of personhood remains wedded to that of civil law. The 'dependence' of workers to employers has no meaning outside of the wider dependence of workers operating within the system of capitalism (and other systems of sociality). Human rights law tends also to draw on liberal legal subjectivity such that the 'rights' of companies will be preferred over the rights of individuals, and collective rights will be interpreted so as to give full effect to freedom of contract. The reality of course is that labour law is necessarily integrated in practice with both contract/tort law and the law of human rights. Hence it is necessary to

[94] Sinzheimer (n 71), 67.

[95] H. Sinzheimer, 'Das Wesen des Arbeitsrechts' in H. Sinzheimer, *Arbeitsrecht und Rechtssoziologie: gesammelte Aufsätze und Reden* (Band 1) (Frankfurt: Europaische Verlagsanstalt 1976), 113.

recognize the limitations of these regimes and seek to modify these rules in the name of the relationality of the subject of labour law. This requires a greater attention to the relationship between individuality and collectivity, and how these intersect in the constitution of the reality of the worker's situation and the construction of self.

Under Sinzheimer's socialist construction of worker status, constitutional change was required in order to recognize the true personality of the worker. The economic system, like the political system, had to be governed in the public interest in order to achieve equality for workers. However, he did recognize that even this system was problematic from the point of view of legal personhood. The operation of economic law required a 'communal' view of the person which had the potential to undermine personal autonomy. Under economic law, the community extends and becomes an 'omnipotence' that covers the complete existence of man.[96] Of course, such a view of personhood is undesirable. We need a view of the person for labour law which understands the importance of individual or personal autonomy while at the same time recognizes the social and material circumstances of the worker and the contribution of those circumstances to autonomy. The next chapter discusses the contribution of feminist theorizations on 'relationality' and 'relational autonomy' to this project and the implications for social justice for workers.

[96] H. Sinzheimer (n 71), 67.

3

Labour Law and Feminist Approaches to Personhood

1. Introduction

It is argued in this book that it is essential that we have a critical theory of social justice for labour law. That critical theory must not only criticize areas where the law does not provide favourable outcomes for workers or fails to strike the correct balance between workers and employers. This can only ever be a superficial enquiry, which does not get to grips with the more fundamental questions which are essential to the understanding and future design of labour law: Why does labour law produce unfavourable outcomes for workers? Why does labour law not cover those workers most in need of protection? Why does labour law recognize only some kinds of work and not others? That is, the key to the understanding of labour law is to analyse not only the *context* in which labour law operates, but also the *construction* of labour law in a particular way which favours some actors rather than others.

This chapter offers a point of departure for building this critical framework. It draws in particular on feminist literature which brings into question the foundations of liberal law as based on the 'liberal legal subject'.[1] The construction of the liberal legal subject of law (a rational autonomous independent – male – being) has been crucial to the consistent and powerful narrative of the liberal scheme of law which has been extremely difficult to challenge and disentangle. This is partly due to the fact that the liberal scheme sits behind a screen of neutrality and rationality, but also because the narrative is fiercely guarded both socially and politically.[2] Any challenge to

[1] The relationship between labour law and liberal law was discussed in the previous chapter. Suffice it to say that although labour law has been presented as an alternative to liberal law, it has always remained complicit in the foundational structures of liberal law.

[2] R. Dworkin, *Law's Empire* (Cambridge, MA: Harvard University Press 1986), 5.

the liberal subject is seen as an attack on neutrality, freedom, and ultimately justice. While the limitations of the liberal legal subject to social justice has been recognized for a long time, it is only recently that the importance and viability of this critique has gained any traction.

This chapter starts with the context of the relationship between labour law and feminist theorizations generally, and an explanation of the failure of feminism and the feminist method to reach the mainstream of labour law theory. It is argued that this represents a missed opportunity for both labour law and social justice. The second section presents the feminist critique of the liberal legal subject and explains why this critique is so important for social justice. The third section suggests ways in which that critique can be positively developed into a social theory for labour law. It investigates the promise of vulnerability theory, and particularly the suggestion that the liberal legal subject should be replaced with the 'vulnerable subject' of law. It then moves to outline the potential of the 'relational' subject and the value of the promotion of relational autonomy for social justice for workers. The limitations of those approaches are then considered, and in particular, the need to incorporate some of the insights outlined in Chapter 2.

2. Feminist theory and labour law

The feminist theoretical project, although influential in some areas of labour law, has generally struggled to gain mainstream traction. There are a number of reasons for this state of affairs, some of which stem from the limited way in which labour law has historically been targeted by feminist theorizing, leading to a lack of recognition of the value of mainstreaming feminist ideas. For example, although the identification by feminist theorists of the particular issues and problems faced by women in the labour market (as opposed to men) has certainly had important policy implications, it has also tended to militate against a wider engagement with the implications of feminist theory for labour law generally. Other reasons for the ambivalence of labour lawyers to feminist theory pertain to the contradictions within and between feminist theorizations. This has tended to lead to a failure to provide a consistent and workable set of solutions to the problems identified. Finally, even the more deeply theoretical projects engaged in by feminist scholars tend to be represented as marginal to the concerns of the core labour law constituency: paid wage labour. The focus on the importance of social reproduction to the operation of labour markets has tended to be viewed as an externality rather than central to the core dilemmas faced in the regulation of paid labour. Recently, there have been calls to reassess the marginalization of feminist discourse in labour law, and a greater recognition of the convergence of feminist theory and labour law.[3] These issues and concerns will be addressed in the following section.

Fudge identifies a key conceptual move in feminist engagements with labour law over time, from a focus on the law's treatment of women towards a more nuanced understanding of the importance of gender as an analytical category which both determines and reflects legal norms. She argues that the literature of the 1970s and 1980s concentrated on women as the neglected subject of labour law. The focus of the literature was identifying women's inequality in labour markets and securing equal access to paid work. The legal frame of reference was therefore anti-discrimination legislation and ensuring the effective contribution of that legislation to tackling occupational segregation, unequal pay, sexual harassment, and pregnancy discrimination. As such, the law provided an instrumental tool to provide a remedy to the social problem of unequal labour market participation, and interest in the law was politically rather than theoretically driven.[4] Although this movement did produce gains for women in terms of securing and extending rights, it became beset with contradictions and conflicts. On the one hand, feminist theorizations sought to highlight the particular position and plight of women in society. On the other they sought to downplay that difference through the promotion of 'universal' citizenship for women on the same level as men. It quickly became clear that these aims were contradictory.

A way out of this contradiction was found by starting not from the plight of women in respect of the labour market, but from the role of the law in shaping labour markets and women's lived experience.[5] The law itself could be seen as a site of gender bias and neglect. Hence, in the 1990s the legal norm of the 'standard employment relationship' was identified as particularly problematic in its implicit gender bias and exclusionary effect. Under this model, only work which conformed to the 'standard' (full-time, permanent work for one employer) was viewed as a suitable site for regulation. This was linked to the post-war social contract which aimed to guarantee the male breadwinner sufficient income to support a dependent wife and child through various statutory and collective bargaining guarantees. This social

---

3 J. Conaghan, 'Labour Law and Feminist Method' (2017) 33 (1) *International Journal of Comparative Labour Law and Industrial Relations* 93.

4 J. Fudge, 'From Women and Labour Law to Putting Gender and Law to Work' in Davies and V. Munro (eds) *The Ashgate Research Companion to Feminist Legal Theory* (London: Ashgate 2013), 2.

5 A. Zbyszewska and S. Routh, 'Challenging Labour Law's "Productivity" Bias Through a Feminist Lens: A Conversation' in A. Blackham, M. Kullmann, and A. Zbyszewska (eds) *Theorising Labour Law in a Changing World: Towards Inclusive Labour Law* (Oxford: Hart 2019), 245.

contract was supported by a gender contract which assumed a female housewife who did not earn wages but took care of domestic and household responsibilities. The standard employment relationship excluded women in two ways. First, it excluded the work of women in the home, which was understood as unpaid and lacking in independent or labour market value. Second, it tended to devalue the labour market participation of women. Those women were disproportionately represented in short-term precarious jobs which did not achieve the standard employment relationship norm. Thus, although the norm of the standard employment relationship was neutral on its face, it operated to marginalize women from the law because of its implicit gender bias.

Implicit in this kind of analysis is a commitment to a social constructivist vision of gender. Instead of treating women and men's different roles and experiences as biologically determined, feminists recognized that gender is socially constructed and dependent on social norms and material conditions. This vision makes gender an important tool in understanding the way labour markets are fashioned and the ways in which those labour markets and supporting state institutions and laws are bearers and reinforcers of gender.[6] A gendered analysis is essential to understand how, considering changing social conditions and the increasing labour market participation of women, the standard employment relationship continues to exclude and disadvantage women. An explanation can be found in the shifting modalities of the gender compromise. Despite the increasing feminization of labour, there persists a gendered division of labour in the family which undermines women's equality. High-quality work continues to be confined to jobs which comply with the standard employment model, and these jobs tend to be less flexible and compatible with caring responsibilities. Hence, women continue to be disproportionately represented in non-standard, precarious work. Indeed, the *absence* of gender from discourse and knowledge producing enterprises concerning the labour market serves only to highlight its social constructivist nature.[7] This absence serves dominant social interests well because it allows gender-based inequalities to persist in the labour market without challenge. Hence, the standard employment relationship persists as a determiner of legal rights, despite its anachronism and the obstacles its produces to social justice (for women).

6 J. Fudge, 'Feminist Reflections on the Scope of Labour Law: Domestic Work, Social Reproduction, and Jurisdiction' (2014) 22 *Feminist Legal Studies* 1, 4.

7 J. Conaghan, 'Work, Family and the discipline of labour law' in J. Conaghan and K. Rittich (eds) *Labour Law, Work and Family* (Oxford: Oxford University Press 2005), 44.

2.1 Care work and affective labour

Feminist analysis has demonstrated how labour markets are gendered institutions, and how gender provides a 'historical, relational and dynamic understanding of how inequality in the labour market is configured, refashioned and challenged'.[8] This analysis has also shown how gender is implicated in the conceptualization of work itself; namely, what does and what does not count as work, and the value attached to certain types of work over others. The characterization of caring work in a family context as 'unproductive' and the commitment to the public/private divide of unpaid verses paid work has limited opportunities for the accommodation of women in the workplace. This is a problem for social justice, which requires a shift in labour law and policy outcomes. As Conaghan argues:

> the reformulation of caring work as 'productive' of economic value and the corresponding repositioning of such productive work as a legitimate 'cost' of doing business, greatly enhances the rhetorical and political power of arguments for better workplace accommodation of child-care and other caring needs, to the obvious benefit of women who remain our primary carers.[9]

With the increased feminization of work and labour markets, the place and value of care work has become a serious point of contention. Feminist economists have identified a number of limits to the 'commodification' of care work, related to the historical labelling of caring and domestic responsibilities as 'private' and 'unproductive'.[10] A salient issue is the relational and affective nature of care work. This kind of work requires emotional investment which is not quantifiable by traditional economic measures.[11] The exchange relation between care giver and care receiver is not easily susceptible to monetary evaluation through which 'productivity' is assessed. Furthermore, the work for profit model does not fit well with the nature of care work. It has been argued that there is little scope for increasing productivity while retaining the quality of care. In the carrying out of care work, it is not possible to substitute capital for labour, or introduce technological innovation to replace human time investment.[12] As a

8 Fudge (n 6), 4.

9 Conaghan (n 7), 56.

10 M. Waring, *If Women Counted* (San Francisco, CA: Harper & Row 1988); K. Rittich, *Recharacterizing Restructuring: Law, Distribution, and Gender in Market Reform* (The Hague: Kluwer Law International 2002), 182ff.

11 A. Hochschild, *The Managed Heart: Commercialization of Human Feeling* (3rd edn, Berkeley, CA: California University Press 2012).

12 Fudge (n 6), 6.

consequence, care workers' wages are continually squeezed, and workers take on the burden of other employer strategies to reduce costs. These strategies are supported by an institutional regime which continues to see care work as low value and 'unproductive'. For example, in the UK the requirement to pay the National Minimum Wage (NMW) under the National Minimum Wage Act and Regulations (NMWR) is currently subject to an exception in respect of hours during which a worker 'by arrangement sleeps at or near a place of work' (Regulation 32 NMWR 2015). The practical effect of this is that care workers who undertake 'sleep-in' shifts can be paid an amount less than the NMW for those hours, apart from for hours when they are 'awake for the purpose of working'. Indeed, in a recent Supreme Court judgment,[13] it was confirmed that any work undertaken during a sleep-in shift (such as decision-making and planning) which is not defined according to a (physical) task is discounted for the purposes of the calculation of the NMW. The division of time in this way is peculiar to care work and reflects the prevailing social and economic assumptions around the lower productivity of this kind of work.[14]

The analysis of the position of care work by feminist scholars has been an important contribution to drawing out the reasons for the continued disadvantages faced by women in the labour market. Feminist scholars have shown how the organization of care work is both constituted by and constituting of capitalist employment relations and the institutions that support it.[15] These constitutive relations operate not just at the local level, but also at the global level through 'global care chains': personal links between people across the globe based on the paid or unpaid work of caring.[16] These transnational processes of the organization of social production have been supported explicitly and implicitly by states keen to move away from public modes of care support. They have also opened up new modes of exploitation and inequality. More than this, the operation of the global regulatory processes around these care chains forces a re-examination of the very epistemology of labour law. Feminist legal scholars who work on global care chains have questioned and challenged the focus on the nation-state as

13 *Royal Mencap Society v Tomlinson-Blake and Shannon v Rampersad and Another* (T/A Clifton House Residential Home) [2021] UKSC 8.

14 D. McCann, 'Temporal Casualisation and "Availability Time": Mencap, Uber and the Framed Flexibility Model' (27 April 2020). Available at SSRN: https://ssrn.com/abstract=3789540 or http://dx.doi.org/10.2139/ssrn.3789540; K. Ewing, 'Tomlinson-Blake in the Supreme Court', UK Labour Law Blog (28 April 2021). Available at: https://uklabourlawblog.com/

15 See S. Fredman, *Women and the Law* (Oxford: Clarendon Press 1997), 413–16 for a discussion of the role of anti-discrimination law in institutionalizing disadvantage.

16 Fudge (n 6), 6.

the appropriate frame of labour law. These networks operate across borders and are able to exploit legislative lacunas in both immigration and labour law which compound the plight of the individuals bound up in these processes. The political economy of care reveals again the importance of gender and social production in understanding problems of social justice and inequality in modern labour markets.

2.2 Failure to reach the mainstream

Despite the shift in the focus of analysis in feminist labour law literature from a concern for the position of women to a more deep and nuanced critique of the gender as tool of enquiry, feminist theorizations have struggled to reach the mainstream of labour law (theory).[17] Certainly, feminist theorizations are viewed as an additional tool in understanding the historical and political context of the formulation of labour market regulation, and the distorted outcomes they produce, but they have not served to supplant the main understanding of labour law as constituted to counteract the commodification of labour and the 'inequality of bargaining power' between employers and employees. As we have seen, this analysis is firmly based in a Marxist understanding of the vulnerabilities faced by workers under a capitalist mode of production, which are perpetuated as a matter of law. A central problem here is the persistence of the perceived dualism between social reproduction on the one hand and industrial production on the other.[18] This dualism has been perpetuated by (early) Marxist-feminist analysis which relied on the understanding 'that women as a group do indeed have a definite relation to the means of production and that this is different from that of men'.[19] Whether or not women participated in wage labour, their exclusive responsibility for 'the production of simple use-values' in the domestic sphere defined their relationship to capital.[20] Hence, on this understanding, issues of gender and social reproduction operate externally to the social justice issues faced by workers in the workplace. Indeed, a traditional understanding of Marx, and one that has not yet been completely supplanted in the field of labour law, is that his focus was squarely on industrial as opposed to domestic production and that he possessed a relative disregard for gender relations.[21] Hence, feminist

[17] Conaghan (n 7), 33.

[18] L. Vogel, 'Forward' in T. Bhattachary (ed) *Social Reproduction Theory: Remapping Class, Recentering Oppression* (London: Pluto Press 2017).

[19] M. Benson, 'The Political Economy of Women's Liberation' (1969) 21 (7) *Monthly Review* 13.

[20] P. Cammack, 'Marx on Social Reproduction' (2020) 28 (2) *Historical Materialism* 1, 2.

[21] Cammack (n 20), 1.

theorizations are either useful in extending Marxist analysis to include this lens, or feminist theorizations have little to say about capitalist relations (and hence labour law theory) in a general sense.

This situation has stifled the feminist contribution to labour law and reduced its influence. There are two responses to this position. The first is to suggest a reading of Marx which does allow for an integration of social reproduction and industrial production. This position has been promoted by the recent work of Cammack, who suggests that Marx was neither blind to gender nor so narrowly focused on industrial production that he rejected the importance of the family and social reproduction to the functioning of the capitalist system and vice versa.[22] According to Cammack, Marx saw capitalist relations of production as fundamentally implicated in these aspects of social life. On this reading, Marx saw the capitalist drive for the production of labour-power as just one further element in its systemic contradictions. At the same time that capitalism needs labour-power, so it remains disinterested in its (social) production, and this leads to practices which threaten accumulation and indeed social reproduction itself. Marx identifies this contradiction in the drive of capital to extend the working day, and suggests that this sets the conditions for the regulation of work:

> By extending the working day … capitalist production, which is essentially the production of surplus-value, the absorption of surplus labour, not only produces a deterioration of human labour-power by robbing it of its normal moral and physical conditions of development and activity, but also produces the premature exhaustion and death of this labour-power itself. It extends the worker's production-time within a given period by shortening his life.[23]

However, the problem with this view for our purposes is that it holds explanatory power as to the operation of capitalist society, but it does not provide a mechanism through which to challenge it. There is the context of the problem of social justice for workers (that everything, including the law, is bound up with the inexorable drive of capitalism in the production of society), but there is no theoretical or epistemological challenge to it. Marx himself was extremely sceptical about the power of the law in overturning

[22] Cammack (n 20), 3.

[23] K. Marx, *Capital: A Critique of Political Economy, Volume One* (tr Ben Fowkes, Middlesex: Penguin 1976 [1867]), 376–7.

the inexorable drive of capitalism, suggesting that social justice could only be achieved through revolution and wider social change.[24]

The second response is to move away from the traditional labour law narrative and to use feminist methodologies not only to study the context of the law, but also to 'destabilize the normative and conceptual infrastructure of the subject'.[25] Just exactly how to do that is difficult given the ambivalence of many feminist scholars towards the transformative potential of the law and scepticism towards 'grand theory'. As Fineman has pointed out, there is the danger that 'the grander the feminist theory, the more it resembles mainstream scholarly format and content'.[26] The power of the law as a 'dominant discourse' drags feminist insights down and feminist sensibilities 'become lost or absorbed into the morass of legal concepts and words'.[27] Once feminist legal theory engages with the mainstream of labour law and theory it 'must adapt to the words and concepts of legal discourse' and this inevitably reduces its power to say anything different or move to protect interests which are not currently protected by the legal status quo.[28] Hence, feminist legal theory loses its guiding light: the insight that law is both a discourse and process of power and the 'neutral' or 'objective' normal created by and enshrined in law are manifestations of power relationships. Social justice for women cannot be created in this environment.

In her early work, Fineman suggested that the limitations of the law and legal discourse for the feminist project determined that feminist legal theory should be developed outside of the constraints of the law. Feminism should remain a political project which served to critique the law but law should never be the 'objective' of feminist theorization as this would 'risk having incompletely developed feminist innovations distorted and appropriated by the institutionalised and intractable dictates of law'.[29] However, her position gradually shifted as she moved to critique the institutionalization of concepts of autonomy and dependence and the foundational conditions of the western social contract from a feminist point of view. Through this critique she moved to reassess the whole way in which personhood is constructed as a matter of (liberal) law through her vulnerability theory. The importance of this theory for the development of the arguments in this book will be discussed in the next section.

---

[24] L. Kutner, 'The Human Rights of Karl Marx' (1979) 55 *North Dakota Law Review* 39, 40.

[25] J. Conaghan (n 3), 100.

[26] M. Fineman, 'Challenging Law, Establishing Difference: The Future of Feminist Legal Scholarship' (1990) 42 *Florida Law Review* 25, 29.

[27] Fineman (n 26), 30.

[28] Fineman (n 26), 30.

[29] Fineman (n 26), 43.

3. Vulnerability theory

Fineman's vulnerability theory arose out of dissatisfaction with the narrative underlying state action in the US. This narrative relied on an extremely individualistic and privatized understanding of state responsibility, heavily weighted in favour of liberty over equality. Under this scheme, individual liberty was understood to mean that individuals must have the autonomy to make choices independent of state interference. Underlying these aims was an idealized understanding of personhood based on rationality, independence, and individual autonomy. Fineman saw that this rhetoric underlies all our economic, legal, and political theories and has pervaded all discussions about the extent and limitation of social welfare. In the legal field, this idea of personhood has informed both the 'subject' of law (to whom law is applied) as well as its outcome (ensuring liberty and autonomy for all).

Fineman saw a number of problems with this scheme for social justice. First, there is a reluctance by the state to deal with or address issues of vulnerability, dependency, and need because these are viewed as externalities or weaknesses which arise in those who do not live up to the ideals of autonomy.[30] Individuals are naturally autonomous, independent, and rational, and the best action of the state is to take no action at all and allow individuals the space to develop their own life projects. Second, 'dependency', need, and vulnerabilities are all socially stigmatized. Policies directed to address 'dependency' or vulnerability thus tend to be either punitive or paternalistic. At its worst, this rhetoric of the 'autonomous liberal subject' has led to herding those who are not viewed as sufficiently capable, independent, and autonomous into 'vulnerable populations' which renders those involved susceptible to stigmatization, monitoring, and supervision.[31]

According to Fineman this model is undesirable and fashioned on unrealistic and unattainable premises. A central problem is the construction of the public/private divide under which dependency is considered to be a private matter. It is the family and not the state or the market which is deemed to have responsibility for the 'inevitable dependent' (the child or other biologically or developmentally dependent person) and the 'derivative dependant' (the care worker or caretaker). The state only steps in when the family fails, and then only providing minimal, grudging, and stigmatized assistance. Fineman agrees with the feminist theorizations which have revealed the falsity of the public/private dichotomy and the revelation that

[30] M. Fineman, *The Autonomy Myth: A Theory of Dependency* (New York: New Press 2005), 34.

[31] M. Fineman, 'Beyond Identities: The Limits of an Antidiscrimination Approach to Equality' (2012) 92 *Boston University Law Review* 1713, 1748.

most things are both public *and* private.[32] At the same time, 'dependency' is deemed to attach only to certain individuals as a result of individual failure. This Fineman identifies as 'puzzling'. She argues that dependency (and later vulnerability), far from being pathological, avoidable, and the result of individual failings, is a natural part of the human condition and 'developmental' in nature. Dependency should be regarded as both universal and inevitable and certainly not deserving of a generalized stigma. Dependency, or 'vulnerability', is much closer to the reality of human existence than the independent autonomous ideal of personhood which informs legal discourse.[33]

From these observations, Fineman manages to cross the divide between the two elements of feminist theory previously viewed as incompatible: the preoccupation with women's experience and the creation of 'grand theory' which reflects feminist aims. Her starting position is the socially embedded nature of law and the problems this creates for those subject to it. This has long been part of the feminist narrative. The difficulty has been how to move from that critique to a deeper engagement with the law without being drawn into its unhelpful and discriminatory narrative. Fineman arguably achieves this by highlighting that the central problem with the law is its incorrect and myopic view of personhood (which does not reflect the experience of women). The law is based on a 'liberal legal subject' which is posited as an autonomous and independent being whose primary demand is for liberty and freedom. This in turn shapes the detail of legal constructions, such as the 'reasonable man', and informs what we consider to be justice. However, we know that this version of justice is very limited, and this can be put down to the exclusion of vulnerability or dependency from our collective legal consciousness. It is only by incorporating the 'messy' aspects of human existence into the law that we can change the way in which society approaches vulnerability and dependency: not as individual problems, but as a natural part of human existence. Once this is accepted, it is possible to build a theory of state responsibility which not only is more effective at reducing inequality but is also closer to the 'truth' of what it means to be human, and why humans should benefit from the law.[34]

Vulnerability theory reflects on the experience of women in accessing the law, and its failure to deal with social reproduction, caring responsibilities, and unpaid work. It also reflects the essentiality of women's experience in relationality and vulnerability. However, in suggesting that vulnerability is *the* truth of the human condition it carries the law beyond a concern just

32 Fineman (n 30), 228.
33 Fineman (n 30), 35.
34 Fineman (n 30), 271.

about women to a concern to all those marginalized by the law. It suggests that replacing the liberal legal subject with the 'vulnerable subject', a legal subject that is primarily defined by vulnerability and need, will engender a disruption of the whole logic of personal responsibility and individual liberty which is a barrier to social justice for all.[35] This will lead to a re-evaluation of the whole social order and lead not only to law but also a society which is built on collective responsibility for ensuring 'resilience'. Vulnerability theory envisages the modification of the social contract. The hope is that the recognition of the collective foundation of human existence will lead to greater collective responsibility and a social justice paradigm which can encompass the whole, and not just part, of society.[36]

4. Vulnerability theory and labour law: positive elements

Vulnerability theory is positive for labour law as it can highlight the failings of current labour law theory. The first area of critique is the failure of current labour law theories to really make a connection between the social and the legal which is helpful for social justice. As explained in Chapter 2, traditional labour law theory recognizes the importance of the social context of law in terms of the systemic effects of capitalism and wider organization of social law. However, it has failed to bring the social to the heart of the law in a number of ways. First, it understands the subject of law as asocial and individualized. Second, rights are understood as bringing individual freedom or emancipation to workers and this freedom or emancipation is viewed as commensurate with the re-establishment of 'humanity' in the Kantian sense. The problem is that law on this scheme has very little fundamental connection with social justice. It is not clear how an individualized asocial view of the law can bring about any equalization of social power. The irony is that labour law becomes an empty shell, subject to an even greater extent to the whims of social power. If the aim of rights is individual freedom, then the argument for rights itself is undermined. Subsequent labour law developments have never been able to resolve these issues, either because they are wedded to an individualistic understanding of rights (human rights and labour law) or they focus on the context rather than the content of the law (feminist legal scholarship).

The second (related) area of critique is the failure of labour law to really focus on the issue of personhood. Personhood is accepted and a given.

35 M. Fineman, 'Vulnerability and Social Justice' (2019) 53 *Valparaiso University Law Review* 341, 342.

36 Fineman (n 35), 368.

Feminist legal scholarship has come the closest to the question of labour law and personhood by showing the difficulties that the law has in dealing with care relationships and relationality. However, issues of identity and personhood have tended to be considered as side issues to the basic inequality of bargaining power and commodification faced by all workers. Identity issues tend to exist in particular silos of equality law. By contrast vulnerability theory suggests that a reconsideration of personhood is fundamental to the operation and effectiveness of labour law. As such, the law can be a force for social justice if it is redesigned to better reflect the reality of personhood.

As well as its general theoretical contribution in challenging the foundational premises of labour law, vulnerability theory also can play a role in practical application to specific areas of the law. Some initial indications of that kind of analysis are provided below.

4.1 Individual employment relations

In applying vulnerability theory to the employment context, it has been argued that the assumption of liberal law that the parties are 'separate, transacting, and contracting individuals, equally capable of agreeing to terms of employment reflecting their respective best interests'[37] is both misleading and divisive. It is misleading because it suggests that employment relationships are 'private' matters, involving individuals free from social, legal, and political constraint. In fact, the employment relationship is imbued with all the assumptions, beliefs, norms, and values governing society as a whole. Law absorbs these norms and values and projects them onto the employment relationship, and thereby acts to constitute as well as modify employer and employee identities. As a result, the employment relationship cannot be seen as a purely 'private' matter. It is constituted by dominant beliefs and assumptions which solidify in state regulation. It is argued that this liberal methodology is extremely damaging to individuals in employment relationships. The liberal assumption of (contractual) equality between parties to employment relationships which informs the regulation of work only serves to reinforce existing distributions of wealth, power, and opportunity. The corollary is that liberal law has failed to respond adequately to issues of subordination and domination in employment relationships and has privileged employer needs over those of employees.[38]

It is suggested on the vulnerability approach, that the liberal subject of law and politics should be replaced by the 'vulnerable subject'.[39] This rejects the

---

[37] Fineman, 'Introducing Vulnerability' in M. Fineman and J.W. Fineman (eds) *Vulnerability and the Legal Organisation of Work* (London: Routledge 2018), 2.

[38] Fineman (n 37), 2.

[39] Fineman (n 30), 267.

notion that individuals are naturally autonomous, rational, and self-sufficient beings. Rather, it suggests that the reality of the human condition is that vulnerability is universal, constant, and inevitable. 'Vulnerability' is inevitable in a biological sense as a result of our corporality. It is also inevitable in a relational sense, given that we are all 'profoundly dependent on others for our physical and psychological well-being'.[40] Vulnerability exists in an institutional sense too. That is, vulnerability is systemic as well as personal.[41] This suggests that although we are all vulnerable, there are certain persons and groups who are particularly vulnerable, and that vulnerability is created as well as ameliorated by societal institutions. The relationship between employees and employers provides one example of a site in which and through which vulnerability is managed and created.[42] It can be a site of vulnerability as a negative experience – a site of injury and harm. However, it can also be a site of vulnerability in the more positive sense, in which work provides the possibility for creativity, human connection, and human flourishing.

This analysis exposes a number of our current labour laws as unnecessarily limited and insufficiently dynamic. Take, for example, employment equality law. This equality law relies on static and historically defined characteristics such as race and sex which have created disadvantage in the labour market. Labour law has stepped in to ensure that employers do not treat employees less favourably because of a particular personal/social characteristic. The vulnerability approach suggests that the current approach to employment equality law will not achieve equality in practice because equality law does not extend to everyone. It only extends to those persons with certain identity characteristics identified in the law.[43] The problem is that privilege is not (solely) distributed along the identity lines suggested in equality law. Deprivation and social disadvantage cut across these lines such that equality law does not address the real problems experienced by labour or their employers. Moreover, equality law is individualistic and relies on empowered individuals to enforce it. It does not recognize the systemic vulnerabilities which affect employees which would prevent such enforcement.

It is further argued on the vulnerability approach that the current equality approach has eclipsed other approaches which might be more successful at achieving equality in practice. It therefore suggests that the structure of equality law needs to be rethought to address a wider range of vulnerabilities.

---

40 J. Herring, 'Defining Vulnerability' in J. Herring (ed) *Vulnerable Adults and the Law* (Oxford: Oxford University Press 2016), 10.

41 M. Fineman, 'The Vulnerable Subject: Anchoring Equality in the Human Condition' (2008) 20 *Yale Journal of Law and Feminism* 1, 11.

42 J. Fineman, 'The Vulnerable Subject at Work: A New Perspective on the Employment-at-will debate' (2013) 43 *Southwestern Law Review* 275, 299.

43 Fineman (n 41), 4–5.

More profoundly, it is suggested that the equality law model has come to dominate the whole of (labour) law. That is, the law is too static and unresponsive to the shifting nature of vulnerabilities to really be a force for achieving justice. The vulnerability approach suggests that both the law and the state should be more responsive to vulnerability.[44] It suggests a valid role for the state in addressing market inequality through protective measures, enhancing arguments for labour law based on this model. This provides new impetus for certain labour laws which have lost out in the marketization of labour law. For example, unfair dismissal law (where it exists) has suffered significant deregulatory pressure in a number of jurisdictions over the law few years. It is viewed as overly protective and an unnecessary restraint on employee and employee autonomy. By contrast, the vulnerability approach has the potential to recognize the value in this kind of law, where it can be shown that vulnerability is experienced in the face of arbitrary decisions by employers.[45]

Vulnerability theory demands that more thought and consideration is given to how vulnerabilities affect labour market participants throughout their life cycle. Workers are seen primarily through the lens of the risks and pressures of human existence, rather than labour market risks per se. For example, it has been argued that labour law has failed to adequately address the lifetime disadvantage suffered by women. Sergeant and Bisom-Rapp identify that despite the fact that women make up nearly half of the workforce in the US, they continue to suffer multiple disadvantages during their working lives which result in significantly poorer outcomes for women in old age than men.[46] The problem has been the lack of a joined-up approach to recognizing those multiple disadvantages and responding to them in law. Policy making has been disjointed and incremental in promoting gender equality as a result of a lack of an overarching narrative to monitor and adjust institutions to ensure persistent disadvantage is eliminated. The authors suggest that vulnerability theory provides such a narrative and instructs policy makers to further strengthen law and policy in light of working women's continued suboptimal experiences.[47]

Indeed, vulnerability theory might be used to suggest that joined-up thinking needs to be applied not just to the measure of labour market

---

[44] Fineman (n 30), 273–4.

[45] J Fineman (n 42), 292.

[46] S. Bisom-Rapp and M. Sargeant, 'Acknowledging but Transcending Gender at Work: applying the model of lifetime disadvantage and vulnerability theory to women's poverty in retirement' in M. Fineman and J. Fineman (eds) *Vulnerability and the Legal Organisation of Work* (London: Routledge 2017), 141.

[47] N. Busby and G. James, *A History of Regulating Working Families: Strains, Stereotypes, Strategies and Solutions* (Oxford: Hart 2020).

disadvantage and the potential effect on the law, but the way in which different laws relate to each other. In vulnerability theory it is accepted that all workers are vulnerable. Such vulnerabilities (illness, incapacity, family commitments) will inevitably mean that workers drop out of the labour law system at some point in their lives. Indeed, all workers retire at some point. If this is the case then it makes sense that the law should be structured in such a way so as to aid transitions not only between jobs, but also between periods of work and non-work. Under vulnerability theory, the aim of legislation is the building of resilience among parties to an employment relationship. This requires that its effectiveness should be judged in terms of its capacity for capability-building among labour market actors. The law should provide 'assets' which allow individuals to survive or recover from the harm or setbacks which inevitably occur over the life course.[48] In order to achieve this for all workers, the relationship between social security legislation and employment legislation needs to be reconsidered.[49] The nature of social 'rights' also needs to be expanded to ensure that even those persons not working have sufficient resources and receive such care to allow them to return to work when personal/social circumstances allow.[50]

4.2 Collective employment relations

The question also arises whether vulnerability theory can be used to embrace and enhance the role of other institutions of value to labour. This is particularly important in the context of the move to view vulnerability as 'potentiality' in vulnerability theory. That is, a recognition of vulnerability as the shared human condition allows us to recognize the needs of others and to recognize that the achievement of justice for one is justice for all.[51] This suggests that solidaristic institutions assume importance as channels for

48 Fineman (n 41), 14.

49 For example, 'workfare' schemes designed to reintroduce individuals to the labour market often involve non-standard work, which itself falls outside some or all labour law rules. The result is that changes in laws on social security which are presented as a way to lessen labour market marginalization may serve only to heighten economic inequality. See C.S. Jydebjerg, 'Vulnerability, Workfare Law and Resilient Social Justice' in M. Fineman and J. Fineman (eds) *Vulnerability and the Legal Organisation of Work* (London: Routledge 2017), 117.

50 This model has been suggested by Alain Supiot in A. Supiot, *Beyond Employment: Changes in Work and the Future of Labour Law in Europe* (Oxford: Oxford University Press 2001), 221.

51 A. Carse, Vulnerability, Agency and Human Flourishing' in C. Taylor and R. Dell'Oro (eds) *Health and Human Flourishing* (Washington, DC: Georgetown University Press 2006), 48.

the potentiality of vulnerability under this new approach.[52] Certainly the value of trade unions has been outlined on a number of occasions in the literature on vulnerability theory.[53] In practical terms, unions can enhance working conditions by negotiating on behalf of workers, promote job protection when jobs are under threat, and provide support for workers in dealing with grievances with their employers both within and outside the court system. Collective bargaining agreements can also serve as a means to equalize pay scales and reduce gender- and race-based pay discrimination.[54] Trade unions can thus be an important way in which worker vulnerability can be recognized its potential be harnessed. This implies that vulnerability theory can not only be a means to enhance legal protection for workers but can also encourage support for institutions which can contribute to worker resilience over the longer term. This analysis is attractive for labour law which has long been concerned with both direct and 'auxiliary' means of ensuring empowerment for workers.[55]

5. Vulnerability theory: negative elements and limitations

One of the major problems with vulnerability theory is that the use of the term vulnerability carries certain negative connotations along the lines of the discourse it tries to escape: a discourse of 'dependency' and 'victimhood'. It has been argued in the literature that vulnerability as human ontology is reductive and is insufficiently connected to positive agency and self-governance.[56] This discourse leads to a paternalistic take on the ways in which to tackle 'vulnerability' and puts too much onus on the state to counteract vulnerability.[57] This is problematic for labour law discourse, given that labour law is so entwined with private law. According to private law, the language of vulnerability is an anathema, making it impossible to cross the private/social law divide. At the same time, the vulnerability narrative

[52] K.V.W Stone, 'Green Shoots in the Labour Market: a cornucopia of social experiments' in M. Fineman and J .W. Fineman (eds) *Vulnerability and the Legal Organisation of Work* (London: Routledge 2017), 54.

[53] R.E. Zietlow, 'The Constitutional Right to Organise' in M. Fineman and J.W. Fineman (eds) *Vulnerability and the Legal Organisation of Work* (London: Routledge 2017).

[54] Zietlow (n 53), 60.

[55] Kahn-Freund outlines a difference between 'regulatory legislation' which lays down rules of employment, and 'auxiliary legislation' which sets the boundaries of trade union action. Kahn-Freund, *Labour and the Law* (London: Stevens 1983), 45.

[56] S. Riley and A. Pele, 'For a Right to Health Beyond Biopolitics: The Politics of Pandemic and the Politics of Life' (2021) *Law Culture and the Humanities* 1, 12.

[57] Riley and Pele (n 56).

runs counter to labour law narratives about the need to equalize social power through collective action. Vulnerability theory understands the need to foster 'resilience' among workers, but resilience and agency comes after the application of the law rather than forming part of our understanding of personhood which informs law's design.

To a certain extent theorists within the vulnerability tradition have sought to address these issues through recognizing vulnerability as a positive trait.[58] While vulnerability may expose us to negative change, it also allows the potential for growth, both personal and institutional.[59] Vulnerability is viewed as 'generative' as it creates in human beings the 'desire to reach out to others, form relationships, and build institutions'.[60] However, quite a lot of work is still required to bridge the connection between vulnerability and resilience, and autonomy and agency. This suggests that a change in language is required if the combination of vulnerability and resilience is to be achieved. In the next section, the language of 'relationality' is explored as a possible alternative to this vulnerability/resilience divide.

Another very worrying feature of vulnerability theory is its willingness to attach vulnerability to inanimate objects, institutions, and even the state. The recognition of institutional vulnerability stems from a desire to contextualize personal vulnerability. That is, personal vulnerability must be seen in the context of the ability of social institutions to respond to individual needs. Further, the recognition of institutional vulnerability forces the realization that institutions are products of society, and hence challenges their separation from the bounds of human existence.[61] As a corollary, social institutions are themselves vulnerable in the wake of market fluctuations, changing international policies, institutional and political compromises, and human prejudice.[62]

On the one hand, this personalization of institutions and their categorization as vulnerable serves useful functions for labour law. First, it enables the role of employer and employee to be viewed as socially constructed. The social construction of those relationships means that law is implicated in *creating* the inequalities and imbalances which exist, rather than merely acting in response to a factual 'truth'. In particular it is recognized that the casting of employees and employers as equals in law does not reflect

58 E. Gilson, 'Vulnerability, Ignorance and Oppression' (2011) 26 (2) *Hypatia* 308, 310; E. Boubil, 'The Ethics of Vulnerability and the Phenomenology of Interdependency' (2018) 49 (3) 183, 184.

59 M. Fineman, '"Elderly" as Vulnerable: Rethinking the Nature of Individual and Societal Responsibility' (2012) 20 *Elder Law Journal* 101, 116.

60 Fineman (n 59), 116.

61 Fineman (n 59), 300.

62 Fineman (n 41), 12.

the differences in their social position, and hence this casting often works to increase rather than reduce social disadvantage.[63] Second, the recognition of employer vulnerability implies an inevitable connection between employer and employee fortunes. Both employers and employees are bound up in the financial and economic system, and hence both need a state response. Of course, the response to employer vulnerability will differ from that in relation to employee vulnerability because the vulnerabilities are qualitatively different. Employers suffer different risks and achieve different rewards. However, state action is empowering for employers just as it is for employees. Law is a major source of resilience, a privilege bestowed on companies in recognition of their particular position.[64] Vulnerability theory challenges the liberal abstractions which dominate the regulation of employment relationships and opens up the space for a greater state responsiveness to both employer and employee needs.

However, assigning vulnerability to companies detracts from moves to ensure a more positive notion of vulnerability as the creation of growth and connectivity between individuals. This is because corporate vulnerability allows vulnerability to be theorized apart from embodiment. This has the potential to undermine the claims under vulnerability theory that there is an intimate connection between embodiment and rationality, embodiment and autonomy, and embodiment and dignity.[65] Companies can achieve vulnerability without *embodied* rationality, autonomy, and dignity. Hence, the potential to read these concepts expansively, beyond the reductive liberal framework, is severely compromised. Companies do not have the corporeal features which imply openness to harm, and correspondingly do not have those features which allow empathy and intimate connections to be forged. The version of vulnerability applied to companies thus appears to be a negative one. This is damaging to the vulnerability project as it suggests that vulnerability is something to be negated and avoided rather than embraced.

Furthermore, it is difficult to see how responses to corporate vulnerability would produce better outcomes for employees than the liberal system of

63 J. Fineman (n 42), 299.

64 J. Fineman, 'A Vulnerability Approach to Private Ordering of Employment' in M. Fineman and J. Fineman (eds) *Vulnerability and the Legal Organisation of Work* (London: Routledge 2017), 29.

65 A. Grear makes a similar claim in relation to human rights. She argues that imbuing corporations with legal personhood, despite their lack of 'embodiment', is one of the reasons why human rights do not function sufficiently well. The implication is that this legal personhood is privileged as a result of the ideology of liberal law. She suggests that, instead, embodied vulnerability should be placed at the heart of the regulation of human rights. See A. Grear, *Redirecting Human Rights: Facing the Challenge of Corporate Humanity* (London: Palgrave Macmillan 2010), 114–16.

law. Certainly, there is a recognition in vulnerability theory that the interests and needs of employers and employees may be different and may contradict each other. However, the solution is to *balance* the needs and interests of the parties to the relationship and 'resolve the contradiction in favour of one or the other'.[66] It has been suggested that the balancing mechanism should be weighted in favour of employees, and this would ensure that the vulnerability approach achieves more favourable outcomes. The 'costs' of employer actions should be viewed more widely, and there should be a recognition of the need to redistribute these costs more fairly to achieve employee resilience. For example, it has been identified that the costs of termination of employment relationships are currently unfairly heaped on individuals and the state. There should be a more balanced approach, whereby the employer should be asked to bear some of the costs of the action of termination. It is suggested that this should be a balancing exercise in recognition of the vulnerability of both employees *and* employers: 'some parity is surely not too much to demand'.[67]

The problem is that the reality of this kind of balancing in the current politico-economic context implies that employer needs win out over those of employees.[68] Employer needs are seen as more pressing, and under the economic efficiency paradigm which dominates the actions of modern neo-liberal states, actions to support companies may also be seen as more efficient than actions to support employees (acting in favour of the employer means that employees will eventually reap the benefits as a result in a raising of living standards as a whole).[69] Indeed, critiques of vulnerability theory identify that the evils that vulnerability theory tries to address – namely, the very individualized understanding of autonomy and the need for independence from the state resulting in negative responses to need – are not evils of liberalism per se. Rather they represent a failure of liberalism to counteract extremist trends towards economism and neo-liberalism. The latter narratives are in fact the most damaging and liberalism can play a role in silencing or modifying them if constructed in a way which better represents human experience.[70]

66 J. Fineman (n 64), 27.

67 Fineman (n 64), 31.

68 S. Garben, 'The Constitutional Imbalance between the "Market" and the "Social" in the European Union' (2017) 13 (1) *European Journal of Constitutional Law* 23.

69 S. Coyle, 'Vulnerability and the Liberal Order' in M. Fineman and A. Greer (eds) *Vulnerability: Reflections on a New Ethical Foundation for Law and Politics* (London: Routledge 2013), 61, 72.

70 L.C. McClain, 'Formative Projects, Formative Influences: Of Martha Albertson Fineman and Feminist, Liberal and Vulnerable Subject' (2018) 67 *Emory Law Journal* 1175.

6. Relationality: agency and social justice in the law

It is argued here that while the methodology of the vulnerability approach is incredibly useful, the focus on 'vulnerability' by itself does not engage a significantly outward, forward-looking, positive notion of personhood. The notion remains individualized and does not represent sufficiently the collectivity of human experience. Furthermore, the evocation of 'institutional vulnerability' serves to undermine the utility of vulnerability theory as this plays into the hands of economic discourses which promote the fragility of markets and the primary need to support their functioning. On this reading, vulnerability theory becomes a balance between competing forces of vulnerability in which the foundational importance of personhood is lost. The centralization of the response to vulnerability in state action is also problematic. This draws the state into the identification of vulnerability or vulnerable persons and aiming to achieve equality or protection rather than on focusing on 'resilience' as suggested on this scheme. Social justice becomes the action of the state on individuals, and this cuts off channels to empowerment.

The question then arises how to combine the insights of vulnerability theory with the traditional concern of labour law with agency and empowerment. It is suggested here that this is possible through adopting a relational approach to personhood. This takes us back to Sinzheimer's understanding of 'Der Mensch in Arbeitsrechts' and the potential of labour law to move away from legal subjectivity based on the atomized independent notion of personhood in civil law. At the same time, it takes us forward. The language of relationality in Sinzheimer's work remains wedded to an understanding of the problem of 'dependence' of individuals in employment relations as a result of their insertion into the capitalist mode of production. This kind of analysis in some ways repeats the negative connotations associated with dependence which vulnerability theory attempts to correct and it also elevates the social relationship of class above all other kinds of 'relationality'. This is problematic for a theory about the complexity of ontology and its meaning. It also tends to negate the value of the law: that real sociality can only be expressed outside of the confines of the law, or that communality can only be expressed through the rejection of capitalism itself. It is argued here that the relational approach, if adopted at the heart of the law, can be a mechanism for the promotion of social justice through labour law (without the wholesale rejection of capitalism). This is achieved through a recognition of the essentiality of collectivity to human existence, the importance of agency even in the context of 'vulnerability', and requiring a rebalancing of labour law towards encouraging relational autonomy.

In many ways, the relational approach aligns with the vulnerability approach. It is couched in a (feminist) contextual understanding of personhood which goes beyond the individuality, independence, and rationality espoused in liberal law and thought. It begins from a recognition of the effects of the asocial and disembodied nature of legal subjectivity on the experience of marginalized groups. Essentially, the abstract and asocial image of persons and personhood leans on the image of White men and serves to exclude women and other social minorities.[71] Women and social minorities are identified with certain physical and social characteristics which mean that they are considered less autonomous or rational and so are exposed to being further marginalized or treated paternalistically.[72] Relational scholars argue that, by contrast, physical and social characteristics must be taken into account as elements of the human legal subject and *constitutive of* their autonomy and rationality. According to Nedelsky, human persons are multidimensional, and cannot be considered apart from their sex, gender, colour, ethnicity, body size, nature, emotions, religion, and so on.[73] Any account which conceptualizes personhood apart from these identity characteristics can only provide a partial account of autonomy and a partial account of rationality.[74] Furthermore, processes of socialization are neglected on the liberal conception of the person. It is argued on the relationality approach that these processes are essential to understanding how individuals make 'autonomous' decisions and whether those decisions are truly autonomous.[75] For example, the decisions of women to be stay-at-home mums and give up their careers, or to apply for less competitive (and less rewarding) jobs, might be considered 'autonomous' on the liberal content neutral account.[76] However, once social norms and 'socialization' are taken into account, it becomes harder to distinguish between genuine 'autonomy' and decisions which are 'forced' upon individuals due to their insertion into a particular social environment.[77]

---

71 Y. Braudo-Bahat, 'Towards a Relational Conceptualization of the Right to Personal Autonomy' (2017) 25 (2) *Journal of Gender, Social Policy and the Law* 111.

72 N. Stoljar, 'Autonomy and the Feminist Intuition' in C. MacKenzie and N. Stoljar (eds) *Relational Autonomy: Feminist Perspectives on Autonomy, Agency and the Social Self* (New York: Oxford University Press 2000), 106.

73 J. Nedelsky, *Law's Relations: A Relational Theory of Self, Autonomy and the Law* (OUP 2011), 158.

74 D.T. Meyers, 'Decentralising Autonomy: Five Faces of Selfhood' in J. Christman and J. Anderson (eds) *Autonomy and the Challenges to Liberalism* (Cambridge: Cambridge University Press 2005), 27, 72.

75 P. Benson, 'Oppressive Socialization' (1991) 17 *Social Theory and Practice* 385.

76 V. Schultz, 'Telling Stories About Women and Work: Judicial Interpretations of Sex Segregation in the Workplace in Title V11 Cases Raising the Lack of Interest Argument' (1990) 103 *Harvard Law Review* 1749.

77 Braudo-Bahat (n 71), 127.

The aim of the relationality approach is to really engage with the relational subject and the sociality and materiality of existence. Contrary to the liberal individualistic approach, the relational conception highlights the relational nature of persons and the development of their identity and autonomy through connections and relationships with others. Individuals are understood to be *constituted* by their interactive relationships with others.[78] This means that 'selves' become who they are – their identities, their capacities, their desires – through the relationships in which they participate.[79] For example, 'autonomy' does not exist for individuals in a way external to their relationships. Rather, persons are embedded in personal and social relationships which either promote or negate their ability to exercise and develop personal autonomy. 'Constructive' relationships are essential to the development of original thinking and creativity. They help to nurture selfhood and self-worth. In turn, that self-worth enhances constructive relationships with others. Constructive relationships and personal autonomy are mutually reinforcing. By contrast, destructive relationships 'limit one's ability to formulate an adequate variety of options, reduce the likelihood of a constructive deliberative process and diminish one's confidence and self-worth'.[80] The question for relational scholars is how to evaluate whether relationships are constructive or destructive and promote interventions which prioritize the former over the latter.

On the relational approach, rationality and autonomy are not given or static. These characteristics emerge through interaction with others, the social environment, and self-reflection. According to Nedelsky, individuals are involved in a 'lifelong dynamic project' of 'finding' their own law.[81] Autonomy is a creative process of self-development and as such is subject to change over time. Autonomy is not binary but can be partial or incomplete or incompletely exercised. This is important for a number of reasons. First, it suggests that creativity is an essential part of autonomy and personhood. It is the human ability to 'act' which both formulates and responds to personal autonomy. Second, individuals who are embedded in destructive relationships may struggle to exercise autonomy, but that does not mean that they can exercise no autonomy at all. Similarly, the existence of constructive relationships is not a guarantee of freedom to pursue a particular life plan. Such constructive relationships may also involve a set of constraints which must be figured into the development of a person's own law. Third, if

78 N. Tuana, 'Viscous Porosity: Witnessing Katrina' in S. Alaimo and S. Hekman (eds) *Material Feminisms* (Bloomington, IN: Indiana University Press 2008), 188.

79 J. Nedelsky (n 73), 4; M. Friedman, 'Relational Autonomy and Individuality' (2013) 63 *University of Toronto Law Journal* 327, 328.

80 Braudo-Bahat (n 71), 133.

81 Nedelsky (n 73), 123.

autonomy can be partial and is built through interactions with others, it follows that autonomy must embed agency in the sense of the possibility for challenge and resistance.[82] The idea that resistance is part of autonomy is potentially empowering for individuals and essential if the law is to embed social justice. It is essential if individuals are able to recognize destructive relationships and seek to escape from or challenge them.

Relationality sets up the imperative for social justice which is necessary for a more responsive law. The liberal legal subject is an 'economic man' – 'a rational self-regarding Hercules'.[83] That version of human nature is a stripped-back and unrepresentative version of what it actually means to be human. This is problematic for law and social justice. If the economic man does encapsulate the true meaning of what it means to be human then we have at the heart of our law a conception of the person who is an 'empathetic, other-regarding weakling': he 'knows everything there is to know about his subjective life, but nothing whatsoever about the subjective life of others'.[84] In that case, there is no role for other-regarding social justice policies which aim towards either recognition or redistribution (or both). Justice is served merely by supporting the interest of the economic man in the 'good life'. Rather, we need a relational concept of personhood because it represents the 'other-regarding' foundation of human nature which sets up the social justice imperative. Reaching out to each other and understanding each other are what make a community and 'without it, we would not crave, much less attain, justice'.[85]

7. Moving forward with relationality

The feminist project is of critical importance if we are to embed social justice in labour law. In a similar way to traditional labour law scholarship, feminist theorizations recognize the centrality of the social, political, and economic environment in both the constitution and the operation of the law. There is an overarching sensitivity to the inequalities and exclusions which are built into the system of capitalism, which are then reinforced through law. This is a problem for all workers, of course, who suffer from an inequality of bargaining power with their employers. However, feminist scholarship recognizes that this is a particular problem for female workers, whose work

[82] Agency can have many meanings. Some feminist scholars suggest that agency is a lesser form of autonomy – the ability to act but without being able to control that action. This is not the sense in which I use it here. See K. Abrams, 'From Autonomy to Agency: Feminist Perspectives on Self-Direction' (1999) 40 *Williams and Mary Law Review* 805.

[83] R.L. West, 'Economic Man and Literary Woman: One Contrast' (1988) 39 *Mercer Law Review* 867, 870.

[84] West (n 83), 870.

[85] West (n 83), 877.

tends to be less valued or not valued at all by the system. Hence, problems emerge for workers, not just as a result of the economic environment, but also the wider social system. That social system is important in terms of the construction of identity which also feeds into worker experience. Without an engagement with identity as part of the human condition then, it will not be possible to understand individual experience at work. More than this, the association of physical and emotional characteristics with the action, constitution, and experience of women is necessarily part of the experience of all workers as people. It is not possible to separate ontology from humanity. This separation is also part of a deliberate political and social mechanism which aims to maintain the status quo (and its inequalities and exclusions).[86]

It follows that we need to engage with the way in which the law and 'humanity' or 'personhood' interact. Fineman identifies the 'liberal legal subject' at the heart of the law as insufficiently reflective of what it actually means to be a person. Legal personhood does not reflect 'humanity' in any real sense. This is of course deliberate: the liberal legal subject reflects a particular construction of 'humanity' which reflects dominant constructions of identity (as male) and the self. This is the 'economic man' which is defined by autonomy, rationality, and independence, and stripped of social context and human ontology. However, this liberal legal subject is not neutral and creates exclusionary effects. In the employment context, this legal subjectivity allows capital to create workers in its own image and promote ideas of freedom, autonomy, and independence which suit its own ends. Hence, greater reference to 'freedom' or 'autonomy' for workers will not bring positive change, without a reconsideration and disruption of these concepts in the first place. Fineman suggests that we need to recognize the 'vulnerability' of workers by the creation of a vulnerable subject of law. This would create a more responsive and socially just response to legal problems.

The vulnerability thesis has its limitations for labour law, particularly because it tends to reinforce ideas of pathological worker dependence at the expense of agency, and also makes insufficient distinction between worker vulnerability and institutional 'vulnerability'. This undermines the importance of the understanding of ontology which is supposedly at the heart of the vulnerable subject. The methodology of inquiry into the 'liberal legal subject' remains important for labour, however. We can use this methodology to consider 'relationality' as the heart of human experience and seek to embed relationality at the heart of legal subjectivity. This is a more positive notion of humanity and a more useful concept in the work context. The next chapters of this book are devoted to a (re)consideration of the relationship between legal personhood and labour law, and the

86 Fineman (n 30), 271.

possibilities of the relational approach. It is hoped that this will 'provide a better framework for identifying what is really at stake in difficult cases and for making judgements about the competing interpretations of rights involved'.[87] Chapter 4 looks at the legal concept of the 'worker' and how this relates to the legal 'person'. Chapter 5 investigates collective rights in labour law and the possibilities of the relational approach in forging a 'collective' subject of law. Chapters 6 and 7 investigate new challenges to labour law in the social/economic/political environment and how far those challenges can be met by a more relational approach to personhood at work.

[87] Nedelsky (n 73), 5; C. MacKenzie, 'Feminist Innovation in Philosophy: Relational Autonomy and Social Justice' (2019) 72 *Women's Studies International Forum* 144.

4

The Worker and the Person

1. Introduction

This book sets out to make two main (and related) claims. The first is that the notion or concept of personhood is essential to understanding the aims and achievement of social justice in labour law. The second is that this conceptualization is dominated by a particular view of personhood based around the liberal legal subject of law: the autonomous, independent, and rational individual. It is argued that this conceptualization is constantly contested and as such modified and reshaped, but it nonetheless endures as the dominant view of personhood at the heart of labour law. It goes without saying that this is not only a *legal* enquiry but is also intensely and necessarily political. The previous chapters have outlined how this liberal legal subject has emerged and its connection to labour law in the abstract sense. This is the liberal subject of civil law from which labour law has never been able to escape. At the same time, labour law theorists have at various times shown themselves open to the critique of this liberal legal subject and have conceived alternative conceptualizations of the 'person' of labour law. Furthermore, alternative conceptualizations of the person which exist outside the mainstream of labour law are also useful in recognizing the limitations of the liberal legal subject and imagining labour law's future.

This chapter moves this project further by investigating the legal person of labour law; namely, the worker/employee. On the face of it, this seems a strange enterprise. The 'worker' or employee of labour law is defined precisely according to antithetical conditions of the liberal legal subject; namely, 'subordination' and 'dependence'. However, as the analysis proceeds, it is possible to see that this subject is shaped by reference to its other; namely, the 'self-employed' person who is assumed to hold all the characteristics of liberal legal rationality. This is problematic for several reasons, and these will be discussed further in this chapter. First, despite the assumptions surrounding self-employed status in terms of its underlying values, in practical terms the experience of self-employment is extremely varied, and its boundaries are poorly defined. Second, there are constant tensions between worker/employee/self-employed status because of their competing ideological underpinnings, and the battleground is intensely political as well as institutionally engrained.[1] As a result, the boundaries of employment status are constantly shifting. Third, the boundaries of employment status are also shifting in response to labour market changes and the practical actions of both employers and employees. The deep battle over employment status in the 'gig' economy is good evidence of these shifting labour market conditions to which the categories of employment status must respond.

This chapter outlines the underlying tensions in employment status which derive from our understandings and commitments to different ideas and versions of personhood. It then proceeds to investigate how these tensions are manifested in the conceptual difficulties and failures around employment status. The chapter will then discuss how the courts have attempted to resolve some of these tensions and some of the reform suggestions in practical terms. The penultimate section outlines an alternative conceptual model for employment status which might address some of the issues raised in this chapter: the softening of the categories and distinctions around employment status through the idea of 'personality in work'. In the final section the limitations of the 'personality in work' model are identified, and an argument made for a more radical solution to the problems of employment status through moving towards a more relational subject of law which incorporates (rather than rejects) dependency.

2. The worker and the liberal legal subject of law

The starting point of this book is that we accept the centrality of the 'liberal legal subject' at the heart of our law. This liberal legal subject complies with the rationalist view of personhood discussed in Chapter 2. The 'person' of the rationalist liberal legal subject is autonomous, independent, and entirely rational. That person is also unencumbered by ontology and is free to act according to 'pure reason'. The ascendance of rationality and autonomy which underscores the liberal legal subject is decidedly Kantian.[2] According to Kant's moral philosophy, the capacity of individuals for moral reason is foundational to personhood. It is this capacity which gives us our

---

1 K. Bales, A. Bogg, and T. Novitz, 'Voice and choice in modern working practices: problems with the Taylor Review' (2018) 47 (1) *Industrial Law Journal* 46, 46; A. Bogg, 'Status update? Why employment status is a political issue' (2019) *Futures of Work*. Available at: https://futuresofwork.co.uk/2019/12/09/status-update-why-employment-status-is-a-political-issue/

2 N. Naffine, *Law's Meaning of Life: Philosophy, Religion, Darwin and the Legal Person* (Oxford: Hart 2009), 64.

essential natures and our inherent dignity. However, although reason defines personhood, it does not lead to dignity unless applied in a certain way. Human beings are under a duty to search for this perfect application of innate reason by attempting to escape 'animality' and focus on the 'establishment of a good will' or set of ends which are the highest practical function of reason.[3] This search starts from innate practical reason which both counsels and commands this action:

> And it is not merely that technically practical reason counsels him to do this as a means to his further purposes (or art); morally practical reason commands it absolutely and makes this end his duty, so that he may be worthy of the humanity that dwells in him.[4]

According to Kant, this process of reason inevitably leads humans to divine the universal truth or universal law of human existence; namely, that individuals must treat other rational beings not as instruments of their own ends, but as beings with their own ends and goals. Reason commands that individuals treat others as autonomous beings with their own life plans because this is consonant with rationality as an end in itself. Humans must be treated as ends and 'never merely as means' to an end because this is to deny their dignity and humanity.[5] To treat people as 'means' rather than 'ends' would be to treat a human being as a 'thing' of lesser moral value which can be traded as any other chattel for a price: 'In the Kingdom of ends everything has either a price or dignity. Humans have dignity.'[6]

This starting point is actually extremely problematic when it comes to thinking about the (moral) status of the 'worker' as a person. This is because Kant tends to portray any dependence or subordination of one individual to another in a negative way. He contrasts autonomous individuals, whose actions are self-willed through the power of reason with individuals in a state of 'heteronomy' who are controlled by or dependent on another. Heteronomous individuals are compromised in terms of their dignity and personhood, and stand outside the moral order of the kingdom of right.[7] The precise application of this position to the status of those in employment relationships is difficult. Kant hardly addresses this precise issue. However,

3 I. Kant, 'Foundations of the Metaphysics of Morals' in L.W. Beck (ed) *Kant Selections* (New York: Macmillan 1988), 261.

4 I. Kant, *Metaphysics of Morals* (tr M. Gregor, Cambridge: Cambridge University Press 1996), 151.

5 I. Kant, *Grounding for the Metaphysics of Morals* (tr J.W. Ellington, Indianapolis, IN: Hackett 1981), 39.

6 Kant (n 5).

7 Naffine (n 2), 145.

Kant did argue that employment contracts concluded on the basis of the ownership of workers must be null and void. Such contracts under which one party completely renounces their freedom for the other's advantage would be 'self-contradictory', since by that contract one person would completely lose their claim to personhood. It appears that Kant envisages not just contracts for 'slavery' within this group, but also contracts under which employees have very little control over their work despite the outward appearance of 'freedom'. Kant does suggest that certain employment contracts could be valid and compatible with the concept of right, but only under certain conditions. An individual might hire himself out 'either as a day labourer or as a subject living on his master's property' as long as the work was 'determined' both as to its kind and its amount.[8] As soon as there was any indeterminacy in the contract either in terms of the quality or quantity of work, there is a risk that 'the subject will in fact have given himself away' as the employer can use their power to subject the individual to their own ends, to which the worker is only a means rather than an end in himself.[9]

Kant's view of the dangers of heteronomy in employment contracts might suggest the need for particular employment regulations which deal with the modification of excessive employer power. In this sense, it is possible for Kant's work to be seen as aligning with the traditional narrative of labour law. Employer control is a threat to worker autonomy and independence and regulation will restore that autonomy and independence to workers. Indeed, Kant's work appears in Sinzheimer's account of the need for labour law. Sinzheimer insisted on a recognition of the injury involved in the subordination of employees to employers (in the context of the subordination of labour to capital).[10] In labour law there was the opportunity to promote the dignity of workers in a Kantian sense. This kind of position has been adopted by more modern labour lawyers to argue that Kant's arguments can be used to justify non-price regulations of the employment contract.[11] For example, Spector argues that Kantian idea of the promotion of equal autonomy could support a number of areas of labour law regulation, including workers' privacy rights, employment anti-discrimination law, and health and safety protection. This could also extend to the prohibition of sexual and moral harassment at work because 'the ban of a non oppressive climate in the workplace is essential to the respect owed to autonomous individuals'.[12]

8 Kant (n 4), 104.

9 Kant (n 4), 104.

10 R. Dukes, 'Constitutionalising Employment Relations: Sinzheimer, Kahn-Freund and the Role of Labour Law' (2008) 35 (3) *Journal of Law and Society* 341, 345.

11 H. Spector, 'Philosophical Foundations of Labor Law' (2005–6) 33 *Florida State University Law Review* 1119, 1146.

12 Spector (n 1), 1146.

However, the argument pursued in this book is that there are distinct problems with using the Kantian scheme as the foundation or justification for labour law. The focus of the argument in this book is the view of personhood which underlies the Kantian scheme is particularly problematic (and indeed Sinzheimer recognizes some of the limitations of the Kantian view of personhood in his later work).[13] Under the Kantian view of the person, autonomy, rationality, and independence (individuality) are prized above all. As outlined previously in this chapter and in Chapter 2, this view of the person has been readily adopted as the prevailing view of personhood at the heart of civil law. However, this is extremely problematic from the point of view of labour and labour law because of the negative view of 'dependence' which is associated with this scheme. Indeed, under the Kantian scheme extreme forms of dependency (heteronomy) are incompatible with personhood altogether. The next section delves into the incorporation of the notion dependency into labour law through employment status, and the difficulties and contradictions this creates.

3. The problem of status and subordination/ dependence

The problem for labour and labour law is that dependency or subordination is central to the understanding of what it means to be a 'worker' or 'employee' and the notion of dependency creates the normative underpinning for the allocation of employment rights.[14] In a descriptive sense, the current model of employee protection in liberal legal systems revolves around the existence of subordinate work as the main characteristic of the employment contract.[15] This is the approach taken by the Court of the Justice of the European Union (CJEU), which understands worker/employee status in terms of (a fairly generous and nuanced notion of) subordination.[16] The notion of

13 H. Sinzheimer, 'Der Mensch im Arbeitsrecht' (1930) in H. Sinzheimer, *Arbeitsrecht und Rechtssoziologie: gesammelte Aufsätze und Reden* (Frankfurt: Europaische Verlagsanstalt 1976), 50.

14 There is a vast literature here. For example, G. Davidov, 'Three Axes of Employment Relationships: A Characterization of Workers in Need of Protection' (2002) 52 *University of Toronto Law Journal* 357; G. Davidov, *A Purposive Approach to Labour Law* (Oxford: Oxford University Press 2016), 35; M. Freedland, *The Personal Employment Contract* (Oxford: Oxford University Press 2003), 23.

15 A. Todoli-Signes, 'The End of the Subordinate Worker? The On-Demand Economy, the Gig Economy and the Need for Protection for Crowdworkers' (2017) 33 (2) *International Journal of Comparative Labour Law and Industrial Relations* 241, 254.

16 Case C-268/99 *Jany and Others* [2001] ECR I-8615, para 34. In the EU context, subordination is compatible with broad notions of control: see N. Kountouris, 'The Concept of "Worker" in European Labour Law' (2018) 47 (2) *Industrial Law Journal* 192.

subordination is also key to UK approaches to employment status, and forms a central point of contention in court decisions. For example, in the case of *Windle*, the employment tribunal (ET) suggested that the individuals were not 'in employment' for the purposes of the Equality Act 2010 because there was a 'lack of direction or subordination'.[17] This finding was upheld in the Court of Appeal, with Underhill LJ stating that it was

> a matter of common sense and common experience that the fact that a person supplying services is only doing so on an assignment by assignment basis may tend to indicate a degree of independence, or lack of subordination, in the relationship whilst at work which is incompatible with employee status even in the extended sense.[18]

Subordination is also key to the 'control test' which underpins employee status in the American legal system.[19]

Importantly, subordination is at the heart of the normative underpinning of employment rights. According to this model, employees under a 'contract of employment' suffer from an imbalance of bargaining power.[20] Labour law is required to step in to equalize that power and negate the effects of dependency on employees.[21] By contrast, self-employed persons working under contracts for services as 'independent contractors' are not in a position of subordination and are not therefore in need of 'protection' by the law. Indeed, they would actively eschew legal intervention because this would potentially affect their autonomy and independence. Rather, self-employed persons operate according to the dictates of the 'just rules of conduct' of the liberal law. They do not expect the law to direct their normal behaviour. Rather, they expect the law only to direct what they can claim and what they must expect to pay if things have gone contrary to expectations.[22] Hence, the comment by the CJEU in *Durre* that those performing an activity 'outside

17 *Windle v Secretary of State for Justice* [2016] EWCA Civ 459, para 17 (citing para 165 of the ET judgment [unreported]).

18 *Windle v Secretary of State for Justice* (n 17), para 23.

19 B. Rogers, 'Employment Rights in the Platform Economy: Getting Back to Basics' (2016) 10 *Harvard Law and Policy Review* 479, 484.

20 This notion of inequality of bargaining power has been more recently extended to intermediate categories of 'worker' status in some countries.

21 Dependence in this context is usually understood as dependence of employees on employers. Of course, it is possible to extend the dependence of employees on employers to incorporate structural dependence (that is, the insertion of workers into capitalist mode of production). See the discussion of Sinzheimer in Chapter 2.

22 O. Kahn-Freund, *Labour and the Law* (London: Stevens 1983), 30.

a relationship of subordination must be classified as an activity pursued in a self-employed category'.[23]

From the point of view of Kantian personhood, this scheme is extremely problematic for workers. In order to be assigned rights, they must prove that they are subordinate to their employers and economically dependent on them.[24] They have to prove that they do not fit the 'ideal' person of liberal law; they are not self-sufficient or independent and their autonomy is limited. In order to gain access to employment rights, workers have to prove that they are not 'persons' (yet). This sets up a number of contradictions and pressures for labour and labour law. First, the stigma attached to dependence means that this concept is constantly contested not just by employers but also by employees or workers. Workers may accept 'self-employed' status on the basis that this appears a more accurate description of their sense of self and empirical experience of work than worker 'dependence'.[25] Employers can latch onto these preferences by structuring employment relationships so that they do not create the appearance of 'dependence' of workers on employers (while at the same time increasing subordination in practice).[26] Second, eschewing dependence in employment relationships contributes to the difficulty of organizing workers around a common interest.[27] This has been seen in the gig economy, where the diversity of working patterns, worker isolation, and employer multiplicity has provided a challenge to unions in accessing this sector.[28] Third, having subordination/dependence at the heart of qualification for labour law is problematic in terms of forging institutional commitment to it, particularly in light of the tendency of many liberal governments to move away from social democratic models of governance

[23] Joined cases C-151/04 and C-152/04 *Durre*, para 31.

[24] It is argued that workers face many kinds of dependency in practice: see G. Davidov, *A Purposive Approach to Labour law* (Oxford: Oxford University Press 2016), 135.

[25] Studies have shown the satisfaction of some gig workers with self-employment status: T. Haipeter and F. Hoose, 'Don't Gig Up: Never!: Country Case Study Report Germany' (May 2023). Available at: www.dontgigup.eu/wp-content/uploads/2023/06/Dontgigupnever_case-studies_GERMANY_ENG.pdf

[26] This is the problem of 'bogus' or 'false' self-employment under which individuals are labelled self-employed but experience low levels of autonomy in practice. See K. Cruz, K. Bales, and T. Sanders, 'False Self-employment, Autonomy and Regulating for Decent Work: Improving Working Conditions in the UK Stripping Industry' (2016) 55 (2) *British Journal of Industrial Relations* 274, 274.

[27] It has been argued that this common interest was present at labour law's inception which gave the system of labour law both collective and individual coherence. See M. Weiss, 'Digitalisation and Basic Principles of Labour Law' in T. Gyulavari and E. Menegatti (eds) *Decent Work in the Digital Age: European and Comparative Perspectives* (Oxford: Hart 2022).

[28] R. Page-Tickell and J. Ritchie, 'Presence and Pretence: Trade Unions and the Gig Economy' in R. Page-Tickell and E. Yerby (eds) *Conflict and Shifting Boundaries in the Gig Economy: An Interdisciplinary Analysis* (Bingley: Emerald 2020).

towards hyper-liberal or neo-liberal models. Under these models of hyper-liberalism, dependency tends to be viewed negatively precisely because it stands in contradistinction to the ideals of autonomy and independence. Hence, in her analysis of the liberal legal system of American individualism, Fineman suggests that:

> The spectre of dependency is incompatible with our beliefs and myths. We venerate the autonomous independent and self-sufficient individual as our ideal. We assume that anyone can cultivate these characteristics, consistent with our belief in the inherent equality of all members of our society, and we stigmatize those who do not.[29]

According to Fineman, under these models of liberalism, there is stigma attached not only to dependence but also to its regulation.[30] This is because individuals are viewed as naturally autonomous, independent, and self-sufficient. Thus, those individuals who have fallen into dependence are those who have failed to take responsibility for their own (economic) welfare. Government intervention will not improve this state of affairs for these individuals but will only increase their reliance on others to meet their own needs. In the American context this leads to arguments against subsidies in the form of social welfare transfers for example. Policy makers arguing for the goals of independence favour the termination of subsidy in order that 'the individual can learn to be self-sufficient'.[31] This kind of rhetoric is certainly present in other liberal legal systems. In the UK, the negative association between state intervention and dependence is pervasive and runs through the whole system of state benefit allocation.[32] It can be seen both in the strict conditionality associated with access to welfare benefits, particularly for those of working age, and in the heavy sanctions attached to failure to meet those requirements.[33]

29 M. Fineman, *The Autonomy Myth: A Theory of Dependency* (New York: The New Press 2004), 34.

30 Fineman's position must be considered in light of the particular political context in which she writes. She describes the foundations and effects of a rather extreme form of liberalism based on American individualism. However, it is possible to argue that the negative view of dependency is common to many if not all forms of liberalism due to its antithetical position in relation to the liberal legal subject.
Fineman (n 29), 50.

31 Fineman (n 29), 49.

32 A. Daguerre, 'The Unemployed and the Moral Case for Benefit Sanctions' (2015) 22 *Journal of Social Security Law* 130.

33 V. Mantouvalou, 'Welfare to Work, Structural Injustice and Human Rights' (2020) *Modern Law Review* 83 (5) 929, 934.

It follows that the association of workers with 'dependence' creates real tensions in the context of promoting employment regulation in these kinds of environment. The policies of (neo-)liberal governments are structured around denying worker 'dependency' and promoting their 'autonomy' at the same time as making access to rights conditional on proving dependency. This creates a deregulatory pressure for labour law. For example, in the UK successive attempts have been made to deregulate working time legislation, on the basis that working time legislation reduces worker autonomy and flexibility, and promotes a culture of dependency. In both 2016 and 2021, Private Members bills[34] were introduced in an attempt to remove working time legislation in the UK, citing the argument that regulation of working time is 'responsible for an enormous lack of productivity and potential in our workforce'.[35] Furthermore, there is constant pressure to limit any (employee) benefits which indicate dependency in the negative sense (while ensuring that workers have to prove 'dependency' to ensure access). This has been the case with the provision of statutory sick pay in the UK. The levels of statutory sick pay in the UK are among the lowest in Europe.[36] The conceptualization of statutory sick pay as a social security benefit rather than a worker 'right' has ensured that statutory sick pay has been neglected as a policy priority and explains the high level of conditionality associated with its access.[37]

There is a further problem for social justice which stems from the association of workers with dependence on this scheme. As we have seen, the state of dependence reduces the worker's connection to the ideal of liberal legal subjectivity or liberal legal 'personhood'. If workers exist in a state of heteronomy, then they cannot also be autonomous

[34] Working Time (Limitation) Bill (HC Bill 46), available at https://bills.parliament.uk/bills/1672 and Working Time and Holiday Pay Bill (unpublished), details available at: https://bills.parliament.uk/bills/2672/publications See also the UK government's recent commitment to (re)introduce rolled-up holiday pay and other deregulatory reforms in relation to holiday pay. See UK Gov, *Retained EU Employment Law: a government response to the consultation on reforms to retained EU employment law and the consultation on calculating holiday entitlement for part-year and irregular hours workers* (8 November 2023).

[35] C. Chope, Hansard 720 18 October 2022, col 546. Available at: https://hansard.parliament.uk/Commons/2022-10-18/debates/8EAA165C-681F-4C1E-B697-B8B36F38AA50/WorkingTimeRegulations(Amendment)?highlight=working%20time#contribution-1BD8FD54-E29D-446E-8118-F2708EE73544

[36] E. Breese, 'How does sick pay in the UK compare to the rest of the world' (April 2023), *Big Issue*. Available at: https://bigissue.com/news/employment/how-does-britains-sick-pay-compare-to-the-rest-of-the-world/

[37] L. Rodgers, 'Going Backwards: Statutory Sick Pay after the pandemic' (12 April 2022), *UK Labour Law Blog*. Available at: https://uklabourlawblog.com/2022/04/12/going-backwards-statutory-sick-pay-after-the-pandemic-by-dr-lisa-rodgers/

or rational. By contrast, their employers, represented by corporations, are much closer to the ideal of the rational, autonomous legal subject. Corporations are autonomous in the sense that they are not under external human control and are therefore free to act according to reason. They are ironically more 'human' than workers under the Kantian scheme because the nature of their disembodiment means that they more easily fit law's representation of the natural living person. Indeed, it has been argued that there is a 'virtually non-existent gap' between the 'human' legal subject and the corporation'.[38] This is problematic for any scheme of law which aims towards social justice for workers, because the scheme starts from corporations enjoying a distinct structural advantage over human beings in the construction of the legal subject. As a result, law 'works in a way which is far more accommodating to corporate persons than human ones'.[39]

The effect of this structural advantage can be seen, for example, in the way that deference is given to employer rationality in the resolution of disputes. Take, for example, unfair dismissal law. Employers are judged against a standard of 'reasonableness' which in practice goes little further than a test of rationality.[40] The courts are asked to judge whether or not the decision made by the employer fell within a band or range of reasonable responses. This band of reasonable responses is judged against the action of the 'hypothetical reasonable employer'. In making this judgment the courts are expressly directed not to substitute their opinion of the reasonableness of the decision for that of the reasonable employer.[41] Essentially the courts are expected to show deference to the expertise of the employer and respect the position and knowledge that the employer had at the time of the dismissal.[42] Interfering in the employer's decision would result in an unjustified curtailment of the autonomy of the employer. This puts the court in a difficult situation in that they have to judge the reasonableness of the decision without being able to reach for their own interpretation of reasonableness[43] and

38 A. Grear, 'Challenging Corporate Legal Humanity: Legal Disembodiment, Embodiment and Human Rights' (2007) 7 (3) *Human Rights Law Review* 511.

39 M. Neocleous, 'Staging Power: Marx, Hobbes and the Personification of Capital' (2004) 14 *Law and Critique* 147, 164.

40 This position is generally but not universally accepted. See D. Cabrelli, 'The Hierarchy of Differing Behavioural Standards of Review in Labour Law' (2011) 40 (2) *Industrial Law Journal* 146 for an alternative opinion.

41 *Iceland Frozen Foods Ltd v Jones* [1983] UKEAT 62_82_2907.

42 A. Baker, 'The "Range of Reasonable Responses" Test: A Poor Substitution for the Statutory Language' (2021) 50 (2) *Industrial Law Journal* 226.

43 Baker (n 42), 263.

have to rely on an industry standard which is necessarily skewed in favour of employers.[44]

In summary, the association of workers with 'dependence' is extremely problematic for workers. This is a negative condition which can run counter to worker experience and (positive) sense of self. It leads to a negative association between labour law and regulation and a preference for employer 'ways of seeing' than that of employees. The next section will drill down more specifically into the determination of status, and the conceptual incoherence which results from the adoption of the employee/dependent versus self-employed/non-dependent model. As it turns out, the notion of subordination/dependence is very bad at capturing actual disadvantage or vulnerability in employment relationships. The suggestion that all employees in subordinate or dependent relationships are to be regarded as disadvantaged or vulnerable, whereas all other workers in non-subordinate or non-dependent personal work relationships are to be regarded as not disadvantaged turns out to be inaccurate and an unhelpful normative ideal for labour law.[45] It follows that the whole scheme of labour law based on worker or employee dependence versus self-employed independence is conceptually suspect and very difficult to apply in practice. The (contested) evolution of this scheme and the conceptual difficulties it creates will be discussed in the next section.

4. Conceptual incoherence of employee/self-employment divide

The binary division between employee and self-employed persons is foundational to the allocation of employment law rights.[46] According to this model, employees under a 'contract of employment' suffer from an imbalance of bargaining power. Labour law is required to equalize that power and negate the effects of dependency on employees. By contrast, self-employed persons working under contracts for services as 'independent contractors' are not in a position of subordination and are not therefore in need of 'protection' by the law. Indeed, they would actively eschew legal intervention because this would potentially affect their autonomy and independence. Rather, self-employed persons operate according to the dictates of the 'just rules

[44] T. Brodtkkorb, 'Employee Misconduct and UK Dismissal Law: Does the Range of Reasonable Responses Test Require Reform?' (2010) 52 (6) *International Journal of Law and Management* 429.

[45] M. Freedland and N. Kountouris, *The Legal Construction of Personal Work Relations* (Oxford: Oxford University Press 2011), 370.

[46] Intermediate categorizations have of course since been added and these will be discussed later.

of conduct' of the liberal law. They do not expect the law to direct their normal behaviour. Rather, they expect the law only to direct what they can claim and what they must expect to pay if things have gone contrary to expectations.[47]

This binary model between employment and self-employment has been extremely enduring and the division is represented to a certain extent in all European labour law systems.[48] As we have seen, this division responds to our deep-seated liberal understandings of personhood and the legitimate scope of legal intervention. Furthermore, this binary division has, over time, become reinforced by a layering of legislative and political compromise which has accepted these baseline assumptions and conditions. For example, the legislative inception of the employee/self-employed divide in the UK can be traced to the development and enactment of the modern welfare state, where it represented or expressed a compromise between the capitalist form of the business enterprise and the new social security system.[49] According to the provisions of the National Insurance Act 1946, workers were classified according to whether they were 'employed earners' or 'working on their own account'. 'Employed earners' were understood as employees under contracts of employment, while individuals working on their own account corresponded to independent contractors working under contracts for services. This division responded to a particular social compromise; namely, 'creating a general, uniform, social security system constructed around the full-time permanent workforce, while nevertheless allowing for the resistance of many professional workers and people in business to being fully absorbed into the state social security system'.[50]

At the same time, the dichotomy is reinforced by the centrality of contractual analysis to labour law. The alignment of employee status with the 'contract of employment' in contradistinction to the 'contract for services' of self-employed status fits nicely into the contractual understanding of the operation of employment relationships. Indeed, this has encouraged an approach whereby personal work relations are viewed as contractually determined and having the character of individual contracts, rather than, say understanding employment relationships as social or collective relationships.[51] However, it is worth noting that this was never a system which was completely conceptually coherent. The distinction between contracts of

47 Kahn-Freund (n 22), 30.

48 Freedland and Kountouris (n 45), 309.

49 S. Deakin, 'Does the Personal Employment Contract Provide a Basis for the Reunification of Employment Law?' (2007) *Industrial Law Journal* 36 (1) 68, 75.

50 M. Freedland, *The Personal Employment Contract* (Oxford: Oxford University Press 2003), 15.

51 Freedland and Kountouris (n 45), 13.

employment and contracts for services was a legislative tool to maintain a particular political compromise; it never did represent an attempt to describe an empirical reality. Concepts such as the 'contract of employment' and the 'contract for services' suggest a unity which has always been false. Even at the height of the Fordist era, the 'standard' contract of employment, based around permanent full-time employment for one employer, remained an ideal type and an aspiration rather than a representation of factual experience. There were always excluded groups as well as difficulties applying the contractual model to relations characterized by hierarchy and organization even for 'employees'.[52]

Likewise, the concept of self-employment and its association with the contract for services lacks conceptual coherence. The self-employed person as the 'other' of employment law is the independent contractor covered by commercial legal norms and whose contracts are judged as transactional.[53] The orthodoxy of the distinction between employees and the self-employed is that self-employed persons carry the financial risk of contractual engagement; for example, in work instability or in the investment of materials. This commercial conceptualization of the self-employed means that for the purposes of academic writing, policy development, and research, the self-employed are grouped together with small and medium-sized enterprises (SMEs) at the far end of the self-employment spectrum.[54] This scheme fits quite nicely with the understanding of the self-employed as possessing the complete or absolute independence of liberal legal personhood. On this model, the self-employed person is represented by the 'economic man' of liberal law in all his abstraction. This is useful to the allocation of employment rights, as the 'self-employed' can be straightforwardly excluded from protection. However, this characterization is problematic both conceptually and empirically. For example, Freedland and Kountouris are sceptical of the claim that self-employment denotes the absence of (relational) dependency. For these authors the binary distinction between contracts of employment and contracts for services is best understood (and only makes sense) as marking out the difference between those work relations which involve one employer over a significant period on the one hand and a more diverse set of work relationships which involve multiple short-term personal work contracts or relations with many different employers or work users over a comparable time period.[55] So self-employment does not represent the absence

52 Deakin (n 49), 75.

53 P. Leighton and M. Wynn, 'Classifying Employment Relationships – More Sliding Doors or a Better Regulatory Framework? (2011) *Industrial Law Journal* 40 (1) 5, 41.

54 Leighton and Wynn (n 53), 41.

55 Freedland and Kountouris (n 45), 343.

of dependency. Rather, for the self-employed, there is a lack of dependence on one particular person during the relevant time frame and hence legislation does not demand or expect that employer offers employment protection or security. Conceptually speaking, self-employment on this model cannot mean the absence of (relational) dependency at all, as this would lead to the very curious and nonsensical proposition that 'persons employed by no others are therefore employed by themselves'.[56]

There is also the very real problem of the 'new' self-employed for the coherence of this scheme. This is a group of individuals identified in the social science literature as adopting the self-employed label, but failing to show those features normally associated with self-employed status:

> The new self-employed do not correspond to the traditional profile of the entrepreneur, given that they work on their own account and without employees, often in professions with only low capital requirements. A growing share of these workers can be found on the one hand in 'modern' service-sector branches (such as education, health, financial and enterprise services) and on the other hand in the construction industry (via outsourcing and contracting). Such types of work are often located at the boundary between self-employment and dependent employment, but mostly they are defined formally as self-employment.[57]

In this literature, it is further argued that the trend towards 'new' self-employment has accelerated as a result of the latest developments in the labour market: on-demand labour, just-in-time labour, crowd work, and work in the sharing or gig economy. These kinds of work depart from the traditional conceptualization of the dependent salaried employment relationship in a number of ways. First, they are often characterized by piecework and are task based. In the case of Amazon Mechanical Turk, for example, 'independent service providers' perform small tasks or fragments of tasks such as proofreading, processing of data, or tagging photographs. Second, the work is completed for a number of different clients, often through an online platform which matches those clients to 'service providers'. In these kinds of situations it can be difficult to identify the 'employer' (the platform is not a legal entity) or 'employment' (the service only involves matching self-employed persons to clients and does

56 Freedland and Kountouris (n 45), 343.

57 K. Schultze Buschoff and C. Schmidt, 'Adapting Labour Law and Social Security to the Needs of the "New Self-Employed" – Comparing the UK, Germany and the Netherlands' (2009) 19 (2) *Journal of European Social Policy* 147, 148.

not have any of the features associated with employment).[58] The problem is, of course, that this kind of work gives rise in practice to precisely the kind of problem which labour law is set up to correct: the 'potential for exploitation in the context of unequal bargaining power between two contracting parties'.[59]

From the above analysis it appears that the categorical and brightline distinction between the self-employed and 'employees' around dependence/subordination is too strong. It is a function of the perpetuation of ideology over common sense and is conceptually difficult.[60] It might be suggested that one means to improve conceptual coherence would be to introduce an intermediate category between employment and self-employment. This might also respond to the very real diversity of contractual types at work in the labour market. In the UK, the intermediate category of 'worker' was introduced in order to address the large and growing gap between those in stable highly paid and well-protected jobs and those at the bottom end of the labour market who suffered from a 'lack of access to fair and basic minimum standards' at work.[61] It was hoped that the introduction of legislation which required individuals only prove 'worker' rather than the more stringent 'employee' status, would extend employment protection to a larger class of workers, and make employment law a more effective tool at reaching those in need of protection. Interestingly, the worker categorization not only stretched the status categorization from the employee end,[62] but also made incursion into the hallowed domain of self-employment status. For example, in the case of *Bates v Winklehof*,[63] Baroness Hale commented that the worker and self-employment categories may overlap; workers must be distinguished 'from *other* self-employed people' in order to determine their employment rights. However, it is to be doubted whether this position really changes the theoretical distinction between self-employed

58 These problems will be discussed further in the next section.

59 V. Daskova, 'Regulating the New Self-Employed in the Uber Economy: What Role for EU Competition Law?' (2018) 19 *German Law Journal* 461, 469. See also A. Todoli-Signes, 'The End of the Subordinate Worker? The On-Demand Economy, the Gig Economy and the Need for Protection for Crowdworkers' (2017) 33 (2) *International Journal of Comparative Labour Law and Industrial Relations* 241, 254.

60 A. Goldin, 'Labour Subordination and the Subjective Weakening of Labour Law' in G. Davidov and B. Langille (eds) *Boundaries and Frontiers of Labour Law* (Oxford: Oxford University Press 2011), 109.

61 Hansard UK, 'National Minimum Wage' HC Vol 314 Col 507 (Margaret Beckett).

62 There has been considerable debate about whether the worker categorization is distinctive from 'employee' status only by degree or also in 'kind'. See J. Prassl, 'Who Is a Worker?' (2017) 133 *Law Quarterly Review* 336.

63 *Bates van Winklehof v Clyde and Co LLP* (2014) 1 WLR 2047, para 39.

and employee/worker status based on autonomy and (in)dependence. In the cases on worker status, it is clear that there is still a need to distinguish workers from the 'genuinely' self-employed on the basis of the absence of entrepreneurial autonomy and freedom.[64]

Indeed, it could not be otherwise. To suggest that a worker (or employee) could be dependent *while at the same time* also autonomous would shake the very foundations of the liberal understandings of the person upon which our system of employment status and rights is based. This would suggest that workers and employees could have a set of aspirations which are distinct and quite possibly contradictory to their employers. The problem is that the worker status categorization speaks most importantly not to some intermediate category of 'semi-dependence' between employees and workers. Rather, the worker category is in reality a category of *hyper-dependence* of an order greater than employees. It is on this basis that the group can be given extra assistance, despite a contractual status akin to self-employment. Thus, in exposing these cases of hyper-dependence, the law has to take into account the embodiment and empirical reality of workers. And where that dependence cannot be explained just by the action of one employer, but by several, this opens questions of structural dependence which are, on the conventional view, best left hidden.

The next section will discuss the problems that the determination of employment status on the basis of the autonomy/dependency divide has brought for the adjudication of employment status in the courts. The section starts with the difficulties that the organization of employment status around dependence/subordination has brought for individuals attempting to access employment rights. In particular it outlines the contradictions and problems from a conceptual and practical point of view of using the contract and contractual terms as determining the content of that employment status. The section then proceeds to outline some of the ways in which the courts have sought to act in a 'purposive' way to ensure that subordination or dependence leads to access to employment rights. The innovative position in the recent case of *Uber* will be discussed in terms of its attempt to suggest that the courts can be involved in an assessment not just of the relationship of dependence between employees and employers, but also a more general assessment of structural dependence of workers/employees as opposed to their employers.

64 A. Bogg and M. Ford, 'The Death of Contract in Determining Employment Status' (2021) *Law Quarterly Review* 137 (Jul) 392, 396.

5. Moving away from liberal legal subjectivity in the courts?

As we have seen, determining access to employment law on the basis of subordination/dependence is problematic because of the negative association between dependence and liberal understandings of personhood, and the conceptual confusion and difficulties this creates in deciding who should be protected under employment law and the extent of protection which should be offered.[65] The idea of dependence at the heart of labour law's conceptualization of the person is also problematic because of the reliance of employment law on contract law for the resolution of disputes in practical terms. This creates a number of contradictions and confusion in employment law disputes and restricts the ability of the courts to really engage with question of dependence, subordination, or vulnerability. The practical consequences and difficulties which arise from tying access to employment rights to employee subordination/dependence will be discussed in this section, and the ways in which the courts have sought to engage with questions of dependence in order to improve individuals' access to employment rights.

Of central concern for this section is the contractual frame of reference for the adjudication of employment rights. At base, a contractual frame of reference does not recognize 'dependence', either individually or structurally/collectively. Contracts are understood as being formed through a meeting of minds which assumes a status equality between the parties. This is why Kant struggled so much with contracts in which there is evidence of 'heteronomy' or inequality between the parties. On Kant's view, such contracts are a nonsense and must be null and void. Furthermore, the law under which contracts are regulated accepts wholeheartedly the understanding of personhood as framed by autonomy, rationality, and independence. The person of contract law is every bit the liberal legal person of rationalist legal thought. This is a problem for labour law because the

[65] A further problem is that subordination and dependence are used simultaneously and understood interchangeably. This tends to lead to a very narrow reading of dependence in employment relationships and what this means for workers. Dependence is understood in terms of economic reliance, and this tends to undervalue the meaning and importance of work for individuals, as well as the connections between worker experience and 'structural' dependence, or the effect of a worker's social position more generally on their experience. These issues will be revisited in the final section of this chapter in which we will consider the potential of alternative conceptualizations of the relationship between labour law and the person.

'contract of employment'[66] or contract for the personal provision of work or services[67] forms the gateway to legal rights. From a conceptual point of view this does not make any sense: the contractual frame of reference, which does not accept dependence, is the starting point for deciding whether there is subordination or dependence on the part of the worker/employee.

There is a further major problem. Contract law is not (or need not be) concerned with questions of 'structural' dependence. Primarily, the law of contracts is concerned with correlative justice between the parties to a contract rather than questions of social or distributive justice. This is not to say that distributive justice concerns cannot be imported into contract law to modify its operation; indeed, this is one way of seeing the role of employment law. Rather, the point is that it is possible to see contract law as having conceptual coherence absent any consideration of distributive justice. Under a system of pure corrective justice, there is no consideration of virtue, just as there is no consideration of need.[68] This is because the question of the 'end' of one person in entering into a contract is not a relevant consideration. Those kinds of consideration are 'internal' to the parties and are not important in the meeting of minds which is at the heart of contract law. All that is important is the *form* of the relationship between the parties; namely, that the parties enter into the relationship on the basis of free choice and reason.[69] If these criteria are satisfied, then there is a valid contract, and the parties are (morally) bound to accept its consequences.

This is extremely problematic from the point of labour law. Many labour lawyers view 'structural' dependence as crucial to understanding the position of workers and the need for their protection. It is the inequality of bargaining power between employees and employers which forms the normative foundation for labour law. The problem is that employment contracts are both a cause and a symptom of that structural dependence.

---

66 In the UK, under section 230 (1) Employment Rights Act 1996 an 'employee' means 'an individual who has entered or works under (or where the employment has ceased worked under) a contract of employment'.

67 In the UK, under section 230 (3) Employment Rights Act 1996:

> 'a worker is an individual who has entered into or works under (or, where the employment has ceased, worked under)—
> (a) a contract of employment, or
> (b) any other contract, whether express or implied and (if it is express) whether oral or in writing, whereby the individual undertakes to do or perform personally any work or services for another party to the contract whose status is not by virtue of the contract that of a client or customer of any profession or business undertaking carried on by the individual'.

68 See the discussion in E. Weinrib, *The Idea of Private Law* (Oxford: Oxford University Press 2012), 57.

69 Weinrib (n 68), 99.

Reliance on the contract of employment leads to a 'refusal to face the main characteristics of all societies, and not least of industrial societies, which is the unequal distribution of power'.[70] Contracts create the appearance of equality while disguising dramatic inequality in practice. Employers can use their social position and superior bargaining power to exploit this position and ensure workers remain in a position of subordination. At the same time, the operation of employment contracts ensures the reinforcement of employer social power over workers as a social class. The law is complicit in this; indeed, it is embedded in the structure of contract law:

> The law does and to some extent must conceal the realities of subordination behind the conceptual screen of contracts considered as concluded between equals. This may partly account for the propensity of lawyers to turn a blind eye to the realities of the distribution of power in society.[71]

The problem for labour law is how to address this problem. Contract law is so embedded in the structure of employment law that it makes it difficult to abandon it altogether. In any event, abandoning the contractual frame altogether does not make sense for workers as the modification of contractual terms and the imposition of implied terms into employment contracts is one of the most effective ways of achieving redress for legal wrongs.[72] Thus there is a constant tension for employees not only in both accepting and denying subordination/dependence but also accepting/denying the contractual frame of reference for employment rights.

This tension plays out in the adjudication of employment status in the courts. On the one hand, the courts are constrained by a contractual framework for allowing individuals access to employment rights. On the other hand, the courts are asked to recognize the 'dependence' of workers which responds to the social reality and social conditioning of employment relationships. These two elements can be difficult to reconcile conceptually and practically. A contractual approach might suggest a technical assessment of the existence of an employment contract which by its nature denies the social reality of the context of employment relationships. A social reality approach suggests that contractual concepts and structures need to be modified, stretched, or even abandoned in order to achieve social justice. Thus, some authors have represented contractual/social reality approaches as

[70] Kahn-Freund (n 22), 15.

[71] Kahn-Freund (n 22), 15.

[72] A. Sanders, 'Fairness in the Contract of Employment' (2017) 46 (4) *Industrial Law Journal* 508.

essentially irreconcilable; there is a choice to be made 'between a contractual approach and one sensitive to the social policy aimed at distinguishing the genuinely independent from the marginal worker'.[73] Fredman suggests that traditionally, courts have preferred a 'contractual and technical' approach to the determination of employment status.[74] She argues that this approach is clear from the imposition of 'mutuality of obligation' as a criteria for individuals to prove employee status in the UK. The imposition of this criteria suggests that the courts are interested only in contractual formalities rather than 'the real social necessities tying … workers inexorably to their employers'.[75]

Certainly, there are examples of the courts adopting a 'social reality' approach in the narrow sense of modifying or stretching contractual tests in order to ensure that individuals get access to employment rights. For example, the courts have introduced the idea of umbrella contracts to allow individuals to join together a series of short-term contracts for the purpose of meeting the continuing of employment requirements for access to employment rights under the Employment Rights Act 1996.[76] The courts have also been willing to interpret the (contractual) tests associated with employee or worker status widely in order to allow individuals access to employment rights.[77] However, in line with Fredman's comment, there remains a great variation in the courts' willingness to stretch or modify contractual tests, with some courts displaying a great reluctance to do so.[78] This has played out, for example, in the interpretation of substitution clauses in employment/worker contracts. In some cases, the existence of a 'genuine' substitution clause has defeated employment (worker) status; in others, the courts have allowed individuals to access employment rights despite the existence (and occasional) exercise of substitution clauses.[79]

---

73 S. Fredman, 'Labour Law in Flux: The Changing Composition of the Workforce' (1997) 26 (4) *Industrial Law Journal* 337, 345.

74 Fredman (n 73), 346.

75 Fredman (n 73), 347.

76 A. Bogg and M. Ford, 'The Death of Contract in Determining Employment Status' (2021) 137 *Law Quarterly Review* 392; D. Brodie, 'Confronting the Gig Economy' (2021) 2 *Juridical Review* 102; J. Atkinson and H. Dhorajiwala, 'The Future of Employment: Purposive Interpretation and the Role of Contract after Uber' (2022) 85 (3) *Modern Law Review* 787; Z. Adams, 'One Step Forward for Employment Status, Still Some Way to Go: The Supreme Court's Decision in *Uber v Aslam* under Scrutiny' (2021) 80 *Cambridge Law Journal* 221.

77 In respect of mutuality of obligations, see *St Ives Plymouth Ltd v Haggerty* UKEAT/0107/08.

78 *Tilson v Alstom Transport* [2011] IRLR 169.

79 *Pimlico Plumbers v Smith* [2018] UKSC 29.

More recently, there has been the suggestion that the social reality approach to employment status is winning out against strict contractual approaches. This follows the case of *Autoclenz* in which the court took a 'purposive' approach to employment status which suggested that the contractual frame could, in some circumstances, be avoided altogether. In the case of *Autoclenz*,[80] the court played down the importance of the wording of contract in the determination of employee status. It stated that the court's role was to determine the 'true agreement' between the parties.[81] In the context of the inequality of bargaining power between employers and employees, that agreement had to be gleaned from 'all the circumstances' of the case, of which the written agreement was only part.[82] Too much focus on the contract had the potential to undermine the statutory purpose of employment protection legislation because employment contracts tended to represent the interests of employers over employees and to obscure the reality of day-to-day working relationships, making it impossible to determine in this way whether an individual was worthy of employment protection or not. Thus, the court was empowered to step behind the contract and look at the reality of the working relationship to determine employment status and rights.

Of itself, this position was not a significant departure from established employment jurisprudence that contractual agreement as to status should not be conclusive as to employment status.[83] More significant has been the way in which *Autoclenz* has been interpreted in the later case of *Uber*.[84] In the *Uber* case, the Supreme Court endorsed the *Autoclenz* approach but suggested that the significance of the approach was not (just) that the court was empowered to look behind the contract in the determination of employment rights. Rather, the significance of the case was the recognition that the 'rights asserted by the Claimants were not contractual rights but were created by legislation'.[85] As employment status was a creature of statute to be *interpreted* by the courts, the key question in status cases was the purpose of the statutory provisions of the Employment Rights Act 1996. In *Uber* this purpose was formulated as the protection of those parties who were vulnerable to contractual exploitation in the work relation. It followed that it might be necessary to abandon the contractual approach to employment rights altogether, given that this could frustrate the statutory purpose behind their introduction:

80 *Autoclenz v Belcher* [2011] UKSC 41.
81 *Autoclenz v Belcher* (n 80), para 88.
82 *Autoclenz v Belcher* (n 80), para 35.
83 *Quashie v Stringfellows Restaurants* [2013] IRLR 99.
84 *Uber BV v Aslam* [2021] UKSC 5.
85 *Uber BV v* Aslam (n 84), para 69.

> The efficacy of such protection would be seriously undermined if the putative employer could by the way in which the relationship is characterised in the written documents undermine, even prima facie, whether or not the other party is to be classified as a worker.[86]

Some authors have attributed great significance to this 'statutory' reading of *Autoclenz* in *Uber.* Bogg and Ford suggest that following *Uber*, the courts are empowered to move from statute to contract rather than the other way around.[87] The courts are empowered to 'examine the degree of control' between employees and employers to *determine* contractual status, rather than determining contractual status and then assessing whether statutory rights should be attached to the relationship.[88] This approach necessarily allows the courts to be more inclusive, and implies a more coherent status regime based on a greater alignment between employee and worker status (based on consideration of subordination or dependency). It will also give the courts a greater freedom to take a broader view of the function and exercise of contractual clauses, allowing those clauses to be disregarded even where they do, to some extent, reflect the operation of the day-to-day employment relationship on the ground.[89]

However, other authors are less convinced by the argument that *Uber* will have 'radical consequences' for employment status. Atkinson and Dhorajiwala argue that *Uber* simply represents a recognition that 'statutory' and 'contractual' (purposive) approaches are at work in the determination of employment status.[90] They suggest that these approaches are mutually reinforcing but apply at different stages of the court's deliberation. The statutory purposive approach applies at the higher level of abstraction in the courts' interpretation of the very broad statutory provisions on employment status. At that level courts are able to determine the kind or type of relationships which should engage employment protection. The contractual analysis is engaged in specific cases, to determine whether contractual documentation reflects the employment relationship, or whether it should be disregarded.[91] Furthermore, Brodie doubts Lord Leggatt's analysis in *Uber* that the rights asserted were in fact statutory rather than contractual at all.[92] Most importantly for our purposes, Adams questions whether the statutory purpose test identified in *Uber* overcomes the problems with the

86 *Uber BV v* Aslam (n 84), para 76.
87 Bogg and Ford (n 76), 394.
88 Bogg and Ford (n 76), 394.
89 Bogg and Ford (n 76), 398.
90 Atkinson and Dhorajiwala (n 76), 797.
91 Atkinson and Dhorajiwala (n 76), 797.
92 D. Brodie, 'Confronting the Gig Economy' (2021) 2 *Juridical Review* 102.

contractual frame of reference for employment rights.[93] The contractual frame of reference suggests that employers can use contracts to create exploitative terms and conditions (despite an appearance of equality). However, if the full implications of structural (rather than individual) dependence of workers on employers are taken into account, the ability to exploit will still be present whether or not a (written) contract exists or not and whatever the 'terms' of its exercise.[94] Exploitation is embedded in the capitalist system of production which creates dependence. This may be reinforced by contractual terms, but it may equally occur 'where there is no express mechanism for specific firms/organizations to exercise control' over workers.[95]

From the previous discussion, it could be argued that progress for workers in access to employment rights lies in a more expansive notion of subordination or dependence which accords with the experiences of workers on the ground. The *Uber* judgment is the start of this process. It allows judges to use arguments around the statutory purpose of employment rights to defeat narrow technical judgments around the particular contractual form expected of a worker or employee and to consider the various manifestations of control that arise in employment relationships. It is possible that this will allow a greater number of individuals to fall within the scope of employment rights. The more nuanced approach to dependence might also lead the way to a greater consideration of the wider 'dependence' of workers in employment relationships; for example, by giving weight to the psychological implications and manifestations of employer control. However, it has already been questioned whether this judgment will really engage with the most important forms of dependence which lie behind the whole system of power relations in employment relationships; namely, the pre-contractual dependence which is part and parcel of the insertion of those relationships into the capitalist mode of production. Furthermore, it does not get to grips with the whole problematic of dependence from the point of view of liberal political and legal systems. In those systems the negative association of law and dependence creates a downward pressure on employment rights and reinforces the ability of companies to avoid legal liability through declassification/misclassification and so on. The next section engages with these issues to suggest that an alternative conceptualization of personhood is required for workers if we are to move forward.

93 Adams (n 76), 221.
94 Adams (n 76), 224.
95 Adams (n 76), 225.

6. The idea of personality in work

This section discusses an alternative conceptualization of personhood for workers introduced by Freedland and Kountouris. They suggest that there should be a normative shift from considerations of subordination or dependence to the more positive notion of 'personality in work'. The final section will introduce a second alternative: moving from subordination or dependence to 'relationality'.

Freedland and Kountouris reject the traditional normative basis of employment law based on the idea of 'redressing [of] the inequality of bargaining power as between employer and employee under the contract for subordinate employment'.[96] They argue that this normative basis is flawed because contracts of employment no longer demarcate those in need of protection in employment relationships (as indicated by 'inequality of bargaining power'). This contractual status does not indicate 'dependency' or 'subordination' in the way envisaged on the traditional model. Indeed, Freedland and Kountouris suggest that it is possible envisage situations where there is 'subordinate' employment under a contract or employment but no discernible inequality of bargaining power between the parties.[97] They also argue that the contractual model is outdated as a way of measuring subordination or dependency as it is based on assumptions of bilateral connections between employers and employees which no longer fit the dominant labour market model. As a result, labour law is insufficiently inclusive and an amendment to its normative basis is required.[98]

In order to correct the insufficiently inclusive nature of the 'contract of employment' as a model through which subordination is judged, Freedland and Kountouris suggest that a broader notion of the 'personal work relation' should be adopted. This notion considers the relevant connections between the parties without giving a privileged position to formal bilateral relations (for example, the 'contract of employment').[99] The domain of personal work relations should be considered as a 'family of relations' rather than as a 'set of concentric circles expanding outwards from a core consisting of the contract of employment'.[100] In order to address the flawed focus on 'subordination' as the generic locator of inequality of bargaining power, the authors suggest that we should focus on a set of 'positive' claims which workers have to certain kinds of treatment. These claims, they suggest, 'underlie the notion

[96] Freedland and Kountouris (n 45), 370.
[97] Freedland and Kountouris (n 45), 370.
[98] Freedland and Kountouris (n 45), 360.
[99] Freedland and Kountouris (n 45), 369.
[100] Freedland and Kountouris (n 45), 434.

of inequality of bargaining power in subordinate work relations, and 'extend in some measure to all personal work relations or profiles'.[101] These claims can be encapsulated by the idea of 'personality in work', and that notion can itself be broken down into the ideas of respect for 'dignity', 'capability' and 'stability'.[102] This move away from subordination to 'personality' in work will allow us to 'depart from the typological separation between dependence and autonomy' and 'to recognize a more homogenous regime for the regulation of personal work relationships'.[103]

In making an assessment of Freedland and Kountouris' work from the point of view of the arguments pursued in this chapter, it is possible to see some broad lines of agreement. Certainly, the difficulties with the 'contract of employment' as the conceptual heart of employment regulation is a common reference point, and particularly the connection between the contract of employment and the notion of 'subordination'. It is also interesting that Freedland and Kountouris recognize the false dichotomy between autonomy and dependence.[104] However, the argument pursued here is that Freedland and Kountouris' scheme is insufficiently ambitious as a critique to allow us to move beyond contract, subordination, and the false dichotomy that exists between autonomy and dependence. At best, Freedland and Kountouris' work is useful as support for the proposition of the Supreme Court in *Uber* that courts are able to use the broad classificatory aims of employment statutes to identify the normative importance of 'dependency' or 'vulnerability', and then move to see how far the internal structure of a particular employment relationship reveals these characteristics (without strict reference to the written documentation).[105] There are two main reasons for this. First, Freedland and Kountouris do not seek to underline the problematic with the *principle* of subordination as the regulating feature of employment relations. Rather, they seek to explain this principle in more nuanced and positive terms. Second, in explaining 'personality in work' as the new basis for the conceptual foundation of employment rights, they rely on well-trodden liberal understandings of notions of 'autonomy' and 'dependence'. For example, dignity is conceived of as a 'conceptual amalgam' between personal autonomy and equality, with autonomy encompassing 'both the ability to take decisions about the life to pursue and the possibility of doing so in the absence of any undue constraints'.[106] The requirements of capability and stability are also shaped by this commitment to worker 'autonomy'.

101 Freedland and Kountouris (n 45), 371.
102 Freedland and Kountouris (n 45), 340.
103 Freedland and Kountouris (n 45), 371.
104 Freedland and Kountouris (n 45), 371.
105 Also suggested by Atkinson and Dhorajiwala (n 76), 796.
106 Freedland and Kountouris (n 45), 374.

Finally, in Freedland and Kountouris' work, there is a distinct separation between individual contracting and collective regulation in the sphere of labour or employment law. The authors are careful to point out that the idea of the legal construction of personal work relations is not 'co-extensive' with 'the whole field of labour or employment' in the sense that it does not embrace the collective regulation.[107] Likewise, the normative idea of personality in work is not intended to 'function as a rationale for labour or employment law as a whole'.[108] Rather they suggest that the idea of personal work relations and personality at work could be seen as part of a scheme of the fair mutualization of risks which could be used conceptually to 'safeguard' the conceptual link between the individual and collective aspects of labour law. On our analysis, this misses a trick. It is precisely the liberal preoccupation with defining autonomy and dignity of the person in ways which do not suggest collective value which creates the underlying but artificial disconnect between the 'individual' and civil society. It is only when we start to see personhood itself in more relational or collective terms that there will be any opportunity to address Freedland the Kountouris' anxiety about the 'supplanting, which is implicit in our work, of the classical rationale for labour and employment law and the corresponding weakening of the bond between the individual and collective in labour law'.[109]

7. Conclusions: moving towards relationality

This book is sympathetic to Freedland and Kountouris' analysis of the problematic of subordination as the defining feature of the employment relationship. However, it is suggested here that it is not the *lack* of dependence of employees/workers, or the failure of the contract to recognize dependence in the right way which is the real problem. Rather, the problem is the failure of the liberal legal subject to recognize dependency as part of the human condition. As we are 'relational beings', dependency is part of who we are. It follows that 'dependency' is a poor mechanism for deciding when to allocate employment rights. The existence of 'dependence' does not indicate that a person is in need of protection because all humans are dependent in some ways or other. Dependency is an omnipresent condition of humanity. At the same time, failing to allocate rights on the basis of an absence of dependence does not make any sense at all. This absence of dependence does not reflect social reality; it reflects only a contractual construction which can be made

107 Freedland and Kountouris (n 45), 439.

108 Freedland and Kountouris (n 45), 439.

109 Freedland and Kountouris (n 45), 439.

(often but not always) to deny a particular social reality, and hence the existence of dependence as part of the human condition.

It is argued here that for a more positive construction of the worker condition based on their humanity, it is necessary to move away from subordination *and* liberal notions of autonomy, rationality, and independence. This is not because we need to deny that 'dependence' and 'subordination' exist, but rather we need to accept that these notions are bound up with worker 'autonomy' and work experience. Dependency cannot be replaced by positive notions of worker claims as suggested by Freedland and Kountouris. Rather, dependency must be accepted *as part of* those worker claims. In doing so, we recognize that the contractual structure of an employment relationship is less important than its reality, and we recognize that employment rights are themselves positive claims which enable individuals to construct their own 'relational' autonomous experience. The outcome of abandoning subordination is a more expansive regime of employment protection.

Interestingly, a group of labour lawyers recently proposed removing subordination from the core definition of employment status as part of the development of the *Manifesto for Labour Law* project, commissioned by the Labour government.[110] In the publication *Rolling Out the Manifesto for Labour Law*, the group proposed amalgamating the 'employee' and 'worker' status categories to produce a new definition of employment status defined according to 'engagement rather than the 'contract of employment' or 'dependence'. The group suggested replacing section 230 (1) Employment Rights Act as follows:

> In this Act, 'employee' or 'worker' means an individual who:
>
> a. Seeks to be engaged by another to provide labour.
> b. Is engaged by another to provide labour.
> c. Where the employment has ceased was engaged by another to provide labour.
> d. Is not genuinely operating a business on his or her own account.[111]

The group argued that removing the requirement of the existence of mutual obligations of a contractual character in order to prove employment status and abolishing the need for 'control' or 'subordination' in order to prove

[110] K. Ewing, J. Hendy, and C. Jones, *Manifesto for Labour Law* (Liverpool: Institute of Employment Rights 2016).

[111] K. Ewing, J. Hendy, and C. Jones, *Rolling Out the Manifesto for Labour Law* (Liverspool: Institute of Employment Rights 2018), 36–7.

employment status would greatly increase the scope of employment rights.[112] It would mean that there was less scope for misclassification by employers and ensure that only those running a genuine business on their own account would be excluded. They also suggested amending the burden of proof such that any person providing labour to another would be assumed to fall within the definition unless proven otherwise. This argument supports the claim in this book that it is possible to imagine a future in which workers do not have to prove (contractual) subordination, and that this future would bring labour law closer to its social justice aims.

112 Ewing, Hendy, and Jones (n 110), 37.

5

Relationality and Collective Personhood

1. Introduction

As we saw in the previous chapter, the 'worker' stands as a contrary figure when it comes to legal personhood. On the one hand, the 'person' of labour law is foregrounded by common or civil law understandings of legal subjectivity based on autonomy, rationality, and independence. These features are a precondition for the entry of workers into contractual relations with their employers and govern the operation of those relations. On the other hand, statutory recognition of the employment relationship seeks to correct some of the failings of the common law for workers, and in doing so appears to adopt a different (but contradictory) understanding of worker status and personhood. Individuals gain access to employment rights through proving an element of 'dependence' or 'subordination' vis-à-vis their employers. It is this subordination which justifies the state stepping in to regulate the employment relation in the worker's favour. To some degree, it is possible to accept this distinction in the context of a strict separation of contractual and statutory rights. The person of contract is distinct from the person of employment, and this speaks to different regimes of regulation. However, this regime starts to break down in the messy world of the adjudication of employment rights, which are necessarily a mixture of common law and statute. In the UK, statutory employment rights require workers to show a contractual relationship with their employer as well as dependence as a feature of that contract. Thus, workers have to be simultaneously 'dependent' and 'independent', 'autonomous' and 'subordinate', show 'rationality' but also the compromise of rationality through employer control.

These features are contradictory under individualistic narratives of personhood. Indeed, while autonomy, independence, and rationality are viewed as constitutive of selfhood, dependence and heteronomy indicate lesser states of being, or that personhood is yet to be achieved. In the UK and American context, these understandings of personhood have been instrumental in demonizing 'dependence' and categorizing dependence as a lack of 'responsibility'.[1] Furthermore, under these narratives, 'dependence' itself is viewed in individual terms. Dependence represents individual failure to reach the heights of autonomy, rationality, or independence. Employment relationships are viewed as correlative power relations between a worker/employee on the one hand, and the employer on the other. There are two main problems with this. First, companies (as a result of their disembodied artificial nature) are much more able to show the features of autonomy, independence, and rationality required of the liberal legal subject than embodied natural persons. Hence, individualized views of autonomy, relationality, and dependence tend to elevate the status of companies over individuals and lead to deference to employers in the adjudication of employment rights. Second, this view of dependence totally neglects the wider social context in which employment relations operate. This neglect of context means that employment rights are (at best) insufficiently protective of workers and (at worst) serve to reinforce existing power patterns rather than challenge them.[2]

This chapter takes forward the debate by considering the impact of narratives of personhood on the design and operation of collective rights. It is argued that our failure to incorporate collective experience into our understandings of the worker/person seriously limits our ability to promote (collective) justice for workers. Section 2 engages with the distinction between individualism on the one hand and collectivism on the other. It is argued in this section that these elements have tended to become severed from each other, and that this has been to the detriment of both collective and individual rights. Section 3 discusses traditional collectivist approaches and their relationship to the law. Section 4 deals with the position of collective rights on the individualist/collectivist divide. The chapter ends with a reflection on the value of attempting to erode the individualist/collectivist distinction identified in the chapter, by more completely engaging with collective or relational views of personhood.

1 See M. Fineman, *The Autonomy Myth: A Theory of Dependency* (New York: The New Press 2004), 9, and the discussion on dependency in Chapter 4.

2 Z. Adams, 'Legal Mobilizations, Trade Unions and Radical Social Change: A Case Study of the IWGB' (2023) 52 (2) *Industrial Law Journal* 560.

2. Individualism, collectivism, and the problem of personhood

The central question to be addressed in this chapter is whether moving beyond individual employment rights and embracing collective rights allows us to promote the importance of relational or collective aspects of personhood for labour. This could be a 'way in' to rethinking personhood as a matter of labour law and the relationship between the worker and the person. However, as straightforward as this question appears, it turns out that this enquiry is fraught with difficulty. A central problem is that this question necessitates an engagement with two ideological traditions; namely, individualism and collectivism. These ideological traditions often stand in tension with each other, both theoretically and politically. This section discusses the problems with the ideological separation of individualism and collectivism, and the implications for thinking about personhood (for labour). The next section discusses the evolution of collectivism and its relationship with the law. The final section investigates the possibilities for combining these different theoretical and political traditions in labour law. In particular it discusses Sinzheimer's ideas around the collective experience of workers as part and parcel of personhood and the feminist take on the relationality of persons as central to the understanding of personhood and rights.

Broadly speaking, 'individualism' champions the priority of 'persons' as the normative ethical foundation of rights and politics.[3] While a commitment to 'individualism' does not presuppose a commitment to any particular political tradition, it sits easily and relatively comfortably within the liberal political tradition which has been central in informing the design of modern Western systems of rights (including 'human' rights). Liberalism is rooted in a commitment to liberty or autonomy. More precisely, liberals give central political place to individual autonomy rather than the liberty of society or the state (albeit that individual liberty may have to be restricted in some circumstances to ensure mutual recognition of equal liberties and opportunities for others).[4] Liberals see individuals as entitled to govern their lives, and to make important life choices for themselves. Indeed, the securing of a moral space within which individuals are free to pursue their own projects is, for these theorists, the chief point of thinking in terms of rights.[5]

3 M. Sandel, 'The Procedural Republic and the Unencumbered Self' in S. Avineri and A. de Shalit (eds) *Communitarianism and Individualism* (Oxford: Oxford University Press 1992).

4 J. Donnelly, *Universal Human Rights in Theory and Practice* (2nd edn, London: Cornell University Press 2003), 47.

5 P. Jones *Rights: Issues in Political Theory* (Basingstoke: Palgrave 1994), 122.

By contrast, collectivism refers to a belief in the importance of collective solidarity and action for the achievement of social and economic goals, and tends to be sceptical of the ascendency of personal liberty in (neo)-liberal thought.[6] For example, Lord Wedderburn suggests that the 'individualist' policies of 1980s Britain were extremely damaging as they were based on the understanding of the moral ascendancy of personal liberty over collective solidarity.[7] He argued that these policies followed the Hayekian view that an employee's freedom depends on choice between employers, and that depends on a competitive market.[8] According to Hayek, the pressures of organized groups such as trade unions distort that market and interfere with personal liberty. Trade unions act to coerce individual workers, upset the market, depress real wages, and increase unemployment, and hence make everyone worse off.[9] On this view, any 'privileges' granted to trade unions in the law must be curtailed, and all relevant freedoms (for example, freedom of association) reconsidered so as to sterilize them against collectivism.[10]

In the labour sphere, collectivism tends to involve the promotion of representative trade unions in the workplace and a commitment to their 'autonomy'.[11] This autonomy is understood as both inward- and outward-facing. Trade unions should have the ability to determine their own affairs without (excessive) state interference.[12] More than this, they should take an active role in workplace management with the aim of the 'joint regulation of working life'.[13] This requires trade union autonomy not only in the negative sense, but also in the positive sense of having agency to really support workers in the workplace. It is the common belief of collectivist scholars that an enhanced role for trade unions and the opportunity for trade unions to be more involved in the 'regulation' of working life will bring benefits for workers.[14] Collective action is seen as an efficient way in which to assuage the conflict between management and labour, and the best means

6 B. Creighton, 'A Retreat from Individualism? The Fair Work Act 2009 and the Re-Collectivisation of Australian Labour Law' (2011) 40 *Industrial Law Journal* 116.

7 Lord Wedderburn, 'Freedom of Association and Philosophies of Labour Law' (1989) *Industrial Law Journal* 1, 22.

8 For the Hayekian view, see: F.A. Hayek, *The Constitution of Liberty* (London: Routledge 2006), 238.

9 Hayek (n 8), 239.

10 See the discussion in F.A. Hayek, *Law, Legislation and Liberty* (London: Taylor and Francis 1982), 293.

11 B. Simpson, 'Freedom of Association and the Right to Organise: The Failure of an Individual Rights Strategy' (1995) 24 (3) *Industrial Law Journal* 235, 249.

12 B. Simpson, 'Individualism versus Collectivism: An Evaluation of Section 14 of the Trade Union Reform and Employment Rights Act 1993' (1993) 22 *Industrial Law Journal* 181.

13 Simpson (n 11), 249.

14 Simpson (n 11), 249.

of securing for workers improved terms and conditions of employment.[15] This has often been associated with a wider political and social agenda concerned with constitutional reform and building a stronger social and political system as a whole.[16]

On the individualist position, there is a strong vein of scholarship which attaches moral significance to 'personhood' which in turn justifies the allocation of rights. In this regard the work of Kant has been extremely influential. On the Kantian tradition, autonomy has normative significance in the establishment of rights because it is a central feature of personhood. Autonomy is a distinctively human capacity and of distinct moral significance. Individuals have rights to basic freedoms because their nature as autonomous beings must be respected. Very many liberal theorists can be located in this tradition, even though they might have significantly different accounts of the content and form of rights that people have.[17] Moreover, the development of the theoretical foundation of human rights has been strongly influenced by this seminal connection between rights on the one hand and personhood on the other. Indeed, human rights have been theorized as 'natural rights' in the sense that they are held simply by virtue of being a person (human being).[18] They are also 'natural' in the sense that they are possessed by individuals whether or not they are embodied in positive law.[19] Human rights have particular characteristics which are determined by their foundation in human nature. They are equal rights, in the sense that each human has the same rights as every other human. They are also inalienable: it is impossible to lose human rights once they have been allocated, given that it is impossible to stop being human no matter how badly a person is treated or behaves.[20] Finally, human rights are universal and 'general', rather than specific.[21] Human rights extend to all human beings irrespective of their assignment or belonging to particular groups or their involvement in particular relationships.

On the individualist tradition then, the nature of 'personhood' is of central theoretical importance and the connections between personhood and the

15 P. Selnick, *Law Society and Industrial Justice* (New York: Russell Sage Foundation 1969), 32.

16 Lord Wedderburn (n 7), 1.

17 C. Taylor, 'Atomism' in *Philosophical Papers* (Cambridge: Cambridge University Press 1985); J. Rawls *A Theory of Justice* (1st edn, Oxford: Oxford University Press 1971). Of course, there are alternative approaches to this even among liberal scholars which will be discussed more fully in later sections of this chapter.

18 J. Donnelly, 'Human Rights as Natural Rights' (1982) 4 (3) *Human Rights Quarterly* 391, 391.

19 P. Jones, *Rights: Issues in Political Theory* (Basingstoke: Palgrave 1994), 98.

20 J. Donnelly, *Universal Human Rights in Theory and Practice* (2nd edn, New York: Cornell University Press 2003), 10.

21 H.L.A. Hart, 'Are There any Natural Rights?' in A. Quinton (eds) *Political Philosophy* (Oxford: Oxford University Press 1967), 60.

law can be neatly and logically pieced together to form a coherent system of law (and politics). By contrast, the connection between collectivism and legal personhood is more obscure for a number of reasons. First, there is a strong vein of collectivist scholarship which is sceptical of the need for law (at all) in the regulation of industrial relations. This is connected to the historical experience of trade unions operating 'outside' of the law, and the radical orientation of this scholarship which tends to reject state-sanctioned legal rules as inimical to worker aims.[22] This means that legal personhood, viewed as the cornerstone of liberal legal (individual) rights, is not of central concern. Second, the focus of collectivist scholarship tends to be on practical outcomes for workers and political change. This means that even where there is an acceptance of the utility of the law, this utility tends to be viewed according to its instrumentality in effecting political change.[23] The values embedded in (liberal) law thus are of lesser importance compared with the outcomes of the broader radical political agenda and social strategy, and ensuring improved terms and conditions for workers in practice.[24] While it is clear (to individualists) that individual rights further the aims of individualism, it is not always clear that collective rights further the aims of collectivism.[25]

Third, the promotion of rights poses difficulties for collectivist scholars precisely because of the primacy of individualist approaches and the difficulties of assigning personhood to collective entities. On the one hand, it is possible for groups to rely on arguments for self-determination or autonomy which are similar to arguments for individual autonomy or self-determination. Assertions of group autonomy might focus on the distinct identity of the collective group which others must respect, or that self-determination is essential to the well-being of its members.[26] However, tensions develop between the individualist normative foundations of liberal and human rights, and the assertion of collective rights.[27] At a fundamental level, collective or 'group' rights can appear to be contrary to (or even undermine) the central normative foundations of human rights.[28] Such group rights cannot be universal because they can only

22 F. Fox Piven and R. Cloward, *Poor People's Movements, Why They Succeed, How They Fail* (New York: Vintage 2012).

23 Adams (n 2), 564.

24 Adams (n 2), 564.

25 B. Simpson (n 11), 249.

26 Jones (n 19), 186.

27 P. Dodh, 'Globalisation and Human Rights in India: A Communitarian and Multicultural Perspective' (2020) 20 (4) *World Affairs* 44; N. Stammers, *Human Rights and Social Change* (London: Pluto Press 2009).

28 Donnelly (n 18), 11.

belong to members of a particular group. They are not 'equal' because they rely on group membership.[29] Furthermore, the identity of those groups worthy of protection can be problematic. Human beings are easily individuated, but the identity of groups as distinct entities worthy of protection can be more difficult to pin down.[30] In the labour context this is assuaged by the formal recognition of 'trade union' status, but it tends to result in legal rules which are antithetical to the recognition of 'new' trade unions and new forms of trade unionism.[31] It can also mean that the admissibility criteria for raising trade union claims are excessively stringent or that the admissibility of such claims is too quickly rejected by the courts.[32] Also problematic is the potential conflict between the recognition of 'collective' rights on the one hand and 'individual' rights on the other. There are concerns that a commitment to collective rights can undermine individual rights. These concerns arise in the context of the over inclusiveness of the group, such that a group's right might extend to curtailing the rights of individuals in the name of some group purpose or forcing individuals into particular courses of action (for example, compelling union membership).[33] These concerns also arise in terms of the exclusiveness of group action. The expulsion of certain trade union members has been challenged in the past on the grounds that it did not respect those members' freedom (of expression).[34] In that sense trade union 'autonomy' can appear to conflict with individual autonomy in a zero-sum game.

It is possible then that this interaction has prevented labour lawyers from reflecting fully on the flaws of individualist notions of personhood and the opportunities of more relational or group/collective approaches. In this section, the relationship between collectivism and personhood will be explored in further detail, beginning with a brief exposition of the relationship between the collectivist tradition and the law (in the UK), and moving on to explore the relationship between collectivist scholarship and human rights, and the potential implications for labour law and personhood.

---

[29] J. Nickel, *Making Sense of Human Rights* (2nd edn, Oxford: Blackwell 2009), 161.

[30] Jones (n 19), 186.

[31] A. Bertolini and R. Dukes, 'Trade Unions and Platform Workers in the UK: Worker Representation in the Shadow of the Law' (2021) 50 (4) *Industrial Law Journal* 662, 677.

[32] K. Ewing and J. Hendy QC, 'The Strasbourg Court Treats Trade Unionists with Contempt: *Svenska Transportarbetareförbundet and Seko v Sweden*' (2017) *Industrial Law Journal* 46 (3) 435.

[33] P. Jones (n 19), 186.

[34] *Associated Society of Locomotive Engineers and Firemen v United Kingdom* [2007] IRLR 361.

3. Collectivism beyond the law

In Kahn-Freund's traditional narrative of labour law, there is an understanding that individual rights for workers by themselves are not sufficient to address the imbalance of bargaining power between workers and their employers. This is because the difference in bargaining power is created and sustained by the structures of contract which are embedded in the inherently unequal social and economic system of capitalism. Kahn-Freund recognized the 'fiction' of the contract of employment which disguised social inequality behind contractual equality; contractual power is also social power.[35] Workers therefore need to build their own social power to counteract and respond to the social power imposed on them by employers (and that of 'organized labour'). According to Kahn-Freund, individual rights must be supplemented by the 'countervailing power of trade unions and of organised workers asserted through consultation and negotiation with the employer and ultimately through withholding labour'.[36] While legal rights can fulfil important functions in the sphere of labour relations, they are secondary to the impact of the spontaneous (non-legal) actions of trade unions to balance that of management.[37]

Kahn-Freund saw an exemplar of this kind of spontaneous trade union action in the British system of industrial relations in existence at his time of writing. He named this system 'collective laissez faire' in recognition of the 'retreat of law from industrial relations and of industrial relations from the law'.[38] Empirically, this was a system defined by a relatively low incidence of 'regulatory law' or individual employment rights. It was also a system in which, for historical reasons, the regulation of collective bargaining through 'auxiliary law' was also limited in volume and non-intrusive in nature.[39] In the most part that law acted only to remove legal obstacles to the smooth progression of the autonomous self-governance of industry. Kahn-Freund was so impressed with the operation of this system of industrial relations that he moved from an empirical observation of the British system to the promotion of a particular collectivist ideology based on a minimum of legal intervention in either the individual or collective labour relation. More than this, collective laissez faire as ideology meant a rejection of legal guarantees by collective bargaining partners and an insistence on the autonomy of industrial forces from 'interference' by the state. This particular collectivist

35 O. Kahn-Freund, *Labour and the Law* (London: Stevens 1983), 24.

36 Kahn-Freund (n 35), 20.

37 Kahn-Freund (n 35), 19.

38 O. Kahn-Freund, *Selected Writings* (London: Stevens 1978), 50.

39 R. Dukes, 'Constitutionalizing Employment Relations: Sinzheimer, Kahn-Freund and the Role of Labour Law' (2008) 35 (3) *Journal of Law and Society* 341, 354.

ideology has been very influential and is often the starting point for the discussion of 'collectivism', in the UK and beyond.[40]

However, this inherited collectivist ideology is problematic for our enquiry. On a practical level, collective laissez faire never provided a strong explanation of British industrial relations. On closer examination, the British system of industrial relations did not in fact operate in the absence of the law. Rather, legislative intervention was 'geared towards encouraging the establishment and maintenance of autonomous regulatory and dispute mechanisms'.[41] There was a particular kind of legislative and political support for collective bargaining and action rather than no support at all. Furthermore, collectivist scholarship related to the collective laissez faire ideal of non-intervention quickly became outdated. Collective laissez faire as an ideal of non-intervention was tied to a particular historical, social, and political compromise. That compromise was gradually eroded by a number of political and social factors, not least the advent of the significant statutory regulation of individual terms and conditions of employment from the late 1960s onwards. Even Kahn-Freund sought to distance himself from the ideology in later years. Attempts to promote the collectivist instinct continued to face difficulty long after because these attempts were viewed as anti-liberal or anti-law.[42] As a result, more recent attempts to revive the collectivist instinct have sought to promote the utility of legal mobilizations for collectivist strategies and the theoretical coincidence between 'individualism' and 'collectivism' in both theoretical and practical terms.[43]

Collectivism tends to adopt a dismissive approach to legal personhood or does not consider legal personhood as worth of attention at all. Marxist understandings of legal form have been very influential in this regard. On this understanding, law must be considered in the context of the social system within which it operates; namely, capitalism.[44] The law develops according to social practices which further capitalist relations of production. In turn, capitalist relations shape the legitimacy of the law and the social practices

[40] Lord Wedderburn, 'Otto Kahn-Freund and British Labour Law' in Lord Wedderburn, R. Lewis, and J. Clark (eds) *Labour Law and Industrial Relations: Building on Kahn-Freund* (Oxford: Clarendon Press 1983).

[41] Dukes (n 39), 342.

[42] Lord Wedderburn, *Labour and the Law* (Middlesex: Penguin 1986), 68. Here Wedderburn describes the threat that the then Conservative government saw in collectivism and their opposition to it: 'For the first time in a century, therefore, labour law policy is directed not towards amendment or reform of the collective bargaining system … It points in a different direction. It does not accept the legitimacy of "collective labour power" in the labour market.'

[43] A. Bogg, 'Individualism and Collectivism in Collective Labour Law' (2017) 46 (1) *Industrial Law Journal* 72.

[44] E. Pashukanis, *Law and Marxism: A General Theory* (London: Pluto Press 1987).

which operate within and around it. The 'equality' of commodity production and exchange which is essential to the function of capitalism becomes embedded as a social practice and is legitimized through law. The 'idea' of the (legal) person as free and equal is part of this system. People come to see themselves as equals with an equal capacity to act autonomously because of the social practices of exchange which are supported and promoted by the state (through legal rules). This idea of the autonomy and equality of the (legal) person serves state ends because it allows the state to escape the social context of the law and, ultimately, to disappear from view. The state only addresses individuals in their abstract capacity as 'equals' and supports their freedom to act as equals towards each other. It has no regard for, and does not need to have regard for, the social context in which individuals operate. Of course, this is inherently contradictory as the state must simultaneously stand outside the social system in order to legitimize its action (in the promotion of freedom and equality between individuals), while at the same acting to reproduce those social practices upon which society and the capitalist system depends. Most importantly, the law's presupposition of a particular kind of legal subject necessarily obscures the fundamental inequalities which exist in capitalist societies as a result of the exclusion of the majority of the population from access to the means of production. The law based on equality leads to inequalities in practice. For Kahn-Freund then, discussion of individual autonomy or 'dignity' is only interesting in terms of the political outcomes of collective bargaining and the value of those outcomes for workers as a matter of social justice:

> By bargaining collectively with management, organised labour seeks to give effect to its legitimate expectations that wages, and other conditions of work, should be such as to guarantee a stable and adequate form of existence and as to be compatible with the physical integrity and *moral dignity* of the individual, and also that jobs should be reasonably secure. This definition is not intended to be exhaustive. It is intended to indicate (and this is important for the law) that the principal interest of management in collective bargaining has always been the maintenance of industrial peace over a given area and period, and that the principal interest of labour has always been the creation and the maintenance of certain standards over a given area and period, standards of distribution of work, of rewards, and of stability of employment.[45]

Furthermore, many collectivist scholars with radical inclination have tended to use the arguments around the abstract and astructural nature of legal

[45] Kahn-Freund (n 35), 69.

personhood to support their rejection of the utility of the law in effecting social change. If the law is based on an ideal of individual freedom and equality which is not determined by social structures, this undermines the idea that structural change is necessary in order to improve the lives of individuals. Indeed, framing a social problem (for example, the inequality of bargaining power between workers and employers) as a legal problem would tend to obscure its very foundations in the socio-economic system.[46] A collective problem becomes an (exceptional) individual one. The legal framing of a social problem also restricts the range of solutions available. Legal solutions only address the narrow way in which a problem is legally framed, rather than the broader structural problem they express. At best, engagement with the law is unlikely to lead to radical social change. At worst, engagement with the law actually undermines solidarity and the very possibility of radical change through turning collective experience into a set of (unconnected) individual issues and the transformative potential of social solutions into rarefied and individualized legal solutions which cut off opportunities for future political action.[47]

This line of collectivist scholarship may be contrasted with other collectivist scholars who suggest that utilizing the law can bring strategic benefits for radical actors despite its (inherent) limitations.[48] The argument here is that the law can have 'radiating' or 'indirect' effects on attempts to mobilize workers and politicize their claims.[49] Framing political demands in legal terms can increase the legitimacy of the claims of marginalized groups and can increase the urgency of dealing with those demands (for example, in the context of threats of legal action). The development of a legal narrative can be useful in building solidarity, and particular legal actions can provide a focal point for campaigning for broader political and social change. This kind of strategic orientation towards the law has arguably informed recent commitments to legal activism among the 'new' trade unions.[50]

Indeed, even at the time of Kahn-Freund's deepest commitment to collective laissez faire, he identified the strategic importance of the common

46 R. Knox, 'Law, Neoliberalism and the Constitution of Political Subjectivity: The Case of Organised Labour' in H. Brabazon (ed) *Neoliberal Legality* (Oxford: Routledge 2016); R. Knox, 'A Marxist Approach to *RMT v The United Kingdom*' in D. Gonzalez-Salzberg and L. Hodson (eds) *Research Methods in Human Rights Law: Beyond the Traditional Paradigm* (Oxford: Routledge 2019).

47 Adams (n 2), 264.

48 T. Colling, 'Court in a Trap? Legal Mobilisation by Trade Unions in the United Kingdom' (2009) No 91 *Warwick Papers in Industrial Relations*; D. NeJaime, 'Winning Through Losing' (2011) 96 *Iowa Law Review Bulletin* 61.

49 Adams (n 2), 565.

50 Adams (n 2), 566.

law and the law of contract in achieving the goals of labour. That is, in order for the system of collective laissez faire to work, there needed to be a 'mechanism by which a set of primarily extra-legal norms could be transposed into existing legal forms and structures both in a theoretical and practical sense'.[51] Labour relations required the 'cornerstone' of the contract of employment to make the system work.[52] This involved a 'difficult concession' on the part of Kahn-Freund, given his awareness of the normative problems with the contract of employment and its enforcement through the common law.[53] On the one hand, the common law or freedom of contract was important to individuals as it ensured the absence of coercion and the avoidance of serfdom. It was also important in the 'protection of the individual against superior social forces', including trade unions.[54] However, the contract as a normative foundation was troubling as it tended to hide social inequalities as well as reinforce those social inequalities because it 'imports a set of hierarchical norms, about discipline and obedience and loyalty, redolent of master-servant relations'.[55] Ultimately, however, he saw those normative concerns as beyond challenge and beyond reach. They were labour law's reality. A more fruitful focus was ensuring the development of collective labour relations and systems of collective bargaining (and worker-protective labour legislation at the outer boundaries of collective labour law).

The result of the uneasy relationship between collectivism and the law is a lack of engagement among many collectivist scholars with the problematic of legal subjectivity and, importantly, a failure to consider alternatives to the particular form of legal personhood which underscores the capital-supporting function of liberal law. It is argued in this book that, rather than being inimical to social justice, engagement with legal personhood is essential to it. This book is sympathetic to collectivist scholarship which argues for the need to engage with the legal system to achieve reform which supports the value of collectivism and collective action (in the achievement of individual goals).[56] However, this book suggests that an engagement with

51 M. Freedland, 'Otto Kahn-Freund, the Contract of Employment and the Autonomy of Labour Law' in A. Bogg, C. Costello, A.C.L. Davies, and J. Prassl (eds) *The Autonomy of Labour Law* (Oxford: Hart 2015), 29.

52 O. Kahn-Freund, 'Legal Framework' in A. Flanders and H. Clegg (eds) *The System of Industrial Relations in Great Britain* (Oxford: Basil Blackwell 1954).

53 Freedland (n 51), 28.

54 O. Kahn-Freund, 'Labour Law' reprinted in O. Kahn-Freund, *Selected Writings* (London: Stevens 1978), 36.

55 Freedland (n 51), 53.

56 For further exposition of the engagement of collectivist scholars with law and legal reform, see A. Bogg, 'The Hero's Journey: Lord Wedderburn and the "Political Constitution" of Labour Law' (2015) 44 (3) *Industrial Law Journal* 229 and the discussion in the next section.

legal *form* is an important part of that process. We need to delve into the structures of the law and legal personhood, and consider the adoption of a more collective or relational approach at this level. This will allow for the promotion of social justice (through rights). The next section will consider how a commitment to collective 'rights' could form a foundation for this approach. The final section considers more radical normative adjustments towards the collective subject of labour law.

4. The promotion of collective rights and implications for personhood

As we have seen in the previous section, the historical scepticism of the labour movement towards the law and legal rights has weakened as a result of the strategic importance of the law in the achievement of social goals. Likewise, many scholars of labour law have promoted the value of rights, and particularly 'collective' rights in allowing trade unions to achieve representative status and act in the interest of workers to improve their terms and conditions.[57] The scheme of justification used in the promotion of those rights is interesting. Some scholars have sought to justify those rights according to 'values of collectivism'.[58] According to Simpson's view, any 'serious' legislative strategy must focus on legal support for the 'joint' regulation of working life through collective bargaining.[59] Only measures which show a 'belief in the benefits of joint regulation will give the law any real role in supporting not just the empty shell of individual freedom of association, but the potential for workers to exercise a real influence over their working lives through collective action'.[60] At times this necessarily involves the promotion of 'collective' *rather* than individual rights; at others, a recognition of the collective dimension of individual rights in order to 'promote the role of representative trade unions in the workplace' and the 'joint regulation of working life'.[61] Simpson's strategy emphasizes the complex and nuanced nature of collective rights and the need to promote them in all their dimensions (which differ from the dimensions of individual rights). First there should be greater provision for trade unions as rights holders. Unions as well as individual workers should be given legal support for their activities, rather than just individual workers. Second, the substantive content of rights should support unions' right to organize, and that substantive right should

[57] Lord J. Hendy and K. Ewing, *Reconstruction after the Crisis: A Manifesto for Collective Bargaining* (Liverpool: Institute of Employment Rights 2013).

[58] B. Simpson (n 11), 251.

[59] Simpson (n 11), 249.

[60] Simpson (n 11), 250.

[61] Simpson (n 11), 249.

be interpreted robustly. Third, collective remedies should be promoted to compensate trade unions where those unions suffer losses (separate from the losses suffered by individuals).

The problem with this kind of analysis is that it can be viewed as anti-liberal or anti-rights. For example, some collectivist scholars have sought to argue that 'positive' freedom of association (the right *to* associate) should be given superior protection to 'negative' freedom of association (the right not to associate or undertake certain forms of trade union action). The argument proceeds that 'negative' forms of freedom of association undermine 'the strongest forms of trade union success'.[62] However, this kind of argument has become increasingly outdated and politically unpalatable. While such arguments are possible under social democratic forms of government, they are not compatible with the neo-liberal emphasis on strong forms of negative freedom of association and enabling positive freedom of association only as desired by individual workers.[63] As a result, there has been an emphasis in the literature on the promotion of the full range of collective rights and their compatibility with individual rights. One stream of this literature focuses on the value of collective rights in promoting individual autonomy. This argument is driven by the 'humanistic' principle espoused by liberal writers such as Finnis and Raz; namely, that in the design of rights it is individual well-being which is of fundamental concern.[64] The promotion of collective institutions and collective rights can fulfil that principle and it is, or should be, the 'primal aspiration of collective activity'.[65]

This view is potentially progressive in terms of the argument in this book. It moves us into the realm of communitarian liberalism which understands the social context of autonomy and 'rights'.[66] For example, on Raz's view, the general culture and structure of society is important in that it creates the possibility and viability of personal autonomy. An autonomous life can only be lived in the context of shared institutions, and an autonomous life is essential element of a good life.[67] As a result, the state has an active role to play in the promotion of 'autonomy' through laws and policies which

62 Simpson (n 11), 236.

63 B. Rogers, 'Three Concepts of Workplace Freedom of Association' (2016) *Berkeley Journal of Employment and Labor Law* 37 (2) 177. Rogers argues that the neo-liberal concept of freedom of association is now ascendant in US law.

64 Bogg (n 43), 74.

65 B. Langille, 'The Freedom of Association Mess and How We Got into it and How We Can Get out of it' (2009) 54 *McGill Law Journal* 177, 188.

66 M. Moore, 'Liberalism, Communitarianism and the Politics of Identity' in T. Christiano and J. Christman, *Contemporary Debates in Political Philosophy* (Oxford: Wiley-Blackwell 2009), 322.

67 J. Raz, *The Morality of Freedom* (Oxford: Clarendon Press 1986), 216.

are geared towards a particular good – autonomy. If collective organization promotes that autonomy, then it should be promoted and encouraged. This is useful because it creates a strong argument for the promotion of collective rights. However, it is limited in that it suggests that collective rights should only be pursued as far as they are coincident with individual autonomy rights. Where collective rights are 'in conflict with the dignitarian rights and economic opportunities of workers' they should be interpreted narrowly, qualified, or abandoned altogether.[68] The problem with this approach is that, while it may be aimed at a better 'balance' between individual and collective rights, the continued primacy of personal autonomy at work in this approach means that there is little defence against the erosion of collective rights in the name of individual liberty. The normative moral ascendancy of individual autonomy (over collective autonomy) is maintained.

The mutual compatibility between collective and individual rights is also recognized in the argument that individual rights uphold and shape collective rights. Lord Wedderburn argued that it is possible to build a collective right to associate out of the 'bricks' of individual employment rights.[69] The problem is that these individual rights are vulnerable to erosion and attack as a result of their weak normative foundations (from a liberal rights point of view). The foundation of these rights lies in the value of positive freedom of association and the promotion of the collective interest. As we have seen, on dominant political understandings of rights, positive freedom of association does not hold greater normative power than the negative freedoms which the individual rights are designed to restrict. Indeed, the 'collective interest' can be seen to undermine private 'autonomy' and freedom of contract. Hence, in the adjudication of these rights, the courts have tended to restrict the scope of these rights, and so weaken their collective value.[70] For example, the recent case of *Kostal*[71] in the UK Supreme Court was concerned with section 145B Trade Union and Labour Relations (Consolidation) Act 1992, which deals with financial inducements by employers related to collective bargaining.[72] It confers an (individual) right on a worker who is a member of a recognized trade union (or one seeking recognition), not to be subject to such inducements where the aim of those inducements is to persuade the worker to give up trade union representation. This individual right has

[68] S. White, 'Freedom of Association and the Right to Exclude' (1997) 5 *Journal of Political Philosophy* 373, 384.

[69] Lord Wedderburn, 'Industrial Relations and the Courts' (1980) 9 *Industrial Law Journal* 65, 85.

[70] D. Brodie, 'Collectivism in Labour Law: Only by Exception' (2022) 5 (2) *Industrial Law Journal* 464, 471.

[71] *Kostal v Dunkley* [2021] UKSC 47.

[72] [2021] UKSC 47.

important implications for collective bargaining and representation because in principle it prevents an employer circumventing collective procedures and making offers directly to workers – a practice which undermines the power and authority of collective representation in workplaces. This right was enacted in the wake of the *Wilson and Palmer* litigation at the European Court of Human Rights (ECtHR), where it was found that the UK government fell foul of its obligations under Article 11 to protect the collective interests of workers by permitting employers to offer inducements to workers to avoid collective bargaining and collective representation.[73]

In the *Kostal* case, the employer tabled a pay offer to the representative trade union (Unite). This pay offer was put to a ballot of trade union members. As a result of the ballot the pay offer was rejected. Soon afterwards, the employer made the same pay offer directly to their employees even though the procedure laid down in the recognition agreement had not been exhausted. The employer made a further offer the following month to those who had not accepted the original offer. The employment tribunal found the employer to be in breach of section 145B. It highlighted the employer's apparent lack of respect for collective bargaining and the collective interests of the employees. The employer lost its appeal in the Employment Appeal Tribunal (EAT), but then appealed further to the Court of Appeal. The Court of Appeal adopted a narrow interpretation of section 145B, restricting its application to situations where there is a permanent surrender of collective bargaining in relation to a term or terms of a collective agreement (as in *Wilson and Palmer*). This restrictive reading was deemed necessary to ensure that trade unions did not acquire a 'veto' over 'even the most minor changes in terms and conditions of employment',[74] and that the autonomy of individuals and employers to bargain individually was not unduly circumscribed. Although the Supreme Court found in favour of the claimants, it was also careful to restrict the applicability of section 145B to avoid an 'effective veto' by trade unions over employer changes to individual terms and conditions of employment.[75]

The problem arises that there is insufficient normative link between individual rights and collective interests to form an effective set of collective 'rights' in this way. Trade union 'autonomy' is deemed a threat to individual autonomy in the determination of terms and conditions of employment. Individual autonomy is served by bargaining with employers, with the

73 *Wilson and Palmer v United Kingdom* [2002] ECHR 552.

74 *Kostal v Dunkley* [2019] EWCA Civ 1009, para 40.

75 A. Bogg and K. Ewing, 'Collective Bargaining and Individual Contracts' in '*Kostal UK Limited v Dunkley:* A Wilson and Palmer for the Twenty-First Century?' (2020) *Industrial Law Journal* 49 (3) 430.

'collective agreement as a mere appendage of individual relationships'.[76] Academic commentary has emphasized the undesirable nature of this balance, which comes down to the failure to recognize the value of collective interest *from the point of view of personhood*:

> Thus the thesis just sketched about the social conditions of freedom is based on the notion, first, that developed freedom requires a certain understanding of self, one in which the aspirations to autonomy and self-direction become conceivable; and second, that this self-understanding is not something we can sustain on our own, but that our identity is always partly defined in conversation with others or through the common understanding which underlies the practices of our society. The thesis is that the identity of the autonomous, self-determining individual requires a social matrix, one for instance which through a series of practices recognizes the right to autonomous decision and which calls for the individual having a voice in deliberation about public action.[77]

It appears that the failure to recognize the importance of the social dimensions of autonomy undermines not only collective but also individual freedoms. This can be seen in the *Deliveroo* series of judgments in the UK. The *Deliveroo*[78] case centred on an attempt by the Independent Union of Great Britain (IWGB) to gain statutory recognition for the purposes of collective bargaining. In order to access the recognition procedure, it was necessary for the IWGB to show that the food delivery drivers concerned were 'workers' under section 296 Trade Union Labour Relations (Consolidation) Act 1992 ('TULRCA'). The case was heard first by the Central Arbitration Committee (CAC), which concluded that the individuals were not workers. It based this decision on the right of substitution in the delivery drivers' contracts, which it found inconsistent with personal service and therefore worker status. The IWGB sought judicial review of the decision in the High Court on the basis that 'worker' status should be interpreted broadly to ensure UK compliance with the freedom of association provisions under Article 11 European Convention on Human Rights (ECHR) (which states that 'everyone' has the right to freedom of association, 'including the right

[76] Per the Chief Justice in *McGavin Toastmaster Ltd v Ainscough* [1976] 1 SCR 718, 719.

[77] Taylor (n 17), 209.

[78] In the Central Arbitration Committee (CAC): *IWGB v Deliveroo T/A Deliveroo*, TUR1/985 (2016) (CAC); in the High Court: *R (The IWGB v Central Arbitration Committee)* [2018] EWHC 3342; in the Court of Appeal: *IWGB v CAC and others* [2021] EWCA Civ 952; in the Supreme Court: *IWGB v CAC and others* [2023] UKSC 43.

to form and join trade unions for the protection of their interests'). This argument was rejected in the High Court and the Court of Appeal.

The Court of Appeal agreed with the High Court that the trade union rights were 'one form or a special aspect'[79] of the rights to freedom of association under Article 11. They apply only to those individuals who are employees or in an employment relationship rather than 'everyone'.[80] The Court of Appeal departed from the High Court in finding that the definition of 'employment relationship' should be interpreted in line with the International Labour Organization (ILO) Employment Relationship Recommendation[81] rather than the definition of 'worker' under national law. That Recommendation suggests that the fact that work is 'carried out personally by the worker' is an indicator of an employment relationship (paragraph 13). The Court of Appeal suggested that it 'follows' that the absence of such an obligation is a 'contra-indicator' of worker status. The CAC was 'entitled' to treat the 'genuine and unfettered right of substitution' as determinative of a lack of personal service between the delivery drivers and Deliveroo. It was also entitled to treat the lack of personal service as 'decisive' on the question of worker status. Personal service is a central feature of the relationship of employer and worker 'as ordinarily' understood, and there was no reason why that position should be any different in the interpretation of the scope of an employment relationship under Article 11.[82]

The Supreme Court agreed with the Court of Appeal's methodology and assessment. It applied a multifactorial test to the question of whether there was an employment relationship between the parties, supported by the indicators of an employment relationship identified in ILO Recommendation No 198. In applying the test, the Supreme Court rejected the appellant's argument that it should adopt a purposive approach, in the sense of recognizing the connection between the lack of power experienced by workers in employment relationships and their corresponding need to have access to collective bargaining. The Supreme Court found that there was 'no support' for this kind of 'purposive' approach to collective rights in the case law.[83] It agreed with the focus of the Court of Appeal on the 'virtually unfettered' contractual power of riders to appoint substitutes as a strong counter indicator of an employment relationship between the parties.[84] It supplemented this

---

79 *Demir v Turkey* (2009) 48 EHRR 54.

80 *Sindicatul 'Pastorul Cel Bun' v Romania* app. no. 330/09 [2014] IRLR 49 ('the *Good Shepherd* case').

81 R198 – Employment Relationship Recommendation 2006 (No 198).

82 *IWGB v CAC and others* [2021] EWCA Civ 952, para 77.

83 *IWGB v CAC and others* [2023] UKSC 43, para 63.

84 *IWGB v CAC and others* (n 83), para 69.

analysis with further counter-indicators of employment status[85] to conclude that the 'riders' did not fall within the scope of an employment relationship for the purposes of Article 11.

There are a number of troubling features of this judgment. First, the ILO Recommendation makes clear that the determination of the existence of an employment relationship 'should be guided primarily by the facts relating to the performance of work and the remuneration of the worker, notwithstanding how the relationship is characterized in any contrary arrangement, contractual or otherwise, that may have been agreed between the parties'.[86] In the *Deliveroo* case, the question of status appears to be determined by the contractual terms first and the exercise of those terms second. The existence of a 'genuine' right of substitution is the most important factor in deciding on worker status, and so long as some delivery drivers have exercised the right at some point that is sufficient to decide the matter. This puts too much emphasis on the contractual arrangement rather than the performance of work in practice (which suggests very little exercise of the substitution right).[87] Second, the ILO Recommendation is couched in terms of 'indicators' which national government 'might include' in determining employment relationships. It gives no priority to any particular indicators. The clear focus on personal service and the contractual power of substitution appears to act contrary to the spirit of the Recommendation.

Third, this case is more harshly or restrictively decided than other cases on employment/worker status in the field of individual rights. This is bizarre in light of the context of the very broad application of Article 11. This situation appears to stem from the greater difficulty of the courts in deciding on a 'purposive' approach to interpretation in this context. In the context of individual rights, the courts have been guided in their interpretation of cases by the need to protect vulnerable individual workers.[88] In cases on collective rights, this interpretative framework does not appear to be either considered or available, and there is a lack of general statement as to the status accorded to collective rights as a matter of public policy.[89] The Court of Appeal did refer to the 'counter-intuitive' nature of the judgment in that the delivery drivers 'might benefit from organising collectively to represent

[85] *IWGB v CAC and others* (n 83), para 72. These counter-indicators included: the freedom to reject offers of work, the ability of the riders to make themselves unavailable, and the ability of riders to undertake work for competitors.

[86] ILO Recommendation R198 (n 81), para 9.

[87] J. Atkinson and H. Dhorajiwala, '*IWGB v Roofoods*: Status, Rights and Substitution' (2019) 48 (2) *Industrial Law Journal* 278.

[88] *Uber v Aslam* [2021] UKSC 5.

[89] D. Brodie (n 70), 471.

their interests as against Deliveroo' but were denied that opportunity.[90] Coulson J conceded that there may be gig-economy cases which would succeed on different facts. However, the Court was not persuaded that these drivers were 'vulnerable', nor that they were denied their rights; they still had residual rights of freedom of association under Article 11, even in the absence of access to the 'special' rights pertaining to trade unions and access to collective representation.

This line of cases appears to give credence to the fears of Lord Wedderburn that the right to freedom of association in Article 11 in fact has 'very little collective content at all'.[91] Freedom of association is akin to freedom of assembly in that it is 'essentially an individual right to meet together, with very little or no protection of any collective purposes'.[92] It is argued here that this is connected to the inability of labour law to give any normative salience to collective action or agency as a matter of collective rights. The next section considers some of the options of embedding this normative collectivity into the heart of (collective) labour rights.

5. Towards a collective subject

We have identified that there are problems with the normative structure of legal personhood from the point of view of individual labour rights. This structure is determined by the contractual view of the person which gives normative salience to equality and autonomy of the person. The 'dependence' or 'subordination' as conditions of personhood are an aberration to be corrected which the law can do by imposing 'rules of just conduct' to ensure equilibrium is restored.[93] This 'equilibrium' is determined by the rule of contract, such that 'equality' can only be partial or incomplete and is often neglected altogether. This view of the subject and the operation of law is extremely unsatisfactory, and many authors have sought to critique its operation. From our point of view, it contradicts that which is implicit in the establishment of labour law; namely, that 'dependency' and 'autonomy' are socially constructed. As explored in Chapter 2 of this book, Sinzheimer suggests that 'Labour law starts from the reality of the person as a class being'.[94] The person as a class being is not free but dependent, and this

90 *IWGV v CAC and others* (n 82), para 86.

91 Lord Wedderburn, 'Freedom of Association or Right to Organise' (1986) *Industrial Relations Journal* 244, 247.

92 Lord Wedderburn (n 91), 251.

93 F.A. Hayek, *Law Legislation and Liberty* (London: Taylor and Francis 1982), 213.

94 H. Sinzheimer, 'Das Problem des Menschen im Recht' (1933) in H. Sinzheimer, *Arbeitsrecht und Rechtssoziologie: gesammelte Aufsätze und Reden* (Frankfurt: Europaische Verlagsanstalt 1976), 59.

dependency is a function of the separation of capital from labour power, and the resulting diversity of life situations between owners and workers. It is the recognition in labour law of the person as a 'dependent being' which sets labour law apart from other disciplines and which allows labour law to create rights that are able to lead to social transformation.

Contract law cannot remove 'dependency' any more than it can construct 'autonomy'. Furthermore, 'dependency' and 'autonomy' are not mutually exclusive. In the condition of work, dependency and autonomy exist side by side. The lack of understanding of this interaction means that liberal legal subjectivity tends to insufficiently incorporate the importance of agency. On the face of it, 'collectivist' approaches to labour law do embed this sense of agency and the importance of worker participation. However, the scepticism of collectivist scholars to the law has meant an insufficient engagement with alternative approaches to legal subjectivity or attempts to embed this agency *within the law*.

From a strategic point of view, it no longer makes sense to promote 'collectivism' outside of the scheme of (liberal) rights. The negotiation of individual and collective rights gives trade unions legitimacy and visibility, and can result in important positive outcomes for individuals. Rather, it is the argument here that any advocate of collective rights can and must reflect on the distinctive nature of the rights so conferred and their particular interaction with other forms of rights. Bogg argues that this reflection should lead to the development of a theory of collective rights that satisfies the constraints of the 'humanistic' principle.[95] On this scheme, those rights should be formulated on the basis of their contribution to individual well-being. Hence, collective rights should be 'individualist' on matters of ultimate value, but 'collectivist' in outcome. This position is useful because we have here an acceptance of the 'social specificity' of individuals commensurate with a communitarian view of liberal rights. This is an important corrective to the view that autonomy is preconditioned and pre-social, and therefore cannot be affected by state action. It means that the state has a role in the promotion of autonomy and the development of workers' capabilities or potentialities:

> More important is the conclusion that if autonomy is an ultimate value, then it affects wide-ranging aspects of social practices and institutions. It is wrong to identify autonomy with a right against coercion, for example, and to hold that right (i.e., the right against coercion) as defeating, because of the importance of personal autonomy, all, or almost all, other considerations. Many rights contribute to making autonomy possible, but no short list of concrete rights is sufficient for

[95] Bogg (43), 74.

> this purpose. The provision of many collective goods is constitutive of the very possibility of autonomy, and it cannot be relegated to a subordinate role, compared with some alleged right against coercion, in the name of autonomy.[96]

However, the adoption of the humanistic principle is limited in a number of ways. First, it tends to de-essentialize collective bargaining. The aim of the humanistic principle is to ensure that all persons are treated as 'capable of exercising and increasing their autonomy, of engaging in valued activities within a private space, and of developing their several potentialities'.[97] If collective bargaining allows individuals to reach this goal of 'autonomy' then it should be promoted, but if this goal can be reached in other ways, then this should be the favoured goal. As has been seen in the *Kostal* litigation, this leads to a situation where the autonomy-enhancing nature of freedom of contract is placed on a par with the autonomy-enhancing nature of collective bargaining. In this situation, there is no independent reason to pursue collective bargaining rights over contractual rights. Indeed, it might be disputed whether it is necessary to consider rights to collective bargaining as 'rights' at all.[98] Furthermore, it is not at all clear that on this view the social situatedness of individuals includes a recognition of the effects of inequalities of power. These inequalities of power are precisely the reason why 'freedom of contract' rarely leads to social justice, but instead serves to reinforce existing power differentials. It is a recognition of these inequalities of power which leads to proposals for the importance of collective action (over other 'freedoms') and why employee collective action may be a prior 'right' to freedom of contract: collective action may be a necessary precondition for autonomous employee choice.[99]

This is all very well, but we are still in the realm of the social and the political here. These are arguments that collective action is important socially and politically, and so should be given extra weight if we are to achieve social goals. The problem has always been that this does not give collective action or actors access to the normative, moral weight associated with legal subjectivity. This is the problematic that Lord Wedderburn identified when he suggested that there is 'little or no knowledge of the dignity that informs collective mutual endeavour in the free association of men and women in society and at work'.[100] There is no collectivist morality in the individualist

96 J. Raz, *Morality of Freedom* (Oxford: Oxford University Press 1988), 206.

97 S. Lukes, *Individualism* (Oxford: Blackwell 1973), 20.

98 J. Raz (n 96), 216.

99 B. Rogers, 'Passion and Reason in Labor Law' (2012) 47 *Harvard Civil Rights – Civil Liberties Law Review* 47.

100 Lord Wedderburn (n 7), 37.

humanity principle. Indeed, a 'collective' morality would be viewed as antithetical to liberal beliefs around autonomy. A collective morality suggests that individuals are not free to formulate or pursue their own goals outside of the collective. This runs counter to the ideal of autonomy at the heart of liberalism, which depends on an absence of coercion and on the imposition of individual will. A 'collective morality' strikes of totalitarianism which implies the absence of autonomy, reason, and independence among its members:

> But within the organisational framework of [totalitarianism], so long as it holds together, the fanaticized members can be reached by neither experience nor argument; identification with the movement and total conformism seem to have destroyed the very capacity for experience, even if it be as extreme as torture or the fear of death.[101]

It is argued here that it is possible to attach morality to collective action without abandoning a commitment to personal autonomy. That is, autonomy remains an 'ultimate value' but that value becomes differently constituted, and with different implications for law. This differential constitution involves recognizing the 'relationality' of individual values. The example here will be a reflection on the transformative nature of 'relational autonomy' given the centrality of autonomy to thinking about collective rights.[102] The argument proceeds that the traditional liberal model which relies on the universality and completeness of autonomy as the ultimate defining characteristic of humanity is deeply flawed. This view of autonomy is exclusionary and serves to reinforce existing power relations by excising social experience from human nature. This social experience goes beyond the recognition of the social situatedness of autonomous practice. Rather, autonomy itself relies on social experience for its own creation, and autonomy is constantly made and remade through this experience. Individual 'selves', their identities and their capacities, are not comprehensible in isolation from their relationships.[103] On a relational view, the persons whose rights and well-being are at stake are constituted by their relationships such that it is only in the context of those relationships that it is possible to define those capabilities, define and protect their rights, or promote their well-being.[104] On this view, the collective is not simply a potential threat to individuals, but it is constitutive of individuals

[101] H. Arendt, *Totalitarianism: Part Three of the Origins of Totalitarianism* (FL: Harcourt 1968), 6.

[102] In other parts of this book, the relationality analysis will be applied to other elements of the liberal legal subject; namely, rationality and independence (Chapters 6 and 7). It is space that dictates that these further issues will not be considered here.

[103] J. Nedelsky, *Law's Relations: A Relational Theory of Self, Autonomy and the Law* (Oxford: Oxford University Press 2011), 121.

[104] Nedelsky (n 103), 121.

and a source of their autonomy. Thus, the objective (of law) is to find the optimal relation between the individual and the collective, and the forms and scope of collective activity that will foster it.

On this view, relational autonomy is a more 'human' version of autonomy and has a greater potential for supporting social justice than traditional autonomy claims. Relational autonomy is more 'human' in that it recognizes the empirical reality that autonomy is partial and often incomplete. Individuals can appear to exercise 'autonomy' in certain aspects of their life and in some decisions but not in others.[105] Workers in employment relationships can be 'controlled' or constrained in certain areas of work, while having considerable freedom and discretion in others. Autonomy is also a process and a state of becoming: people must develop and sustain the capacity for finding their own law, and the task is to understand what structures of power, patterns of relationship, and person practices foster that capacity.[106] Both of these elements underlie the importance of 'autonomy' for social justice. Autonomy implies a process of 'creative interaction' because autonomy is a process which is both individually engineered and socially mediated. That creative interaction implies the possibility of not only personal development and empowerment but also social transformation: the possibility of 'new engagement, breaking or transforming received patterns, giving rise to and acting on one's own distinctive perceptions, insights and forms of engagement'.[107] In autonomy there is the potential for action and disruption which is essential for social justice.

The moral salience of relational autonomy could be used to bolster claims for collective rights. Using the relational autonomy approach might make it easier to push back against the moral ascendancy of 'freedom of contract' in freedom of association cases. It could also underscore an expansive interpretation of status classifications for the purpose of individual access to trade union representation in the workplace. The ability to access these constitutive relationships is central for the forming of personal autonomy in the relational sense. There are further possibilities for the relational autonomy approach. This approach could constitute a starting point for a rethinking of the current interaction between contractual doctrine and collective agreements, and open the door for a greater role for trade unions in enforcing contractual terms.[108] Most of all, it gives the judiciary access

---

105 K. Abrams, 'From Autonomy to Agency: Feminist Perspectives on Self-Direction' (1999) 40 *Williams and Mary Law Review* 805, 807.

106 Nedelsky (n 103), 123.

107 Nedelsky (n 103), 167.

108 See the recent case of *SSHD v Cox* [2023] EWCA Civ 551 in which it was held that a trade union could not be a third party to a contract because that was not the 'intention of the parties'.

to normative reasons for the support of 'collectivist' outcomes through the law without compromising the central commitment to personal autonomy. Indeed, there is the possibility on this approach of a greater coincidence between 'individualist' and 'collectivist' outcomes for workers.

There is a note of caution to sound here. In the work environment, trade unions can be important vehicles for the construction of personal autonomy in the relational sense. They are, broadly speaking, collectivities of workers who aim to improve the terms and conditions under which workers have to work. However, trade unions have not always been and are not always helpful in fostering relational autonomy among all workers. Unions have been guilty of prioritizing the needs of certain groups or deprioritizing certain member interests on the basis that they are 'individual' rather than collective problems. For example, Crain explains that trade unions in the US have tended to accept the judicial division between 'collective' economic rights on the one hand and individual rights to be free from discrimination on the other. This has prevented action on key issues that contribute to women's economic subordination; namely, occupational segregation by sex, associated pay inequalities, and sexual harassment.[109] Ultimately the relationality scheme requires that collective organizations also reflect on the ways in which their laws or norms foster personal autonomy in the relational sense.[110] It is also cognizant that relationships are not always constructive, but are always constitutive. It remains the case that questions of rights are best analysed in terms of how they structure relationships, because this is more likely to present solutions which come closer to social justice (for workers).

6. Conclusion

Individualism has tended to dominate the intellectual ground where the theorization of legal personhood is concerned. This can be explained on the basis of the easy intellectual link between the values of individualism on the one hand and individual rights on the other. Individualism promotes autonomy, rationality, and independence as its central values, and these are the same values which underlie the liberal legal subject. On the other hand, the values of collectivism are group-based. In terms of labour, collectivism is concerned with group loyalties, and the opportunities of workers to organize together in protection of their occupational (class) interests and against organizational exploitation in a pluralist democracy. Under this scheme, the link between collectivism and collective *rights* is more difficult.

---

[109] M. Crain, 'Sex Discrimination as Collective Harm' in D.S. Cobble (ed) *The Sex of Class: Women Transforming American Labor* (New York: Cornell University Press 2011), 100.

[110] Nedelsky (n 103), 33.

Fundamentally, there tends to be a scepticism towards the law in the furtherance of collective aims or a belief that true change will only come about through non-legal action. So, while it is clear (to individualists) that individual rights further the aims of individualism, it is not always clear that collective rights further the aims of collectivism.[111] Indeed, the aims and commitment of 'collectivists' tend to reach beyond the law and towards political solutions (which may then have repercussions for legal regulation):

> For labour law this must inevitably mean – like it or not – in conventional terms an era of intense politicisation. Assumptions are no longer freely shared. The game has been moved off the old board and no player can have his bid heard, let alone capture the lead, who is shy about casting his principles to 'stand the hazard of the die'.[112]

This tends to mean that collectivists do not consider deeply the nature of personhood. This is considered to be outside of the collectivist domain and/or of little value in the furtherance of their cause. This is a real problem because it means that collectivist ideals and collective action can be dismissed as less fundamental and/or pressing than individualist concerns. Individualists speak to the fundamental liberal concerns around individual well-being whereas collectivists attempt to subvert individual well-being through the promotion of the group over the individual. This problematic has led some labour lawyers to reassert individualism as the moral foundation not just of individual rights but also of collective rights. For example, Bogg argues that the 'humanistic principle' – namely, the furtherance of individual well-being – could legitimately form the basis of both individual and collective rights. However, this only serves to reinforce the individualist/collectivist divide. Rather, if there is to be any rapprochement between individualism and collectivism there needs to be a consideration of whether personhood itself has relational or collective elements. It needs to be considered whether legal subjectivity could incorporate 'relational autonomy' and whether, in doing so, the aims of labour law and the needs of labour are more completely realized.

---

111 B. Simpson, 'Freedom of Association and the Right to Organize: The Failure of an Individual Rights Strategy' (1995) 24 (3) *Industrial Law Journal* 235, 249.

112 Lord Wedderburn (n 7), 37.

6

The Challenge of the COVID-19 Pandemic

1. Introduction

The COVID-19 pandemic challenged our most basic assumptions about our 'selves' at work, and (hence) the relationship between labour law and social justice.[1] First, it involved unprecedented government intervention through furlough schemes and lockdowns. Governments imposed 'stay at home' orders or requests on the basis that it was unsafe to travel to work or mix with other workers in a work environment. Health and safety came to dominate, at least for a short while, the experience of workers and the work that could be undertaken. Second, working from home mandates meant that homeworking increased exponentially.[2] This disruption was exacerbated by the closure of nurseries and schools such that childcare and work had to happen side by side. This resulted in a sea change in the way in which private life and work life, and the balance between them was experienced. The separation of work and private life which had been taken for granted was no longer possible and had to be reimagined.[3] Third, there was a forced reflection on the 'vulnerability' of persons at work. The corporeal nature of individual workers could no longer be ignored in the context of the very real

---

1 B. Langille and A. Trebilcock, 'Introduction: A Framework for Thinking about the Future of Social Justice' in B. Langille and A. Trebilcock (eds) *Social Justice and the World of Work: Possible Global Futures* (Oxford: Hart 2023), 2.

2 Between October to December 2019 and January to March 2022, homeworking in the UK more than doubled from 4.7 million to 9.9 million people. ONS, 'Homeworking in the UK – regional patterns 2019–2022' (11 July 2022), available at: www.ons.gov.uk/employmentandlabourmarket/peopleinwork/employmentandemployeetypes/articles/homeworkingintheukregionalpatterns/2019to2022

3 L. Vyas, 'New Normal at Work in a Post-COVID World: Work–Life Balance and Labor Markets' 41 (1) (2022) *Policy and Society* 155.

risks to workers in attending places of work. The reflection on reasonable adjustments which were previously confined to certain classes of individuals (those who were classified as disabled, for example) now applied to all workers, regardless of gender, disability, race, sexual orientation, and so on. Fourth, the traditional schisms between the 'mind' and the 'body', 'nature' and 'reason' were brought into question. Both during and in the aftermath of COVID-19, the world faced a mental health crisis of unprecedented proportions due to the isolating effects of lockdowns and stress and trauma from the experience of the disease personally and among loved ones.[4]

The COVID-19 pandemic showed the breadth of possibility for intervention in employment relationships in order to ensure corporeal protection for workers. Government reaction to the pandemic was often strong and deep and employers were forced to follow suit. In other ways, the legal environment turned out to be a poor mechanism for worker protection in practice. First, governments were able to deregulate some of the most basic legal protections in the working environment; for example, working time.[5] Second, existing labour law protections turned out to be too inflexible to meet the challenges of the experiences of workers during the pandemic. Third, the more that individuals were drawn to the health and safety regime for their protection, the more its limitations were revealed. Employees had to rely on health and safety protections which were unable to cope with the changing environment (for example, working from home) or were based on a system of risk assessment which was outdated and in any event allowed employers to get away with conducting a set of actions which did not ensure safety in practice, but ensured only that an individual was not able to counter the rationality of the employer's action.[6] Who counted for these purposes was also very controversial: those most at risk in the labour market turned out to be the least protected in terms of labour law or health and safety. The impact of the COVID-19 pandemic was to increase already existing

4 Mind, 'Coronavirus: the consequences for mental health' (July 2021), available at: www.mind.org.uk/media/8962/the-consequences-of-coronavirus-for-mental-health-final-report.pdf

5 In March 2020, the UK government introduced regulations to ease the requirements on businesses to ensure that workers take their annual leave in any one year –Working Time (Coronavirus) (Amendment) Regulations 2020. Two exceptions to the working time rules were enacted. The first exception permitted employers to require workers to carry over leave where it was not 'reasonably practicable' for them to take it due to the coronavirus emergency, and the second allowed the outstanding leave to be carried over into the two years immediately following the relevant leave year.

6 P. Andersson and T. Novitz, 'COVID-19 at Work: Exposing How Risk Is Assessed and its Consequences in England and Sweden' (2022) *Bristol University Research Papers* 31, available at: bristol.ac.uk/law/research/legal-research-papers

inequalities and accentuate pre-existing disadvantage.[7] Finally, the reversal of government mandates for worker protection happened in a reactionary way, focusing on the perceived needs of employers, and neglecting the position of workers.[8]

This chapter investigates these issues and their implications for social justice. In particular, it concentrates on how the COVID-19 pandemic has accentuated the individualist and rationalist conception of the person at the heart of the law of the workplace, and the obstacles that this conception has caused for regulating the workplace both during and post-COVID. This approach has led to the erosion of collective and negotiated solutions, the equation of employee and employer struggles, and the inability of the law to protect those workers most in need. Indeed, the experience of the COVID pandemic has been a tightening of the grip of traditional approaches on law and the person despite the potential for the disruption of those narratives.

2. COVID-19 and the social justice challenge

In this book, various assertions are made about the operation and potentiality of legal personhood in labour law. The first set of assertions is that it is not sufficient to adopt a 'legalistic' approach to personhood. Under the legalist approach, adopted by scholars such as Hans Kelson, the 'legal person' has no natural or metaphysical foundation. The legal person is simply a heuristic device used to allocate rights and duties to various entities and its function is entirely internal to the law. The legal person is a complete abstraction and has no relationship to any natural persons outside of the law. However, the position adopted in this book follows Naffine's argument that, while attractive, the legalist position in relation to legal personhood is necessarily insufficient. Law 'must operate with some understanding of what we are and why we matter in order to do its work in regulating society'.[9] This is unavoidable. In law and in the making and designing of the law, there is always a decision to be made about who counts for the purposes of the law and this is a normative and not just a factual decision.[10]

The second set of arguments is that labour law is dominated by the rationalist conception of the legal person. This rationalist liberal conception

---

7 ILO, 'ILO Monitor: COVID 19 and the World of Work, 7th edition' (25 January 2021) 20, available at: www.ilo.org/wcmsp5/groups/public/-dgreports/-dcomm/documents/briefingnote/wcms_767028.pdf

8 A. Arkwright, 'Can your employer force you back into the office' (September 2021), available at: www.tuc.org.uk/blogs/can-your-employer-force-you-back-office

9 N. Naffine, *Law's Meaning of Life: Philosophy, Religion and the Legal Person* (Oxford: Hart 2009), 45.

10 Naffine (n 9).

relies on the liberal political creation story of contract and the emergence of the modern autonomous individual. It is a story of Enlightenment: from unequal natural relations to social relations formed freely through the mechanism of contract. It is also a story of morality. Legal rights and duties attach to individuals as a result of their capacity for moral decision-making; it is the human ability to make intelligent choices and to be accountable for those choices which allow those decisions to have both legal and moral standing. It is argued in this book that despite opportunities to depart from this conceptualization, labour law remains wedded to it. In large part this is a result of the inability of labour law to release itself from the ties of civil, private law; namely, contract and tort. It is suggested in this book that the rationalist conception of labour law is damaging and limiting. This conceptualization tends to rely on Kantian hierarchies of mind and body. According to Kant, it was the human capacity for reason which gave humans their essential nature and their inherent dignity.[11] He emphasized the need to contain the body for the benefit of reason. For Kant, the body was a potentially disruptive force and the best way to contain that disruption was for individuals to maintain physical separation and thereby respect autonomy.[12] Once the boundaries of autonomy were broken between individuals, there was the risk of subordination and heteronomy which rendered individuals unfree.[13] A person who was not free had no sense of self and lost his human essence:

> Having failed to achieve that autonomy which alone commands the respect of rational beings, he stands outside the moral order, unfree, subservient, diminished in his very personhood, and in his respect for himself.[14]

This scheme is problematic for a number of reasons. First, this scheme suggests that subordination negates humanity. If this is the case, then there does not seem much to separate employment relationships from slavery. Second, the body disappears from view. This disappearance denies the truth of human existence; namely, that we are all embodied and bounded individuals. We have a conception of the legal person which purports to represents 'humanity', but which is missing vital parts. The rationalist conception of the person denies human vulnerability, sensitivity, and relationality, or

11 I. Kant 'Foundations for the Metaphysics of Morals' in L.W. Beck (ed) *Kant Selections* (New York: Macmillan 1988), 261.

12 I. Kant, *The Metaphysics of Morals* (tr M. Gregor, Cambridge: Cambridge University Press 1991), 244.

13 Kant (n 11), 261.

14 R.A. Scruton, *A Short History of Modern Philosophy: From Descartes to Wittgenstein* (London: Routledge 1989), 155.

makes those characteristics of humanity undesirable and exceptional. The implications are that individuals are misunderstood, and legal protection is aimed at the wrong kinds of injury and the wrong kinds of persons. The law creates divisions rather than resolves them,[15] and completely misses problems that are the most pressing for social justice. Indeed, on this scheme, the law is set up to embed pre-existing power relations and accentuate problems of social justice rather than address them. It turns out that powerful economic actors, such as companies, are most able to follow the logic of the legal scheme and gain access to rights, as these actors can separate 'rationality' and 'autonomy' from embodiment in a way that human 'workers' are not able to do.[16] Finally, resistance to these entrenched power relations is hampered by a commitment to individualization, separation, and non-interference on the basis of 'autonomy'. Collective means of organization are not given any priority on this scheme.[17]

One of the most interesting elements of the advent of COVID was that it brought (bodily) vulnerability to the fore. Government mandates required great swathes of workers to stay at home on the basis that travel to work and the workplace posed a serious threat to worker health. It was thus impossible to ignore the bounded and embodied nature of workers. It was also interesting that vulnerability pertained across the board. The virus could affect any worker (or anyone) regardless of wealth, class, or ethnic background. Embodiment and vulnerability were unavoidably entwined. This led to a narrative around worker protection which included everyone; hence, Rishi Sunak's famous phrase that 'we are all in this together'.[18] This is important for the purposes of the narrative in this book, because it shows the reality of vulnerability and embodiment on the ground. This lends weight to the claims of feminist writers that vulnerability and embodiment are important for understanding personhood rather than, for example, abstract rationality. Furthermore, it follows that we should seek to further understand that embodiment and vulnerability in order to better regulate society. Knowledge of our human limitations is also part of understanding our powers; acceptance of our species nature can lead to greater self-knowledge and self-direction.[19]

---

[15] K. O'Donovan, *Sexual Divisions in Law* (London: Weidenfeld and Nicolson 1985).

[16] A. Grear, *Redirecting Human Rights: Facing the Challenge of Corporate Humanity* (London: Palgrave Macmillan 2010), 68.

[17] See the discussion in Chapter 5.

[18] E. Conway, 'Coronavirus: we are all in this together – but some more than others' (4 May 2020), Sky News, available at: https://news.sky.com/story/coronavirus-were-all-in-this-together-but-some-more-than-others-11981917

[19] K. Savell, 'The Mother of the Legal Person' in S. James and S. Palmer (eds) *Visible Women: Essays on Feminist Legal Theory and Political Philosophy* (Oxford: Hart 2002), 29.

The experience of COVID-19 also brought to the fore the reality of worker relationality, which is denied on rationalist accounts of personhood. The experience accentuated the fact that the narrow relationship between employer and employee does not exist in isolation from other relationships involving the worker. This became evident in the struggles of working men and women attempting to juggle work and childcare in the context of the closure of schools and nurseries, and the fears of workers forced to attend work who lived with elderly relatives particularly susceptible to the disease. Previously accepted boundaries, between public and private life, between home and work, between self and others were manifestly fragmenting and breaking down. This was an important moment and opportunity for reflection on our understanding of the relationship between workers and personhood. It cast new light on the desirability of worker autonomy as self-determination and freedom through 'boundaries against others'.[20] In the context of the messiness of coronavirus, the artificiality of the bounded self came to be experienced not just by the other of market interaction (women outside the labour market). This experience became part of the experience of even those who had previously felt themselves immune from the reality of the intersecting boundaries of human nature.

It became evident during the pandemic that work was a social determinant of health in the sense that 'what we live, what we eat and why we become ill; all [are] related in part to where we work, what we are paid and the nature of the conditions in which we work'.[21] In the context of coronavirus, it soon became clear that the notion that we are 'all in this together' was a mere chimera.[22] There were dramatic disparities in experience according to particular (worker) vulnerabilities. For example, the distribution of mortality rates from COVID-19 was starkly uneven. In the most deprived areas mortality rates were far higher than wealthy areas. Mortality rates were also far higher among older persons, those with underlying health conditions, and ethnic minorities. Thus, although on the face COVID-19 was the great leveller, and did not discriminate on the basis of social position or personal characteristics, the reality was that it revealed and accentuated pre-existing socio-economic and racial characteristics across the UK and around the world.[23] More specifically in the context of work, this inequality of experience was exacerbated by the disproportionate exposure to risk in relation to the virus among 'key' or 'critical' workers; namely, those required

20 J. Nedelsky, 'Reconceiving Autonomy' (1989) 1 (1) *Yale Journal of Law and Feminism* 7.

21 K. Ewing and Lord Hendy, 'COVID-19 and the Failure of Labour Law: Part 1' (2020) 49 (4) *Industrial Law Journal* 497, 499.

22 Ewing and Lord Hendy (n 21), 500.

23 R. Horton, 'Independent Science Advice for C-19 – At Last' (9 May 2020) *The Lancet*.

to keep essential services operating.[24] Those key workers were some of the lowest paid in the workforce[25] and also worked in professions which were disproportionately female and/or disproportionately represented by ethnic minority groups in comparison with the workforce as a whole. For example, in the health care sector, almost 80 per cent working in social care are women.[26] The health and care workforce in England is also significantly over-represented by people from British, Asian and Minority Ethnic (BAME) groups: 40 per cent of doctors, 20 per cent of nurses, and 17 per cent of social care workforce are from BAME groups.[27] In London, nearly 50 per cent of the NHS and Clinical Commissioning Group (CCG) staff come from a BAME group (44.9 per cent). Often, BAME workers are in lower-paid roles within the NHS, which mean that these roles cannot be done remotely, and this leads to greater exposure with other members of the community.[28]

In summary, the pandemic has been important in re-emphasizing the corporeal nature of the worker; a nature which is separate and distinctive from the nature of employers. In some ways, it temporarily raised the status of 'critical' workers on the basis of the role that they play in maintaining and sustaining us, while at the same time emphasizing their (corporeal) plight. However, despite the heightened public awareness of (worker) vulnerability and relationality, this has not so far translated into any adjustment in the labour law scheme when it comes to the adjudication of rights. In fact, labour law has hunkered down into a rationality approach which has favoured employers to a greater extent than employees. There are two ways in which this has come about. The first is that the courts have measured employer rationality according to the (low) standards of

[24] This group of workers included those working in: (i) health and social care; (ii) education and childcare; (iii) key public services (including public sector broadcasters but not private news agencies); (iv) local and national government (but only those dealing with COVID-19 or delivering essential public services, such as the payment of benefits; but not MPs); (v) food and 'other necessary goods' (including production, processing, distribution, sale and delivery); (vi) public safety and national security (including police, MI5 and MI6, fire and rescue, and prison staff); (vii) transport (including those 'keep[ing] the air, water, road and rail passenger and freight transport modes operating during the COVID-19 response'); and (viii) utilities, communication, and financial services (such as the oil, gas, electricity, and water sectors, including sewerage), and postal services and delivery.

[25] C. Farquharson, I. Rasul, and L. Sibieta, *Differences Between Key Workers*, Institute of Fiscal Studies, London (22 April 2020).

[26] Skills for Care, 'The State of the Adult Social Care Sector and Workforce in England' (2023) 84, available at: www.skillsforcare.org.uk/Adult-Social-Care-Workforce-Data/Workforce-intelligence/documents/State-of-the-adult-social-care-sector/The-State-of-the-Adult-Social-Care-Sector-and-Workforce-2023.pdf

[27] Public Health England, 'Beyond the data: understanding the impact of COVID-19 on BAME groups' (June 2020) 22.

[28] Public Health England (n 27), 22.

government pronouncements on COVID safety. Second, in the context of the 'crisis' of COVID, employees have had real difficulty in measuring their response against any standard of rationality at all. Employees have, on the one hand, been assumed to exaggerate their emotional responses to the disease or have failed to show that those responses fall into the categories traditionally protected by labour law.

3. Labour law cases in the pandemic

The pandemic presented a novel set of challenges for both employees and employers. The negotiation of these novel conditions gave rise to a number of labour law claims which tested the boundaries of traditional labour law. The scope of discrimination law and unfair dismissal law was brought into question in a number of cases. Furthermore, provisions which existed in labour law but had been rarely used prior to the pandemic now became important for workers; for example, the provisions in the Employment Rights Act 1996 which allow employees to take certain action where they reasonably believe there is 'serious and imminent' danger to their health and safety – section 100 (1)(d) and sections 44 (1)(d) and (e). This section examines the response of the courts to these claims.

3.1 Discrimination law

In some instances, discrimination law proved flexible enough to accommodate the conditions in which individuals found themselves, and still find themselves in the post-COVID world. For example, it is clear that it is possible for individuals suffering from the conditions of 'Long COVID'[29] to fall within the scope of disability discrimination law. This is important given the widespread[30] and debilitating nature of this disease[31] and the inadequacy

29 Long COVID is defined as the continuation or development of new COVID symptoms three months after the initial SARS-CoV-2 infection, with these symptoms lasting for at least two months with no other explanation. See WHO, 'Post-COVID-19 Condition (Long COVID') (7 December 2022), available at: www.who.int/europe/news-room/fact-sheets/item/post-covid-19-condition

30 Long COVID continues to affect more than 2 million people in the UK: ONS, 'Prevalence of ongoing symptoms following coronavirus (COVID-19) infection in the UK' (2 February 2023), available at: www.ons.gov.uk/peoplepopulationandcommunity/healthandsocialcare/conditionsanddiseases/bulletins/prevalenceofongoingsymptomsfollowingcoronaviruscovid19infectionintheuk/2february2023

31 Long COVID displays a mixture of both physical (joint pain, breathing difficulties) and psychological symptoms (brain fog, confusion) as well as symptoms which are difficult to classify as either physical or mental (exhaustion, fatigue).

of many employer sickness absence policies in managing the condition.[32] In the case of *Burke v Turning Point Scotland*,[33] the court accepted that an employee suffering from Long COVID was disabled for the purposes of section 6 Equality Act 2010. The court found that the physical effects of Long COVID in this case (fatigue, severe headaches, sleep impairment) amounted to a 'physical impairment' and that the impairment had an adverse effect on the ability of the claimant to carry out day-to-day activities (for the period under examination he was unable to undertake household chores, walk to the shop, sleep through the night, or concentrate for any length of time). Although the severity of the symptoms varied over time, the court accepted that the adverse effect was substantial, and on the evidence, long-term. This decision is to be welcomed, although its utility is limited in the sense that individuals will have to prove that Long COVID is a disability on the facts. Furthermore, Long COVID has still to be recognized by the government as giving rise to access to the Industrial Disablement Scheme (IDBS).[34] This scheme offers compensation to individuals for disablement because of an accident at work, or because of one of over seventy prescribed diseases known to be a risk from certain jobs. Sufferers of Long COVID can still apply to the scheme, but success depends on showing, on the balance of probabilities, that the disease was contracted at work. This has created difficulties for some claimants.[35]

In relation to the law on religion and belief, the claimant in *Wierowska v HC-One Oval*[36] was able to show that her refusal to have a COVID vaccine was a religious belief and therefore protected under section 10 Equality Act 2010. The claimant was a lifelong Roman Catholic and raised a number of objections to the vaccine which she linked to her faith. The respondent's representative argued that the claimant's opinions on the vaccine were

---

32 For example, new guidelines for dealing with the management of Long COVID in the NHS were drafted in July 2022. See NHS, 'Guidelines for Supporting our NHS People affected by Long COVID' (7 July 2022), available at: www.england.nhs.uk/wp-content/uploads/2022/02/C1672_Guidelines-for-supporting-our-NHS-people-affected-by-Long-COVID_July-2022.pdf

33 Case No: 4112457/2021.

34 Long COVID is not on the list of prescribed diseases for the purposes of access to the Industrial Disablement Scheme (IDBS). See 'Industrial Disablement Scheme: Technical guidance' (updated 11 July 2023), available at: www.gov.uk/government/publications/industrial-injuries-disablement-benefits-technical-guidance/industrial-injuries-disablement-benefits-technical-guidance#appendix-1-list-of-diseases-covered-by-industrial-injuries-disablement-benefit

35 Royal College of Nursing, 'Long COVID: how the RCN can help you' (10 January 2023), available at: www.rcn.org.uk/magazines/Advice/2023/Jan/Long-COVID-benefits-support

36 Case No: 1403077/2021.

not in fact religiously motivated but were rooted in her scepticism of the vaccine and the limited evidence of its effectiveness. The tribunal disagreed, stating that vaccine refusal could be a religious issue. This issue had troubled the 'worldwide Catholic Community', leading to a pronouncement by the Pope (even though the Pope did not mandate vaccine refusal). In any event, the tribunal accepted the evidence that the claimant's religious beliefs determined her action, and so the belief was protected by the Equality Act. By contrast, in *Dimitrova and others v Barchester Healthcare*,[37] the tribunal was much more sceptical about the claimant's evidence that their religious beliefs determined their failure to accept the vaccine. There was the question of evidence, in that the claimants here had not mentioned their religious beliefs in their communications with their employers about the vaccine refusal. The tribunal (unlike in the *Wierowska* case) also thought it significant that there was disagreement about the desirability of accepting the vaccine in the religions under question. It was stated here that the fact that '[c]learly, members of the Christian and Muslim faith have accepted the vaccine in huge numbers'[38] undermined the claimants' case.

in *X v Y*[39] the question arose whether the claimant's 'belief' in fear of catching coronavirus (and subsequent need to protect herself) was protected under the Equality Act 2010.[40] This was a question of 'philosophical' rather than religious belief and so the (stringent) *Grainger* criteria had to be applied. The employment tribunal applied the criteria in *Grainger* and found that the case failed on two main grounds. First, the fear of catching COVID did not amount to a belief; it was an opinion or viewpoint on the particular dangers of COVID as understood at the time. Second, the 'belief' as claimed by the claimant did not relate to a 'weighty or substantial aspect of human life or behaviour'. Rather, the fear of catching COVID was 'time-specific' and related only to the current danger that she considered her (and her husband) to be in if she attended work.[41]

These cases demonstrate the difficulty of attempting to use labour law where matters of social justice are at stake. It is clear that COVID-related fears were real, and beliefs strongly held. These fears were weighty and substantial in the sense that they affected what people could do and their ability to work and to attend work. However, evidentially, in order for these beliefs to be protected they either had to be 'religious' or pass the stringent criteria of the *Grainger* test. In some instances, tribunals have been willing

37 Case Nos 1803315/2021, 1803339/2021, 2601442/2021 3207353/2021, and 3205334/2021.

38 *Dimitrova and others* (n 37), para 321.

39 Case No: 2413947/2020.

40 J. Moseley, 'Coronavirus (COVID-19) Employment Cases' (London: LexisNexis 2023).

41 Case No. 2413947/2020, para 20.

to accept the link between religious beliefs and COVID-related action or fear, even where there is no obvious connection to the pronouncements of the mainstream faith. In others, there has been more scepticism about this connection. The time-specific (albeit severe) nature of the COVID crisis and the lack of evidence available at the time all served to increase the pressure on claimants, but reduce the effectiveness of the law in protecting those claimants' beliefs.

Even where claimants have managed to fall within the scope of discrimination law, proving their discrimination claims has been problematic. This is particularly the case for indirect discrimination. In the context of government pronouncements on safety issues and the need to protect all staff, mandatory rules (such as the requirement to wear masks) have been found to pursue a legitimate aim and to be proportionate, even where this has caused difficulties for some workers. Employers have faced a low hurdle to prove the rationality of their actions in this context. For example, an individual claimed indirect disability discrimination on the ground that the rule that all employees should wear a mask was a provision, criterion, or practice with which she could not comply due to her disability (vertigo).[42] The tribunal accepted that the claimant had a disability but found that the refusal of the respondent to relax the mask wearing rule was justified on the basis of the need to protect all staff and preserve business operations (providing life-saving medication to its clients).[43]

3.2 *Unfair dismissal*

It could be argued that fears around the safety of workplaces during COVID are not properly discrimination claims. These kinds of issues should be dealt with under the auspices of health and safety law (see Section 4) or unlawful dismissals or detriments under the Employment Rights Act 1996. There are certainly instances where individuals have been able to show unfair dismissals for COVID-related reasons and have received compensation as a result. The success of these cases has in large part been determined by the extent to which employers engaged with health and safety guidance at the time. In *Gibson v Lothian Leisure*[44] the tribunal held that a chef had been unfairly dismissed for refusing to attend work. The claimant chef had a vulnerable father at home, and he was concerned that his attendance at work presented a serious and imminent threat to his father's health. The tribunal

42 *Shields v Alliance Healthcare Management Services* Case Nos: 4110642/2021 and 4101741/2022.

43 Case Nos (n 42), para 164.

44 Case No: 4105009/2020.

was persuaded of this danger, given the lack of safety measures in place at the restaurant at the time. It was also persuaded that the claimant had taken steps to avert the risk by raising the issue of the lack of personal protective equipment (PPE) with the employer. Similarly, in *Best v Embark on Raw*,[45] the claimant successfully argued that she had been unfairly dismissed for making 'protected disclosures' about unsafe working practices at the pet shop where she worked. Although there were safety measures in place these were not enforced by the employer and were frequently breached by other members of staff. The complaints made by the claimant were not taken seriously by the employer and ultimately led to her dismissal.

By contrast, where employers did engage with safety measures, it is very difficult for claimants to successfully argue unfair dismissal under section 100 Employment Rights Act 1996. In the case of *Rodgers v Leeds Laser Cutting*,[46] the question arose whether the claimant had been automatically unfairly dismissed for his failure to attend work. His argument was that he did not attend work because he (reasonably) believed that his workplace posed a 'serious and imminent' danger to his health (and that of his vulnerable children) and so was unfair under section 100 (1)(d).The case failed on its facts at first instance and again on appeal (in particular the inconsistency of action and evidence by the claimant). However, the case was interesting because the Employment Appeal Tribunal (EAT) and the Court of Appeal made it clear that where an employer has taken the recommended measures to reduce the risk of infection (as mandated at the time), it will be much harder for an employee to show that the danger posed by coronavirus in that workplace was either 'serious or 'imminent'. In this case the 'effective measures' taken by the employer militated against the reasonableness of the belief in the danger posed by coronavirus. A similar situation was seen in *Kubilius v Kent Foods*,[47] in which dismissal for a failure by the employee to wear PPE at the customer's request was seen as reasonable employer behaviour and the claimant's unfair dismissal claim failed.

As in a number of other areas examined in this book, apart from a few short-term 'wins' and minor legal adjustments, labour law remains a long way from escaping the rationalism of civil law and legal subjectivity based on autonomy, freedom, and independence. This has created problems for workers in trying to utilize labour law to deal with the employment issues that they faced as a result of the pandemic. The case law reveals that labour law was completely unable to deal with the challenge to legal subjectivity that arose. For example, employers have been able to prove the rationality of their

[45] Case No: 3202006/2020.
[46] [2022] EWCA Civ 1659.
[47] Case No: 3201960/2020.

actions due to government pronouncements about employer expectations during the pandemic. As long as employers attempted to follow those rules, their action has largely passed the test of rationality for the purposes of labour law. For employees and workers, their responses have largely failed the test of rationality despite the very real threats and concerns that arose in the context of the pandemic and the competing pressures that workers had to manage. This in itself shows the lack of recognition of the complexity of the 'multidimensional' self which is the reality of worker existence. The next section will outline a further set of potentialities for the recognition of the sociality and relationality of workers which arose in the context of the pandemic. This is the recourse to health and safety law.

4. Health and safety and labour law in the pandemic

With the advent of the pandemic, health and safety 'law' and enforcement came to represent a more visible and central part of the experience of workers than had hitherto been the case in the UK.[48] COVID-19 changed the risk profile of workplaces, such that many workplaces which were previously considered 'low risk' under the health and safety regime suddenly became 'high risk' for the purposes of COVID-19 transmission and therefore subject to higher levels of intervention.[49] Furthermore, COVID-19 made health and safety a daily concern for all workers and managers seeking to comply with government pronouncements on safety requirements for workplaces to limit COVID transmission. These wide-ranging government safety measures were modelled on the provisions of health and safety law – namely, the Control of Substances Hazardous to Health (COSHH) Regulations 2002 (as amended)[50] – one of the 'six-pack' of regulations which implemented

[48] Traditionally in the UK, health and safety law had been focused on certain 'high risk' industries where the risk of injury was highest and so many employees or workers did not have day-to-day or regular interaction with health and safety law. See C. Sirrs, 'Risk, Responsibility and Robens: The Transformation of the British System of Occupational Health and Safety 1961–74' in T. Crook and M. Esbester (eds) *Governing Risks in Modern Britain* (Basingstoke: Palgrave Macmillan 2016).

[49] ONS, 'Which occupations have the highest potential exposure to the coronavirus (COVID-19)' (11 May 2020), available at: www.ons.gov.uk/employmentandlabourmarket/peopleinwork/employmentandemployeetypes/articles/whichoccupationshavethehighestpotentialexposuretothecoronaviruscovid19/2020-05-11

[50] All employers have a duty to manage workplace risks caused by biological agents under the COSHH Regulations. Section 7 provides that every employer shall ensure that the exposure of his employees to substances hazardous to health is either prevented, or, where this is not reasonably practicable, adequately controlled. Under section 7 (2), the employer should consider the removal of the biological agent. Where that is not possible, the COSHH Regulations suggest certain protection measures including: (a) the design and use of appropriate work processes, systems, and engineering controls and the provision

European Directives made under the general 1989 Health and Safety Framework Directive.[51] Provision of PPE during the pandemic was regulated through the PPE Regulations[52] – another set of regulations derived from the European health and safety directive. The guidance and management of COSHH, PPE, and COVID regulations were carried out by the Health and Safety Executive (HSE), which was also in charge of enforcing those provisions. Hence, worker experience of and subjection to health and safety regulation in the workplace dramatically increased during the pandemic.

This is interesting for the purposes of this book. It is possible to argue that the health and safety regime in the UK (and health and safety regimes in general) is more 'relational' than the labour law regime. There are several reasons for this assertion. First, the understanding of the scope of protection is broader than under labour law. Under health and safety law, self-employed persons fall under the scope of the employers' duties to take reasonable care (to a certain degree). There is as a result less focus on 'dependence' as forming the gateway to employment protection, or a recognition that vulnerabilities arise even where 'dependence' is not a key feature of a relationship. Second, through the ethos of 'risk management', there is a greater level of proactivity built into the law than for other areas of workplace regulation. This is potentially a more 'relational' approach in that the focus is on building constructive relationships at work with the involvement of the law, rather than only seeking to mitigate the effects of destructive employee/employer relationships after they have broken down. Third, there is a sympathy to collective engagement in the tradition of health and safety law in the UK and specific legal provisions for encouraging employee representation on health and safety issues in the workplace. Employers are expected to consult with employees on health and safety issues in a proactive manner and safety representatives are given quite wide-ranging powers under the law. The potential of these elements for a more 'relational' approach to regulation are discussed in this section, as well as the limitations of the regime experienced in practice during the pandemic.

---

and use of suitable work equipment and materials; (b) the control of exposure at source, including adequate ventilation systems and appropriate organizational measures; and (c) where adequate control of exposure cannot be achieved by other means, the provision of suitable PPE.

51 Directive 89/391. The other regulations are: Provision and Use of Work Equipment Regulations 1992, Manual Handling Operations Regulations 1992, Personal Protective Equipment at Work Regulations 1992, Workplace (Health, Safety and Welfare) Regulations 1992, Health and Safety (Display Screen Equipment) Regulations 1992, Management of Health and Safety at Work Regulations 1993/1999, and Control of Substances Hazardous to Health Regulations 1994/1998.

52 Now the Personal Protective Equipment at Work (Amendment) Regulations 2022.

4.1 Greater relational inclusivity

The public-facing nature of health and safety in the workplace means that the general duties under the Health and Safety at Work Act 1974 (HSWA) have always covered not only employees but also workers and others affected by an employer's activities. Under the HSWA an employer must 'ensure, so far as reasonably practicable, the health, safety and welfare at work of all his employees' (section 2). The duties of employers extend to self-employed persons in a limited way under section 3 HSWA which provides that employers must 'conduct their undertaking in such a way as to ensure so far as reasonably practicable, that persons not in his employment who may be affected thereby are not thereby exposed to risks to their health and safety'. This duty is supplemented by the provisions of the Management of Health and Safety at Work Regulations 1999 (MHSWR) which require that every employer makes a 'suitable and sufficient' assessment of the health and safety risks to which employees are exposed while at work. Under the MHSWR employers must also make this suitable and sufficient risk assessment in respect of the health and safety of persons not employed by an undertaking but who may nevertheless be affected by its conduct (section 3).

This is a more relational approach to employment status than the approach in labour law. The scope of the law depends on judging the sphere of influence of the employer and its impact on individuals rather than focusing on contractual status as such. This is particularly important in the context of the pandemic, given that some of the individuals most exposed to COVID transmission were also the ones with the most precarious contractual status.[53] For example, the contractual status of 'critical workers' fed into and exacerbated their negative experiences during the pandemic.[54] Many workers in the 'gig economy' were classified as 'key workers' and so were required to carry on working and travelling throughout the pandemic. The precarity of their legal status is well known.[55] Hence, the expansion of status provisions to bring 'self-employed' persons within the scope of the law might increase the visibility of these key workers and expose the destructive elements of the employment relationships within which they are embedded. It would also give them access to those resources necessary for their protection and development.

However, there were a number of reasons why the promise of this regime was not realized in practice during the pandemic. First, there were changes to the law in 2015 which reduced the scope of the application of

---

[53] Ewing and Hendy (n 21), 499.

[54] Ewing and Hendy (n 21), 508.

[55] A. Rosin, 'The Right of a Platform Worker to Decide Whether and When to Work: An Obstacle to Their Employee Status' (2022) 13 (4) *European Labour Law Journal* 530.

health and safety law in relation to the 'self-employed'. Section 3 HSWA was amended such that self-employed persons were tasked with making an assessment of whether their undertaking posed a 'risk' to others. Only those self-employed persons who considered their activities risky would now have an obligation to take (reasonably practicable) steps to ensure that they, and other persons who may be affected by their activities, were not exposed to risks to their health and safety. Ostensibly, the intention behind the law was to reduce the burden of health and safety compliance in the name of increased autonomy.[56] However, the effect was to take responsibility for health and safety protection even further away from employers and increase the opportunities for employers to escape health and safety liability in situations of 'bogus' or 'false' self-employment, which is widespread in certain sectors; in particular, the gig economy.[57]

Second, although the general duty under health and safety law provides for a more expansive scope, specific regulations within the health and safety regime maintained a very restrictive approach to employment status. For example, the status provisions in the PPE Regulations were extremely problematic. The PPE Regulations were formulated on the basis that they applied only to 'employees' and not to 'workers'. This caused many difficulties for groups of workers at particular risk of COVID transmission. For example, a detailed study of the experience of platform workers during the pandemic (many of whom would not qualify for 'employee' status due to the nature of their employment) found that these workers had struggled to get consistent access to PPE during the first year, with employers only providing 'one-off' PPE provision or none at all.[58] For these gig economy workers, there was no opportunity to seek recourse for these failures through the law. Indeed, the Independent Workers Union of Great Britain (IWGB), a union representing low-paid migrant workers and other casual labour was so concerned about the lack of access to PPE among its members that it brought a legal claim against the government challenging the narrow scope of the Regulations.[59] It argued that the government's implementation of the PPE Regulations failed to meet the requirements of EU law; namely,

56 UK Gov, 'Explanatory Memorandum to the Deregulation Act (Health and Safety at Work) (General Duties of Self-Employed Persons) (Consequential Amendments Order) 2015', available at: www.legislation.gov.uk/uksi/2015/1637/memorandum/contents

57 S. Smith, 'How Bogus Self-employment is Harming Workers', available at: huckmag.com

58 Fairwork, 'The Gig Economy and COVID-19: Fairwork Report on Platform Policies' 9 (April 2020), available at: https://fair.work/wp-content/uploads/sites/17/2020/11/COVID19-Report-Final.pdf

59 *The Independent Workers' Union of Great Britain v The Secretary of State for Work and Pensions & Ors* [2020] EWHC 3050 (Admin) (13 November 2020).

that those regulations should cover all 'workers'. The court agreed, and this eventually led to an amendment of the PPE Regulations to include both employees and workers within its scope.[60]

4.2 Risk management and proactivity in the law

The ideology of risk management is central to the operation of health and safety law. Employers have a general duty to control risks 'so far as reasonably practicable' under the HSWA and this is supplemented by a scheme of risk assessment and management under the MHSWA.[61] This approach is interesting from the point of view of the project in this book. The scheme of risk management is primarily proactive rather than reactive. It is based on the identification and removal of risks prior to those risks causing harm. Inherent in this ideology is the recognition of corporeality and the threats to bodily integrity created by workplace activities. Also inherent in the health and safety system of risk management is the recognition of the individual as a social subject who exists not just in the private sphere of the employment relationship. Issues arising in the private sphere of the employment relationship can spill over into public life and vice versa. For example, injury created by industrial activity is a 'public' issue in a number of ways. First, the visibility of injury and the dramatic consequences for individuals make this issue one of the highest moral and constitutional standing.[62] Second, industrial accident and disease have an impact beyond the workplace. Members of the public can be directly affected by industrial accidents and disease, and all are indirectly affected by the burden of industrial accident and disease on the public insurance, public enforcement, and social security system.[63]

A good example of the possibilities of the operation of the risk management model is provided by the system of the provision of PPE at work. Employers in the UK have a duty to assess the health and safety risks of a particular work environment for employees and respond by providing 'suitable' PPE.[64]

---

[60] For further discussion, see L. Rodgers and A. Davies, 'Towards a More effective Health and Safety Regime for UK Workplaces post COVID-19' (2023) 52 (3) *Industrial Law Journal* 665, 681.

[61] Section 2 HSWA 1974.

[62] Early factory legislation was justified on strongly moral grounds. Lord Ashley, who presented the Factories Bill 1933, was clear on the humanitarian motivations of the Bill: that such a Bill was necessitated on the basis of the deep commitment of mankind to prevent the 'unjust sufferings' of innocent children. HC Deb 03 April 1833 vol 17 cc79-115, col 90.

[63] L. Rodgers and A. Davies (n 60), 669.

[64] SI 1992/2966, reg 4.

Given the evidence of the effectiveness of high-quality PPE on the prevention of transmission,[65] the provision of adequate PPE was a central measure to ensure a basic level of protection for all workers during the pandemic, and enhanced protection to those particularly exposed to the disease. However, ensuring access to PPE during the pandemic was extremely problematic. Particularly in the early stages of the pandemic, there were shortages of PPE. The government had failed to maintain or replace outdated stocks of PPE prior to the pandemic and was thus forced to rely on buying PPE on international markets in the context of dramatically reduced levels of international trade.[66] The lack of PPE led to a greater transmission risk for frontline workers, experienced particularly dramatically in the healthcare sector.[67] There were also recurrent problems with the quality of PPE through the pandemic. In the healthcare sector, PPE was supplied which did not meet the required safety standards, and thus workers were not adequately protected, or supplies were abandoned. There was also a particular problem in the social care sector where the quality requirements for PPE were not as stringent as for other areas of healthcare.[68] Finally, there was a distinct failure on the part of the HSE to prosecute those organizations falling short of the required standards on the provision of PPE.[69]

More generally, the system of risk management in operation in the UK health and safety regime tended to work more in favour of employers rather than employees during the course of the pandemic. Indeed, the 'public' nature of the coronavirus disease did not lead to greater liability for employers – quite the opposite. This public nature served to allow employers to distance themselves from responsibility for death or injury caused by workplace transmission of the virus. Indeed, under the HSE's reporting mechanisms, COVID infections were only required to be reported in very limited circumstances. For example, the reporting obligation did not extend to cases where an employee was infected by another employee through

65 UK Gov National Institute for Health and Care Research (NIHR): 'The effectiveness of PPE in reducing the transmission of COVID-19 in health and social care settings: December 2021 update' (12 December 2021), available at: www.gov.uk/government/publications/nihr-the-effectiveness-of-ppe-in-reducing-the-transmission-of-covid-19-in-health-and-social-care-settings-december-2021-update-12-december-2021/nihr-the-effectiveness-of-ppe-in-reducing-the-transmission-of-covid-19-in-health-and-social-care-settings-december-2021-update-12-december-2021

66 Ewing and Hendy (n 21), 501.

67 D. Oliver, 'Lack of PPE Betrays NHS Clinical Staff' (2021) *British Medical Journal* 372.

68 Public Accounts Committee Oral evidence: 'COVID-19: Government procurement and supply of personal protective equipment HC 928 Thursday 10 December 2020 Ordered by the House of Commons to be published on 10 December 2020', available at: https://committees.parliament.uk/oralevidence/1373/default#page=9

69 Ewing and Hendy (n 21), 525.

'general transmission' in the workplace, unless it could be shown that the worker was infected by a person known to have coronavirus; for example, in a health or social care setting. Of course, this led to the situation where workplace transmission and COVID deaths at work were dramatically underreported and created ongoing problems for workers in trying to assign responsibility for long-term effects of the disease.[70]

There was also the problem that the risk management scheme was limited in its ability to promote the recognition of risk stratification in an individualized or context-sensitive way.[71] The system of risk management in operation during the pandemic presented the risks from coronavirus as standardized across industries and any flexibility in the operation of COVID-secure rules was downplayed. Even where particular individual vulnerabilities were identified by employers, the guidance issued during the pandemic distanced itself from providing any specific role for employers in identifying or addressing that vulnerability. During the height of coronavirus restrictions, guidance for employers stated that 'there are currently no expectations of additional controls specifically for [vulnerable] groups'. Instead, the HSE recommended ensuring that existing controls (social distancing, good hygiene and cleaning, ventilation, supervision, and so on) were applied strictly to help vulnerable workers, and that those individuals who considered themselves vulnerable should 'have individual discussions with their managers around their particular concerns, in which the risk management measures in place at the workplace should be pointed out and emphasised'.[72]

Furthermore, under the risk management system employed by the HSE, the toleration of COVID risk[73] was high. The high toleration of

---

70 It has been recommended by the Industrial Industries Advisory Council (IIAC) that certain complications arising from COVID-19 infection should be recognized as giving rise to recovery under the UK Industrial Disablement Scheme. This implies a recognition of the causal connection between the occupation disease contraction. See IIAC, 'COVID-19 and occupational impacts', available at: www.gov.uk/government/publications/covid-19-and-occupational-impacts/covid-19-and-occupational-impacts#recommendations However, this recommendation has yet to be implemented: UK Gov, 'Industrial Injuries Disablement Benefits: technical guidance' available at: www.gov.uk/government/publications/industrial-injuries-disablement-benefits-technical-guidance/industrial-injuries-disablement-benefits-technical-guidance

71 TUC, 'Coronavirus (COVID-19) Guidance to Unions (Updated January 2021) Activist Template', available at: tuc.org.uk [last accessed 6 December 2023].

72 HSE, 'Protect vulnerable workers during the coronavirus (COVID-19) pandemic', available at: www.hse.gov.uk/coronavirus/working-safely/protect-people.htm

73 The tolerability of risk framework adopted by the HSE is set out in the following: HSE, 'Reducing Risks, Protecting People: HSE's decision-making process' (Norwich: HSE 2001), 3. According to this framework there are three kinds of risk: unacceptable, tolerable, and broadly acceptable. A tolerable risk 'refers to a willingness by society as a whole to live with a risk so as to secure certain benefits in the confidence that the risk is one that

COVID-related risk was influenced by the unprecedented level of social restrictions in place during the pandemic and the detailed guidance to which employers were already subject. Those social and private restrictions shifted the balance in the risk toleration model towards risk acceptance (a willingness of society to live with the risk) on the basis that the risk was already subject to tight control, and further duties on employers to manage the risk would be disproportionate.[74] However, for workers, this meant that employer actions during the pandemic were difficult to challenge. The government set out a formalistic set of guidelines which each employer should take in order to make their premises COVID secure. Employers who followed these guidelines were considered to have taken sufficient steps to eliminate the risk of COVID transmission, despite the reality of the remaining substantial risk of workplace transmission and the wider fall-outs of the disease (for example, in terms of worker mental health). This situation has led some commentators to suggest that the engagement of employers with COVID risk assessments was merely a defensive device to avoid liability, rather than a real effort to avert or eliminate risks for workers.[75]

The weak response of health and safety law in the context of the pandemic was exacerbated by the fact that, in terms of enforcement, the decision was taken by the HSE only to classify COVID as a 'significant' rather than a 'serious' risk.[76] This decision was taken on the basis of the argument that exposure to the virus resulted in a range of different experiences, with the majority of workers experiencing only 'mild' symptoms and exposure only resulting in death in a small percentage of cases. This had an important influence on the nature of the scrutiny and inspection of suspected COVID breaches, as well as the enforcement options available to inspectors on discovery of a breach. The 'significant' rather than 'serious' risk posed by COVID meant that inspectors were not directed to consider prosecution as an enforcement option for COVID safety breaches.[77] An improvement notice would be the most severe option open to them.[78] Moreover, there would be no basis under the system of risk management for issuing a prohibition

is worth taking and that it is being properly controlled. However, it does not imply that the risk will be acceptable to everyone, ie that everyone would agree without reservation to take the risk or have it imposed on them.'

74 HSE (n 73), 3.

75 P. Anderson and T. Novitz (n 6), 31.

76 HSE, 'HSE's enforcement of guidelines on coronavirus (COVID-19) in workplaces', available at: www.hse.gov.uk/coronavirus/regulating-health-and-safety/enforcement-coronavirus.htm

77 HSE (n 76), Tables at para 61.

78 HSWA 1974, s 21.

notice (to order the employer to stop a dangerous activity)[79] if an inspector were to find breaches on visiting a workplace.[80]

4.3 Collective structures

The UK government has been more open, in general, to the value of collective consultation in the field of health and safety than in other areas.[81] Some authors put this openness down to an understanding of a natural 'identity of interest' between workers and employers in the elimination of accidents and illness in the workplace, first identified in the 'Robens report' on health and safety.[82] This Robens report, which continues to be celebrated today,[83] identified the importance of consensus and tripartism (the involvement of government, industry, and trade union representation) in the successful management of health and safety issues in the workplace. The idea was that health and safety should proceed through a system of 'self-regulation' under which there was a centralization of health and safety in industrial management, with clear responsibilities for all actors in a particular industrial setting. This should be supported by written safety policies, detailing safety arrangements in the workplace. There should also be clear consultation arrangements between employers and employees to deal with health and safety matters.

The result of this openness to the value of collective consultation has been the development of legal provisions in the UK which provide relatively stringent duties on employers in terms of health and safety negotiation, and relatively extensive powers to trade union representatives in the investigation of health and safety issues and in the reporting of breaches to the HSE. The main legal provisions are set out in the Safety Representatives and Safety Committee Regulations,[84] which give recognized trade unions the power to appoint employees to act as safety representatives for the purposes of consultation with an employer. Employers must consult with safety representatives on the introduction of new measures which might affect health and safety, the implementation of procedures to mitigate health and safety risk, and the planning and organizing of health and safety training.

---

79 HSWA 1974, s 22.

80 HSE (n 76), paras 30–4.

81 Z. Adams, C. Barnard, S. Deakin, and S. Fraser-Butlin, *Deakin and Morris' Labour Law* (Oxford: Hart 2021), 885.

82 Adams et al (n 81), 885. See also *Report of the Committee on Safety and Health at Work*, Cmnd 5034, 1972.

83 IOSH Magazine, 'The Robens Report: 50 years on' (May/June 2022), available at: www.ioshmagazine.com/2022/04/26/robens-report-50-years

84 SI 1977/500.

The powers of safety representatives are also relatively wide ranging. They are empowered to investigate potential hazards in the workplace as well as looking into dangerous occurrences and the causes of accidents after they have happened. They can also represent employees in discussion with HSE inspectors and set up a health and safety committee to monitor health and safety matters at work.[85] There are specific protections for health and safety officials in terms of raising health and safety concerns, and this supports the consultative backdrop of the legislation.[86]

As originally enacted, the consultation requirements only applied to those employers with a recognized trade union for collective bargaining purposes. However, the duty to consult was extended by the Health and Safety (Consultation with Employees) Regulations 1996.[87] These regulations introduced an obligation on employers to consult any elected employee (or directly with the whole workforce where there is no representative) 'in good time' on health and safety matters.[88] Employers are required to provide these 'representatives of employee safety' with such information as is necessary for them to fulfil their statutory functions and participate fully and effectively in health and safety consultation.[89] However, the functions of these representatives are less extensive than trade union-elected health and safety representatives and they have less power. For example, they do not have the right to conduct workplace inspections or investigate potential hazards or dangerous occurrences in the workplace. They also do not have the power to demand the establishment of a safety committee. These changes have been met with concern by some commentators who have questioned the independence of these representatives and their ability to effectively negotiate with employers in the light of a lack of union backing.[90] These commentators also worry about the value of 'direct' consultation for workers, and the contribution of these provisions to 'regulatory degradation' of consultation requirements in the field of health and safety.[91]

Interestingly, there is some evidence to suggest that health and safety representation increased during the pandemic. In a study of health and

85 SI 1977/500, reg 9.

86 ERA 1996, s 44 (1)(a) and (b), s 100 (1)(a) and (b).

87 SI 1996/1513.

88 SI 1996/1513 (n 87), s 3.

89 SI 1996/1513 (n 87), s 5.

90 M. Cai, S. Moore, C. Ball, M. Flynn, and K. Mulkearn, 'The Role of Union Health and Safety Representatives during the COVID-19 Pandemic: A Case Study of the UK Food Processing, Distribution, and Retail Sectors' (2022) 53 *Industrial Relations Journal* 390, 392.

91 S. Tombs and D. Whyte, 'A Deadly Consensus: Worker Safety and Regulatory Degradation under New Labour' (2010) 50 (1) *British Journal of Criminology* 46, 50.

safety representation in the food and distribution sector in the UK, it was discovered that union representation increased by 2 per cent at the union level and non-union representation also increased. A 10 per cent rise in the use of health and safety committees was reported in food retail with a larger increase in food distribution.[92] The formal legal infrastructure helped to foster greater informal communication between union representatives and employers on health and safety matters. The pandemic appeared to be an issue that union representatives and management could work on together 'enhancing relationships and encouraging interactions'.[93] There was evidence that managers recognized both the legal status and expertise of health and safety representatives, and this helped to embed them further in the labour process.[94] However, the increase in representation did not pertain across the board, and the existence of safety representatives or health and safety committees did not *guarantee* effective engagement by employers on matter of health and safety. According to a TUC survey in 2021 only 15 per cent of participants reported that safety representatives were fully involved in risk assessments, and 27 per cent said that safety representatives were not involved at all in this process.[95] Also, despite the advent of the pandemic, many representatives reported a lack of 'facility time' to work on health and safety matters and very few reported strong triangulation between employers, safety representatives, and the HSE in relation to the risks posed by coronavirus.[96] In addition, the advice produced by the HSE in respect of consultation during the pandemic suggested that this activity was optional and did not specifically mention the role of safety representatives. In managing risk, the HSE suggested only that employers should 'involve your employees as they will usually have good ideas'.[97] In a pamphlet produced during the coronavirus pandemic, entitled 'Talking to your workers about preventing coronavirus', consulting health and safety representatives was presented as an option only once and was not central to the scheme.[98]

Moreover, the experience of the pandemic has not led the UK government to lend more support to collective negotiation or action. In fact, since the pandemic, the government has introduced legislation to restrict the

92 Cai et al (n 90), 396.

93 Cai et al (n 90), 397.

94 Cai et al (n 90), 398.

95 TUC, 'Union Health and Safety Reps Survey' (2020–21) 16, available at: www.tuc.org.uk/sites/default/files/2021-03/Safety%20reps%20survey%202021.pdf

96 TUC (n 95), 30.

97 HSE, 'Risk assessment: steps needed to manage risk', available at: https://www.hse.gov.uk/simple-health-safety/risk/steps-needed-to-manage-risk.htm

98 See www.hse.gov.uk/coronavirus/assets/docs/talking-with-your-workers.pdf, cited in P. Andersson and T. Novitz (n 6), 25 (subsequently removed).

right of 'key workers' to undertake industrial action.[99] The justification for this legislation is that the pandemic has revealed key workers as 'truly the lifeblood' of the country, such that their services are required at all times to support the public and should not be disrupted by strike action.[100] Of course, the irony is that this 'lifeblood' status does not appear to merit government investment in ensuring inflation-matching pay rises for those workers, or government commitment to the ability of those workers to fight for improved terms and conditions at work.[101]

Thus, despite the inherent recognition of corporeal vulnerability and relationality in the design of health and safety law, there are a number of tensions in the administration of health and safety protection which undermined its effectiveness and ability to achieve social justice for workers in the pandemic. The potential for an expansive reading of the scope of health and safety law was undermined by secondary legislation and restrictive new provisions. The risk management model at work in the law on health and safety tended to be interpreted in ways which downgraded its effectiveness. Fundamentally, the 'risk' presented by coronavirus tended to be downplayed. Risk assessment standards were often low and focused on industry-wide guidelines rather than particular worker vulnerabilities. There was the further problem of enforcement which, due to years of underinvestment in the HSE and the misclassification of the risk posed by COVID, was wholly inadequate to the task.[102] Finally, while industry engagement with health and safety issues did increase during the pandemic, this engagement was not routinely negotiated through collective means. This was a missed opportunity given the evidence of the benefits for both workers and employers of this kind of engagement.[103]

5. Conclusion

The advent of COVID-19 provides an important point at which to reflect on the relationship between personhood, labour, and the law. The pandemic made visible the corporeality of human subjects at work and the importance of sociality and relationality to worker experience. This was subsequently reflected in the law by government intervention which mirrored health

[99] The Strikes (Minimum Service Levels) Act 2023.

[100] Grant Shapps HC Deb, vol 725, col 432 (10 January 2023).

[101] I. Katsaroumpas, 'Crossing the Rubicon: The Strikes (Minimum Service Levels) Act 2023 as an Authoritarian Crucible' (2023) 52 (3) *Industrial Law Journal* 513, 551.

[102] P. James (2021) 'HSE and COVID at work: a case of regulatory failure (IER)', available at: www.ier.org.uk/product/hse-and-covid-at-work-a-case-ofregulatory-failure/

[103] G. Davidov, 'Collective Bargaining: Purpose and Scope' (2004) 20 *International Journal of Comparative Labour Law and Industrial Relations* 81.

and safety provisions. This was a proactive and inclusive engagement which elevated the importance of worker protection and diminished the importance of inconvenience to employers. The pandemic also revealed the value and importance of collective engagement on health and safety issues on the basis of the communality of interest between employers and employees in the prevention of workplace disease and injury. It also increased the possibilities for reasonable adjustments for employers and employees seeking to manage the difficult balance between work and family life.[104]

However, there were a number of reasons why the possibilities for greater reflection on the relationship between personhood, labour, and the law raised by the pandemic have not been realized. First, the pandemic has been characterized as a 'national crisis' and so temporary in effect.[105] Once the threat of COVID-19 subsided and the immediate health and safety concerns diminished, the law defaulted to the pre-pandemic status quo and any learning was lost.[106] Second, the greater incursion of health and safety provisions into the workplace during COVID often did not operate in practice to support workers. The provisions were often badly managed and inconsistently applied. Years of government underinvestment in the system of health and safety meant that in practice legislative provisions were watered down or discretionary and poorly and patchily enforced. Third, the scepticism of successive governments to collective bargaining processes has reduced institutional support for union negotiation in the workplace on health and safety issues. Hence, there was little comeback to employers who refused to engage with these processes.

Outside of a catastrophic event such as the pandemic, there is little political appetite for embedding corporeality or relationality more firmly in the law. If anything, the pandemic served to heighten the government's commitment to the separation of the public and private elements of worker experience,[107] the limitation of employer responsibility for worker safety,[108]

---

104 ACAS, 'Reasonable Adjustments at work' (November 2022), available at: www.acas.org.uk/reasonable-adjustments

105 C. Estlund, 'Book Review: For Labor to Build On: Wars, Depression, and Pandemic by William B. Gould IV (Cambridge University Press 2022)' (2023) 52 (3) *Industrial Law Journal* 834.

106 According to Estlund (n, 105) 838: 'For one thing, instead of producing some semblance of national unity—through either bipartisan cooperation or, in the Depression, a huge electoral wave in favour of labour's Democratic allies—the pandemic seemed to harden political polarisation and deepen legislative paralysis. Far from the pathbreaking reforms of those earlier periods of crisis, organised labour in the pandemic era failed (again) to achieve even relatively modest legal reforms.'

107 See the provisions of the Strikes (Minimum Service Levels) Act 2023.

108 The government recently rejected proposals to re-introduce third-party harassment into the Equality Act 2010. The proposals of the original Bill – the Worker Protection (Amendment of Equality) Bill 2023 – are discussed here: J. Tait, 'Third-party harassment: haven't we

and the pushing of risks from employers onto workers. The importance of effective enforcement highlighted in the pandemic has not led to further commitments to funding of enforcement bodies. Furthermore, the courts have tended to rely on very strict and asocial interpretations of rationality and autonomy in the interpretation of COVID cases. This all points to the need for a greater engagement with the moral project of embedding relationality at the heart of labour law.

---

been here before?' (28 April 2023), available at: www.peoplemanagement.co.uk/article/1821211/third-party-harassment-havent-before

7

AI, Technology, and Work

1. Introduction

The increasing incursion of artificial intelligence (AI) into our workplaces is viewed as one of the most pressing ethical and social issues of our time.[1] The issues that arise depend on the way in which 'AI' is defined. At one level, concerns surround the role of 'narrow' AI in job automation. 'Narrow' AI performs specific tasks using information from specific data sets to assist and enhance the functions carried out by humans, such as speech or facial recognition.[2] Narrow AI is already widely used in workplaces.[3] The crisis narrative surrounding 'narrow' AI focuses on the social threat of job displacement and mass unemployment as a result of the automation of functions previously carried out by humans.[4] The argument proceeds that 'AI' will increase job automation and this will lead to workers losing their jobs. Job automation will also mean that there are fewer jobs to go around, making it more and more difficult for new entrants onto the job market.[5]

---

1 UNESCO, 'Recommendation on the ethics of artificial intelligence' (23 November 2021), available at: https://unesdoc.unesco.org/ark:/48223/pf0000381137 [last accessed 20 November 2023]. The UNESCO Recommendation recognizes (at 5) the 'profound and dynamic positive and negative impacts of artificial intelligence (AI) on societies, environment, ecosystems and human lives, including the human mind, in part because of the new ways in which its use influences human thinking, interaction and decision-making and affects education, human, social and natural sciences, culture, and communication and information'.

2 C. Manning, 'Artificial Intelligence Definitions' (September 2020), available at: https://hai.stanford.edu/sites/default/files/2020-09/AI-Definitions-HAI.pdf

3 The uses of these kinds of AI tools (or algorithms) are discussed fully in section 2.

4 D. Autor, 'Why Are There Still So Many Jobs? The History and Future of Workplace Automation' (2015) 29 *Journal of Economic Perspectives* 3.

5 The apocalyptic nature of this forecasting has been largely discredited. It has been suggested that these studies overestimate the direct link between automation and job loss and underestimate human and job adaptability to technological change. See E. Dahlin, 'Are Robots Really Stealing our Jobs? Perception verses Experience' (2022) 8 *Socius* (online).

On the other hand, the development of 'strong' or 'general' AI is seen to pose a more existential threat. This kind of technology describes a system that can reason, analyse, and achieve a level of understanding that is on a par with humans.[6] The development of 'strong' AI for use in the workplace is thought to raise huge ethical questions about the interaction between work and humanity, and the ways in which that interaction could be regulated. For example, authors question the wisdom of allowing machines legal status,[7] and how far AI can be 'autonomous' in a way traditionally only associated with human beings.[8]

However, there is an increasing recognition that even 'narrow' AI can generate ethical concerns.[9] These 'ethical considerations' have been broadly construed, and include challenging or undermining the respect of certain values in the workplace such as 'privacy, fairness, agency, transparency and accountability'[10] as well as issues which might traditionally be associated with 'social justice': heightening the risks of automation, increasing inequalities between workers in the labour market and changing the relationship between employers and employees in the workplace.[11] It appears that when it comes to the regulation of AI in the workplace, ethical and social justice concerns are difficult to distinguish and are often coincidental. Furthermore, there is a recognition in the literature that the 'ethical' issues raised by (narrow) AI in the workplace 'may not be dramatically different from the concerns raised by other digital technologies, or traditional, non-digital, workplace management practices'.[12] AI can 'extend and systematize ethical failings' in the system of workplace practice, but the failings are already present in existing management practices.[13] This is important in the context of this book,

6 Manning, (n 2).

7 V. De Stefano, 'Negotiating the Algorithm: Automation, Artificial Intelligence and Labor Protection' (2019) 41 *Comparative Labour Law and Policy Journal* 15, 19.

8 P. Moore, 'AI Trainers: Who Is the Smart Worker Today' in P. Moore and J. Woodcock (eds) *Augmented Exploitation: Artificial Intelligence and Work* (London: Pluto Press 2021), 15. See also UNESCO (n 1) 10 in which it is claimed that 'in the long term, AI systems could challenge human's special sense of experience and agency, raising additional concerns about, inter alia, human self-understanding, social, cultural and environmental interaction, autonomy, agency, worth and dignity'.

9 A. Salvi del Pero, P. Wycoff, and A. Vourch, 'Using Artificial Intelligence in the Workplace: What Are the Main Ethical Risks?' (2022) OECD Social, Employment and Migration Working Papers No 273.

10 OECD 'Tools for Trustworthy AI: A Framework to Compare Implementation Tools for Trustworthy AI Systems', OECD (2021) 312 *Digital Economy Papers* 312.

11 S. del Pero et al (n 9), 23.

12 del Pero et al (n 9), 23.

13 del Pero et al (n 9), 23.

given the book's contention that ethical concerns are always central to understanding the experience of workers and the operation of labour law in the workplace.

What this literature does not do, however, is to make an explicit connection between concerns around 'personhood' which arise in the context of 'strong' AI and the ethical concerns which arise from the incorporation of 'narrow' AI practices into the workplace. This chapter aims to fill this gap. This chapter discusses how the introduction of (narrow) AI into the workplace at once confirms and challenges our inherited understandings of the relationship between personhood and labour law. This introduction confirms this understanding in the sense that AI is easily incorporated into our patterns of regulation. AI can meet the standards of 'rationality, autonomy and independence' set by the law. On the other hand, the ease at which AI can fit these standards of personhood presents a challenge to our legal framework. It suggests that our view of the person at the heart of labour law is not 'human' at all. This has ethical implications, but it also has social justice implications: the incorporation of AI easily into labour law's schematic means that it can act to reinforce the managerial prerogative and undermine its social justice imperative. AI serves to increase rather than decrease inequality for workers, and the law is implicit in that process.

Section 2 of this chapter identifies the potentially disruptive nature of the digitalization of workplaces in terms of our understanding of the 'self' at work. Traditional divides around work and private life, mind and body, and machine and human are increasingly being reshaped by the introduction of certain kinds of technology into the labour market. The next section outlines how these changes might be conceptualized on the traditional labour law narrative and its limitations. Section 4 investigates the issues which arise from the introduction of AI into the workplace according to our inherited understanding of 'personhood'; namely, the effect of AI on worker 'rationality' and 'autonomy'. Section 5 discusses the implications of changing our approach to 'personhood' in a theoretical sense and section 6 explores how the alternative vision of personhood might be adopted to increase the effectiveness of the regulation of AI in the workplace.

2. New technology in the workplace and the experience of work

The application of new technology in the workplace has profoundly affected the experience of work. Communication technologies have made it possible for an increased flexibility around the location of work. Workers are not confined or restricted to working in large-scale factory, office, or university settings, but have greater flexibility to choose their work location, and increasingly work from home.[14] Technological innovation has been the driving force behind the growing 'platform' or 'gig' economy through which workers connect directly with customers through online apps. Within the platform economy there are a number of ways in which work can be organized.[15] For example, work can be organized 'on-demand via an app' and performed in a traditional way (transport, cleaning) or work can be performed entirely online through 'crowdwork'. Indeed, the range of forms of platform work make this increasingly difficult to define and categorize. Platform work covers the whole range of skill levels from low-skilled workers completing simple tasks to much more complex platforms where highly skilled persons are confronted with complex tasks. Some authors have suggested that these 'game-changing' technologies, such as app-based management, have hollowed out the distribution of jobs into either high-paying skilled positions or low-paying routine positions through the destruction of middle-level tasks in clerical occupations and on factory floors. This in turn has led to the polarization of labour markets to the detriment of (some) workers.[16]

At the same time, AI tools are changing the way in which work is organized within workplaces. Firms are increasingly using technology to monitor workers, both on and off the job. Information technology and AI allow for the monitoring of workers' activities to an extent unthinkable in the past.[17] Daily activity tracking software such as the WorkSmart Productivity Tool allows companies to monitor remote workers by taking screenshots of their computers and measuring any interruptions or breaks. It is also possible for companies to measure web history and bandwidth utilization; essentially, how much the worker is online. There are increasingly reports of workers being supplied with wearable work instruments that track their movement and location as well as measuring their work pace.[18] GPS systems allow for the tracking of the speed and position of individuals engaged in a range of transport and delivery work. Data collected through this software and these wearable devices are then

---

14 B. Robinson, 'Remote work is here to stay and will increase in 2023', available at: www.forbes.com/sites/bryanrobinson/2022/02/01/remote-work-is-here-to-stay-and-will-increase-into-2023-experts-say/

15 M. Weiss, 'Digitalisation and Basic Principles of Labour Law' in T. Gyulavari and E. Menegatti (eds) *Decent Work in the Digital Age: European and Comparative Perspectives* (Oxford: Hart 2022).

16 Eurofound, *Automation, Digitalisation and Platforms: Implications for Work and Employment* (Luxembourg: Publications Office of the European Union, 2018).

17 De Stefano (n 7), 23.

18 S. del Pero et al (n 9), 25.

analysed through the use of AI to gain a picture of a workers' productivity or performance.[19]

Another important development is the use of technologies in workplaces to track not only physical performance but also measure 'mental' activity or employee 'wellness'. Indeed, Fitbit's market share was secured in 2015 largely because of its new corporate wellness packages.[20] Employers now have a number of options to measure 'performance' outside of the workplace or outside of work time through a range of self-tracking software and other monitoring techniques.[21] Even at the hiring stage, employers can use software to evaluate the suitability of potential employees by analysing applicants' behaviour through their online profile, ultimately rejecting candidates who demonstrate 'lifestyle concerns'.[22] All of these technologies mean that the opportunity for worker and workplace surveillance has dramatically increased.

The increased ability of employers to survey and monitor their workers is directly feeding into the way in which the workforce is managed. Data collected as part of 'electronic performance monitoring' is used through AI tools to rate workers and ultimately to sanction those falling short of the required standard. This kind of algorithmic management has become synonymous with work on digital labour platforms. On these platforms, algorithms can control almost all aspects of the labour process.[23] For example, Uber drivers must adhere to the platform's rules and regulations on acceptance and cancellations when logged on to the app. This means that drivers are constrained by how often they can decline or cancel rides and receive warnings if they do not accept a ride or cancel the ride after acceptance. Most online platforms include rating systems which allow clients of the platform to make assessments of worker performance. On platforms such as Uber and Amazon Mechanical Turk, reputation systems are used to remove poor performers from association with the platform. This kind of algorithmic management is no longer limited to online platforms; its use is in fact widespread in 'offline' industries such as retail, call centres, hospitals, and warehouses.[24]

---

19 V. De Stefano, 'The Rise of the Just in Time Workforce: On-Demand Work, Crowdwork and Labour Protection in the Gig Economy' 37 (2016) *Comparative Labour Law and Policy Journal* 471, 477.

20 P. Moore, *The Quantified Self in Precarity: Work Technology and What Counts* (New York: Routledge 2018). 6,

21 Moore (n 20), 6.

22 S. Sunder and A. Siibak, 'Employers as Nightmare Readers: An Analysis of Ethical and Legal Concerns regarding Employer-Employee Practice on Social Networking Sites' (2017) 10 *Baltic Journal of Law and Politics* 76, 82.

23 J. Berg, 'Protecting Workers in the Digital Age: Technology, Outsourcing and the Growing Precariousness of Work' (2019) 41 *Comparative Labour Law and Policy Journal* 96, 80.

24 Berg (n 23), 81.

A number of labour lawyers have suggested that these changes are bad for workers. Employers hide behind the supposed neutrality and objectivity of 'data' in making unfair and biased decisions. The 'accuracy' and 'precision' and 'impartiality' of code-based governance systems guarantee only the infinite replication of hidden flaws generated by the (White male)-dominated environment in which they are created.[25] In such systems, the possibility of discriminatory outcomes is exacerbated by the impossibility of halting feedback loops, and the low transparency in the way in which data are both collected and used. From a worker perspective, interaction with a 'system' rather than humans deprives them of opportunities for discussion or negotiation with their supervisor or management team.[26] Ultimately this means that workers have little opportunity to challenge the decisions which profoundly affect their working lives. It has also been asserted that the incorporation of digital technologies into the workplace has brought a step change in the operation of the managerial prerogative. Workers are subject to ever tighter control. The control mechanisms of the digital environment operate in different and more insidious ways, but they have allowed management to control and direct more of what workers do both inside and outside of work, as well as eroding the accountability for decisions either to workers or the law.[27]

3. The theoretical challenge

It is possible to theorize these changes using a traditional labour law approach. The use of AI in the workplace can be seen as a tool to increase the alienation or subordination of the worker which reinforces or extends the inequality of bargaining power between employers and employees (workers). These processes can also be explained in terms of the acceleration of 'commodification' of workers driven by the role of technology in the acceleration of capitalist processes. These processes of commodification are examples of the dehumanizing power of the insertion of individuals into the capitalist relationship of production. The introduction of technology and AI into the workplace tends to accelerate these trends and as a result individuals are in greater need of (labour law) protection than ever before.[28]

Put in Marxist terms, the rise of technology in the workplace is a way for capitalists to accelerate processes of capital accumulation. The capitalist's

25 A. Aloisi, 'Automation, Augmentation, Autonomy: Labour Regulation and the Digital Transformation of Managerial Prerogatives' in T. Gyulavari and E. Menegatti (eds) *Decent Work in a Digital Age: European and Comparative Perspectives* (Oxford: Hart 2022), pt III(B).

26 Aloisi (n 25), pt III(B).

27 Aloisi (n 25), pt III(B).

28 De Stefano (n 7), 21.

goal is to earn profit by removing personal value from work and by owning labour and all the application of labour power. New technologies provide new tools through which to achieve this. Capitalists are now able to own not only work performance and outputs, but also conscious and unconscious motivations and desires. Through technology they are able to transform greater fields of 'concrete' work and life into something abstract over which they can own all the tools of measure. The quantification of work denotes an abstraction which can be used to control work life. This process has been described by Marx to the extent that he identifies the impact of machines on work life and experience. In Marx's *Fragment on Machines* he identifies how processes of industrialization turned 'living labour into a mere living accessory' to machinery, with machinery able to absorb the 'labour process in its material character as a mere moment of the realisation of capital'.[29] The power of machines lay in their capacity for the quantification and division of labour, which in turn enabled the greater absorption of workers into the capitalist labour process. The introduction of machines ensured that 'the worker's activity, reduced to a mere abstraction of activity, is determined and regulated on all sides by the movements of the machinery, and not the opposite'.[30]

Indeed, some authors have suggested that the rise of AI and technology in the workplace represents a new phase of (accelerated) capital. Thrift uses the phrase 'knowing capitalism' to describe this new phase.[31] Knowing capitalism depends on technologies that generate knowledge in the form of data and on the commodification of those knowledges. Digital data as a form of knowledge has become extremely profitable and hence has been developed and appropriated by capitalists in order to control even more of the 'surplus' of labour power. It is no longer just workers' bodily labour which is commodified, and the profit extracted. Rather workers' desires, moods, and emotions can also be commodified. Furthermore, digital technologies shorten the link between 'production' and 'consumption', as people interacting with online technologies and other digital devices simultaneously consume and create digital content. As a result employers have even greater opportunities to control the life of workers within and beyond work.[32]

Some authors have described these conditions as contributing (or creating) a new precariat, or 'precarity 4.0.' Moore argues that the experience

[29] K. Marx, 'Fragment on Machines' in K. Marx (ed) *Grundrisse: Foundations of the Critique of Political Economy* translated with a forward by M. Nicolau (London: Penguin 1858/1993), 693.

[30] Marx (n 29), 693.

[31] N. Thrift, *Knowing Capitalism* (London: Sage 2005).

[32] D. Lupton, *The Quantified Self: A Sociology of Self-Tracking* (Cambridge: Polity Press 2016), 35.

of precarity among workers has risen with the increasing infiltration of technology into the workplace.[33] That technology has accelerated the opportunities for companies to create unstable and non-standard forms of work. These forms of work typically represent greater risks of work insecurity, with casual work and bogus self-employment exhibiting the highest level of insecurities and risk, and thus offering the lowest job quality. Through these various forms of 'precarious' work employers have successfully shifted risk away from enterprises and onto workers who provide work for those enterprises.[34] Moreover the prevalence of precarity and insecurity in all forms of work, brought about by the pernicious use of technology by employers, means that 'precarity' is not just experienced while at work, but is experienced as a life condition. At the same time as workers are increasingly controlled by capital their insecurity leads to dependence on capital for survival, disposability, and a 'hell of the absence of guarantees'.[35]

The problem for labour lawyers is where to take this in terms of solutions. A strong insight outlined by Marx is the implication of the law in capitalist labour relations. Not only do capitalists control the means of production, they also control the 'ideologies' which surround the system of capitalist accumulation. They therefore have the power to create laws which serve to legitimate the system and thereby sustain practices of accumulation and exploitation.[36] Of course, labour law does recognize to some extent the inequalities which arise as part of this system and serves to correct them. However, it can be argued that this correction is itself constitutive of capitalist relations.[37] This is because inherent in the system of capitalist relations is the tendency towards over-exploitation, which in the end is detrimental to capitalist accumulation. Essentially the downward pressure on the value of labour power created by the capitalist system threatens the capacity of workers to produce in the longer term. Without mechanisms capable of counterbalancing these tendencies then social reproduction will be compromised to the extent that capital accumulation will be limited. So, labour law steps in to limit the social ills of overexploitation and equalize the contractual conditions which have tipped too far in favour of the employer. Labour law does not challenge as such the unfair premises upon which law has been created, nor does it serve to address social inequality in general. Rather, labour law only serves to make the outcomes of those premises

33 Moore (n 20), 79.

34 Berg (n 23), 75.

35 Moore (n 20), 84.

36 A. Giddens, *Capitalism and Modern Social Theory: An Analysis of the Writings of Marx, Durkheim and Weber* (Cambridge: Cambridge University Press 1971), 41.

37 Z. Adams, 'Labour Law, Capitalism and the Juridical Form: Taking a Critical Approach to Questions of Labour Law Reform' (2021) 50 (3) *Industrial Law Journal* 434, 442.

more palatable to workers and to ensure the support of the capitalist system in the longer term.[38]

This analysis suggests that the introduction of AI into the workplace accelerates social justice problems, and that the law is in some way implicated.[39] The law has the effect of attempting to correct social justice problems but is so infiltrated by the structures of power that the law can never be an effective means of social justice for workers. This is important of itself, but on this Marxist analysis, there is little that the law can do outside of revolutionary political and social change. The next section suggests an alternative way of analysing the social justice challenge which arises from the adoption of AI in the workplace: the relationship between AI and 'personhood'. To some extent, labour lawyers have already risen to this challenge, as they have indicated that AI compromises both worker 'autonomy' and 'rationality'. As we know from earlier in this book, these are central pieces of the Kantian puzzle of personhood which have infiltrated into our law. However, this analysis necessarily has limitations as a result of all the problems that arise from the association of the worker person with the Kantian rationalist legal person. Section 5 will stick with the personhood analysis but will suggest that an alternative reading of personhood is required in the law if it is to be a means to achieve social justice for workers. Section 6 discusses the potential for the incorporation of this alternative vision for personhood in the regulation of AI.

4. AI and the theorization of the person

The digitalization of the workplace has presented a challenge to the way in which we understand the boundaries of 'self' at work, and the way in which personhood is constructed in the work environment and in the regulation of work. There is the suggestion that the introduction of new technologies and digitalization of the work environment is detrimental to the 'humanity' of the worker. These new technologies are applied in such a way as to erode the worker's sense of self by reducing the sphere of worker autonomy through ever increasing managerial control. This is accelerated by the move towards using machines not just to use data descriptively but also prescriptively. Prescriptive algorithmic tools have the ability to shape worker conduct and choice as they create an 'environment in which there are no alternatives to performing the work as described'.[40] Although

[38] Adams (n 37), 443.

[39] M. Weiss, 'Digitalisation and Basic Principles of Labour Law' in T. Gyulavari and E. Menegatti (eds) *Decent Work in a Digital Age: European and Comparative Perspectives* (Oxford: Hart), ch 2.

[40] Aloisi (n 25), pt IIIB.

this model leaves workers with the impression that they own their own actions, they in fact lose opportunities for autonomy and self-reflection.[41] Furthermore, as targets for workers are increasingly being set and directed by machine through people analytics and algorithmic governance, there is the risk that '[v]arious groups of workers are on the verge of experiencing not replacement by machines but treatment as robots'.[42] If workers are viewed only in terms of their ability to match to the data-driven aims of a particular business, then there is nothing to set the abilities of workers apart from the abilities of machines. This is a dehumanizing process which goes to the core concerns of labour law.[43] This section investigates how the notion of self as it is incorporated into the law facilitates these trends, but how these trends also present a challenge to the law. This is a complex dialectic, but one which is essential to understand if the future of work is to be 'human-centric' in both a theoretical and practical sense.[44]

4.1 AI and rationality

As has been argued in earlier chapters of this book, both employees and employers are judged according to standards of rationality. This stems from the centrality of 'rationality' to legal subjectivity and the 'liberal' legal subject. Take, for example, unfair dismissal law. Employers are judged against a standard of 'reasonableness' which in practice goes little further than a test of rationality.[45] The courts are asked to judge whether or not the decision made by the employer fell within a band or range of reasonable responses. This band of reasonable responses is judged against the action of the 'hypothetical reasonable employer'. In making this judgment the courts are expressly directed not to substitute their opinion of the reasonableness of the decision for that of the reasonable employer.[46] Essentially the courts are expected to show deference to the expertise of the employer and respect the position and knowledge that the employer had at the time of the dismissal.[47] Interfering

41 Aloisi (n 25), pt IIIB.

42 Aloisi (n 25), pt IIIB.

43 De Stefano (n 7), 21.

44 C. Casalone et al 'Human-centric AI: From Principles to Actionable and Shared Policies', September 2021, available at: www.g20-insights.org/policy_briefs/human-centric-ai-from-principles-to-actionable-and-shared-policies/

45 This position is generally but not universally accepted. See D. Cabrelli, 'The Hierarchy of Differing Behavioural Standards of Review in Labour Law' (2011) 40 (2) *Industrial Law Journal* 146 for an alternative opinion.

46 *Iceland Frozen Foods Ltd v Jones* [1983] UKEAT 62_82_2907.

47 A. Baker, 'The "Range of Reasonable Responses" Test: A Poor Substitution for the Statutory Language' (2021) 50 (2) *Industrial Law Journal* 226.

in the employer's decision would result in an unjustified curtailment of the autonomy of the employer. This puts the court in a difficult situation in that they have to judge the reasonableness of the decision without being able to reach for their own interpretation of reasonableness[48] and have to rely on an industry standard which is necessarily skewed in favour of employers.[49] Ultimately this has led to the erosion of the reasonableness standard towards a situation where the question is no longer whether the employer has acted within a band of reasonableness, but rather whether the employer has taken a decision which no reasonable (rational) employer could take. The standard of rationality turns out to be a very low hurdle for employers to reach.[50]

This is very important in the context of the introduction of AI into the workplace. The use of AI would not, on the face of it, appear to make the decisions of employers less rational. Indeed, the use of AI is considered hyper-rational because it depends only on the manipulation of facts and evidence in the form of objective data.[51] The modes and means of decision-making by AI are more 'rational' than human intervention as they are pre-programmed according to a set of criteria which are logical and stable. Machines do not make mistakes in the same way as humans. In the context of work, it has been argued that automated HR practices eliminate the possibility of individual biases of supervisors or managers and hence lead to decisions which are more objectively rational, and ultimately fairer.[52] Furthermore, wearables which track worker behaviour are a way of ensuring that decisions rely on the maximum data set. The use of customer rating systems as a means to score performance are much fairer because they are based on data collected 'on the ground'.[53] Decisions made on the basis of this data might therefore be considered 'rational' and in the interests of workers. The argument proceeds that AI is the perfect manifestation of the 'truth' of universal rationality and so its increasing infiltration in the workplace brings benefits both to workers and employers.[54]

---

48 Baker (n 47), 263.

49 T. Brodtkkorb, 'Employee Misconduct and UK Dismissal Law: Does the Range of Reasonable Responses Test Require Reform?' (2010) 52 (6) *International Journal of Law and Management* 429.

50 A. Freer, 'The Range of Reasonable Responses Test – From Guidelines to Statute' (1998) 27 (4) *Industrial Law Journal* 335.

51 S. Wiblen and J.H. Marler, 'Digitalised Talent Management and Automated Talent Decisions: The Implications for HR Professionals' (2021) 32 (12) *International Journal of Human Resource Management* 2592.

52 D. Ravid, D.L. Tomczak, J.C. White, and T.S. Behrend, 'EPM 20/20: A Review, Framework, and Research Agenda for Electronic Performance Monitoring' (2019) 46 (1) *Journal of Management* 100, 102.

53 Ravid et al (n 52), 106.

54 Ravid et al (n 52), 102.

Labour lawyers have consistently pointed out the dangers of the assumptions of AI rationality and that AI 'rationality' necessarily brings benefits to workers.[55] For example, many labour lawyers have pointed out that management by algorithm does not necessarily lead to more objective or bias-free HR practices. These HR systems merely replicate the biases of their human programmers or reflect embedded institutional bias.[56] Furthermore, the data collected are often partial and selective, and this disrupts the objectivity of decision-making.[57] The result is that algorithm-based decision-making, far from being rational or objective, 'may be biased, may reflect cultural, gender and other prejudices and preferences and may contain errors'.[58] A number of further studies have shown the side effects of 'rationality' monitoring, including increased stress and decreased job satisfaction among workers.[59] What this analysis does not bring out so starkly is the problematic nature of rationality itself as a standard of analysis or adjudication. Rationality as a standard contributes to the dehumanization or sterilization of the issues which arise from increased use of AI in the workplace, and paralysis in legal response. These issues will be discussed further in Sections 5 and 6.

4.2 AI and autonomy

It is widely recognized that AI causes shifts in the autonomy balance between employers and workers. There has been some interesting analysis on whether the introduction of AI into the workplace increases or decreases employer autonomy and the impact on workers and their autonomy. On the one hand, technology in the workplace is seen as a good thing for workers. It can improve job quality by automating some routine and unpleasant tasks, and hence increasing job satisfaction. It can boost worker 'autonomy' in the sense that workers have more opportunities to apply their own ideas in more creative tasks.[60] It can also lessen the physical burden of some jobs, as well as the physical risks associated with those jobs.[61] On the other hand, new

---

55 De Stefano (n 7), 22.

56 A. Aloisi and E .Gramano, 'Artificial Intelligence Is Watching You at Work: Digital Surveillance, Employee Monitoring and Regulatory Issues in the EU Context' (2019) 41 *Comparative Labour Law and Policy Journal* 95, 99.

57 De Stefano (n 7), 28.

58 De Stefano (n 7), 28.

59 R. Siegel, C. König, and V. Lazar, 'The Impact of Electronic Monitoring on Employees' Job Satisfaction, Stress, Performance and Counterproductive Work Behaviour: A Meta-Analysis' (2022) 8 *Computers in Human Behaviour Reports* 1.

60 De Stefano (n 7), 16.

61 De Stefano (n 7), 16.

technologies and the digitalization of employment carry a number of risks for workers in terms of job quality and experience. It has been suggested that new technologies are dangerous because they increase the possibility for employers to control workers and exercise the managerial prerogative. For example, the devolution of managerial functions to algorithms can increase the ability of managers to control their workers, and decrease the channels through which workers can make sense of or challenge that control.[62] The digitalization of the work environment is also dangerous because employers are able to monitor and record details of worker activity which might previously have been considered 'private'; for example, calorific take, physical activity levels outside the workplace, and sleep 'success'.[63] Moreover, employers are now able to track the 'affective' aspects of labour, such as emotional and mood responses and stress levels.[64] All of this suggests that rather than worker autonomy increasing through digitalization, such autonomy is actually decreasing, and employees and workers are subject to ever increasing managerial control.

Furthermore, there are questions about the increasing 'autonomy' of AI decisions. AI itself is increasingly being defined on the basis that it autonomous. In 2019, the OECD's 'Recommendations on the Council on Artificial Intelligence' stated that AI could be differentiated from other technologies on the basis that 'AI systems are designed to operate with varying levels of autonomy'.[65] As a result, AI represents a good opportunity for 'augmenting human capabilities and enhancing creativity, advancing inclusion and underrated populations, reducing economic, social, gender and other inequalities, and protecting natural environments, thus invigorating inclusive growth, sustainable development and well-being'.[66] Likewise, the European Commission's definition of AI also refers to autonomy. In its 2018 Communication, it stated that AI 'refers to systems that display intelligent behaviour by analysing their environment and taking actions – with some degree of autonomy – to achieve specific goals'.[67]

The 'autonomy' of AI has been viewed as contributing to worker well-being. The more sophisticated the AI, the greater scope there is for worker tasks to be delegated to AI, leaving workers to develop their own creative

62 Aloisi (n 25), pt IIIB.

63 Moore (n 8), 16.

64 Moore (n 8), 16.

65 OECD, 'Recommendation of the Council on Artificial Intelligence' (2019), para I, available at: https://legalinstruments.oecd.org/en/instruments/OECD-LEGAL-0449

66 OECD (n 65), 7.

67 European Commission, 'Communication from the Commission: Artificial Intelligence in Europe' (25 April 2018) COM (2018) 237 final, available at: https://eur-lex.europa.eu/legal-content/EN/TXT/HTML/?uri=CELEX:52018DC0237&from=EN

capacity. More and more functions can be delegated to AI, including middle-management functions previously out of the reach of digitalization. The argument proceeds that this creates a more efficient business environment which creates benefits for workers in the longer run.[68] There is also the possibility that more autonomous AI mechanisms could involve increasing sensitivity to workers; AI systems can record and factor in a greater range of worker personal data (including data on mood, emotion, and so on) than a traditional employer with a large and heterogeneous workforce might manage.[69] This can lead to more sensitive decision-making and a greater ability to achieve fairness for workers. On the other hand, it can be argued that the 'autonomy' of AI presents even greater challenges for workers. This autonomy dictates that AI decisions will become increasingly less transparent while at the same time allowing employers to escape accountability for AI decisions. Indeed, the 'control' exercised by AI is already indirect; algorithmic control is exercised in a myriad of ways, often eschewing direct orders or explicit instructions.[70] More complicated programming structures and the use of 'machine learning' technologies means that the process of decision-making becomes ever more diffuse, while at the same time subjecting workers to increasing levels of control. Indeed, it has been argued that the greatest asset of autonomous AI systems is to increase the control over workers, while at the same time scrupulously avoiding the appearance of traditional employer control.[71]

4.3 AI and the personhood analysis

The analysis of the effects of AI on worker and employer rationality and autonomy are important considerations. They bring to the fore the challenge to personhood brought about by the introduction of AI into the workplace. However, it is argued here that there are also conceptual limitations with this kind of analysis. It is the argument in this book that this kind of analysis must proceed with a more careful appreciation of the context and construction of 'autonomy' and 'rationality' as conceptual frameworks for the analysis of worker experience and the aspirations for their future. The concepts of 'rationality' and 'autonomy' can themselves be problematic. The construction of AI as 'autonomous' should ring alarm bells because

68 M.T. Bodie et al, 'The Law and Policy of People Analytics' (2017) 88 *University of Colorado Law Review* 961, 971.

69 Bodie et al (n 68), 1011.

70 J. Adams-Prassl, 'What if Your Boss Was an Algorithm? Economic Incentives, Legal Challenges, and the Rise of Artificial Intelligence' (2019) 41 *Comparative Labour Law and Policy Journal* 123, 139.

71 Adams-Prassl (n 70), 145.

this suggests that autonomy can extend to non-human entities and thus is not such a useful construct in the analysis of worker experience. The fact that non-human entities are able to meet the criteria of 'rationality' much more easily than workers should also be a point of reflection. If non-human entities are able to meet the criteria of 'humanity' much more easily than human workers, does this not imply that there is a problem with the way in which we characterize the worker/person as part of our law?

The next section outlines in more detail the problematic of personhood and labour law. It suggests that it is not enough to think about the challenge of AI to 'autonomy' and 'rationality' without thinking more deeply about the connection between 'rationality and 'autonomy', and legal subjectivity in labour law. Indeed, if we want to have a law which deals with the ethical and social justice challenges presented by AI, we must move to a different conceptualization of legal subjectivity: the relational subject of law.

5. Moving beyond the liberal legal subject

In Chapter 2 we saw how the nature of 'personhood' and the incorporation of 'personhood' into legal subjectivity is a vexed question for labour law. Labour law at once accepts a non-rationalist view of the person in raising the issues of 'inequality of bargaining power' and 'commodification', and seeking to correct the failings of liberal law. At the same time, labour law is tied to the structures and operation of 'civil law' which does adopt a rationalist/reductive view of the person through the 'liberal legal subject.' The result is that labour law is forced to adopt the liberal legal subject at its heart, despite the intuition that this adoption constrains labour law and makes it impossible for it to achieve its own aims (for example, 'de-commodification'). The liberal legal subject is an individualistic and individualized representation of personhood. Its adoption means that not only is the input of labour law too individualized but also the outcomes are too individualized – that is, 'independence', 'autonomy', and ultimately 'freedom'. Labour law is not able to address social inequality or deal with social injustice as it manifests itself in employment relationships as a result. Moreover, the liberal legal subject is insufficiently human. Its characteristics – autonomy, rationality, and independence – can be applied and extended to a range of non-human entities. This is seen as an advantage in some areas of the literature as it brings companies and other institutional agents (AI) within the scope of the law.[72] However, this state of affairs carries with it real risks and challenges

[72] J. Vincent, 'Giving Robots Personhood Is Actually about Making Corporations Accountable', *The Verge* (19 January 2017), available at: www.theverge.com/2017/1/19/14322334/robot-electronic-persons-eu-report-liability-civil-suits

for social justice. Essentially powerful groups in society are able to gain legal protection without personal risk.

As we have explored in this book, the liberal legal subject and the values it promotes are not 'neutral' because they hold within them a particular world view which reflects the adulation of individuality over collectivity, mind over body, and rights over experience. Modern power operates not by ignoring individuals, but by claiming to have arrived at the 'truth' of the individual and thereby limiting the individual to a set of very specific patterns.[73] This form of power 'categorises the individual, marks him by his own individuality, attaches him to his own identity, imposes a truth on him which he must recognise, and which others have to recognise in him. It is a form of power which makes individuals subjects'.[74] The determination of this subjectivity has operated in our society to create an ethos of individuality to which we all must aspire, but which does not accurately reflect our 'humanity'.

According to feminist critique, universal reason and rationality are phallocentric concepts embedded in a hierarchical division of mind and 'nature'.[75] On the one side of the division there is masculine reason and intelligence, and on the other there is the embodied condition which is essentially feminine. Reason and rationality form the basis for standards of morality on which legal systems can be built.[76] Embodiment complicates reason and rationality and so this is a hindrance to the creation of universal principles upon which law relies. However, feminists argue that embodiment is inescapably part of the human condition and worker experience.[77] Indeed, the introduction of AI by employers to capture, record, and track 'emotional' or 'affective' labour demonstrates these essential features of human nature. This kind of AI can be alienating for workers precisely because it involves the creation of schisms which are artificial and destructive of the multidimensional 'self'.[78]

It is the argument of feminist writers (and others) that the construction of the self in terms of individual rationality and autonomy is divisive and

73 M. Foucault, 'The Subject and Power' (1982) 8 *Critical Enquiry* 777.

74 Foucault (n 73), 781.

75 Y. Braudo-Bahat, 'Towards a Relational Conceptualization of the Right to Personal Autonomy' (2017) 25 (2) *Journal of Gender, Social Policy, and the Law* 111, 123. For a full discussion, see Chapter 3 of this book.

76 Braudo-Bahat (n 75), 119.

77 M. Fineman, 'The Vulnerable Subject: Anchoring Equality in the Human Condition' (2008) 20 *Yale Journal of Law and Feminism* 1, 2.

78 A. Hochschild, *The Managed Heart: Commercialization of Human Feeling* (3rd edn, Berkeley, CA: University of California Press 2012); P. Brook, 'In Critical Defence of Emotional Labour: Refuting Bolton's Critique of Hochschild's Concept' (2009) 23 (3) *Work, Employment and Society* 531, 532.

disempowering.[79] First, these standards are disempowering because they are insufficiently 'human'.[80] Non-human entities are much more able to meet these standards than humans precisely because their 'autonomy' or 'rationality' is not socially contingent or physically bounded in a way that it is for embodied human beings.[81] Second, the liberal legal subject internalizes an idea of the transhistorical self under which self-hood is static and predetermined. This is seen as its great value, as it ensures impartiality and equality of treatment for all individuals. However, this narrative is disempowering because it implies that individuals are stuck with a version of self which cannot be changed or developed. 'Autonomy' and 'rationality' are part of the metaphysical, not the political. This severs the link between autonomy and collective action, and means that selfhood and social justice stand in opposition. If 'autonomy' cannot be built, then the question arises why it is worth fighting for.[82] As a result, critical scholars argue that rationality and autonomy can only be a force for political resistance or opposition if those notions themselves are reclaimed:

> The political, ethical, social, philosophical problem of our days is not to try to liberate the individual from the state, and from the state's institutions, but to liberate us both from the state and from the type of individualization which is linked to the state. We have to promote new forms of subjectivity through the refusal of this kind of individuality which has been imposed on us for decades.[83]

It is suggested in this book that in order to recapture the dynamic nature of self and for the possibility for resistance to be incorporated into labour law, an alternative conceptualization of the legal person is required: the relational self. The argument proceeds as follows. According to the relationality analysis, selfhood is best represented by multidimensionality.[84] A person has a myriad of physical and identity characteristics in addition to intelligence and reason. All of these characteristics are important to understanding selfhood. They not only mark individuals out as unique, but they also represent a person's relationality or social experience. Furthermore, the complexity of a person is what constitutes their ability to build relationships and achieve

79 Braudo-Bahat (n 75), 122.

80 A. Grear, *Redirecting Human Rights: Facing the Challenge of Corporate Humanity* (London: Palgrave Macmillan 2010), 41.

81 Grear (n 80), 85.

82 A. Kritzman (ed) *Politics, Philosophy, Culture: Interviews and Other Writings 1977–1984* (London: Routledge 1988).

83 Foucault (n 73), 785.

84 Braudo-Bahat (n 75), 137.

'creative interactions with others'.[85] Hence, any account which ignores the myriad dimensions of a person conceptualizes personhood and autonomy in a 'partial, superficial and inaccurate manner'.[86] Indeed, the fact that AI is able to achieve the status of 'autonomy' shows how dangerous this failure is.

Accounts which do not recognize the relational nature of autonomy (and rationality) also tend to demonize 'dependence' as an aberrant and dehumanizing experience. According to this scheme, dependency is a threat to both rationality and autonomy; it interferes in the ability of individuals to engage in rational decisions and make plans which are truly autonomous. As a result, the task of the law is to avoid creating or exacerbating problems of 'dependence' through excessively paternalistic or interventionist policies.[87] Of course, this leads to legal paralysis in labour law: the best action for the law is to do nothing at all.

On the relationality analysis, the non-interventionist position does not make sense. Every human is necessarily 'dependent' in some ways because all are constituted by a set of (both good and bad) relationships. The law does not create 'dependence' through intervention. Rather sensitive policy making should ensure the encouragement of the development of good relationships which are autonomy building while recognizing the destructive nature of others. Good laws will recognize the multidimensional and relational character of human nature and ensure that each individual is able to 'find one's own law'.[88] Importantly, the adoption of this alternative approach to subjectivity necessarily upgrades the importance of collective action and group-based support. On the relationality scheme, there is a direct link between the availability of collective structures and the ability to achieve 'autonomy'. Indeed, collective experience marks us out as human.[89] As a result, collectivities can no longer be seen as extra legal and a part of 'social' experience outside the realm of law. If the law is to be 'human-centric', then the law must play a role in legitimizing and encouraging those collective structures and accepting their central role (in worker experience).

The relationality analysis is very important in the context of AI (and its regulation). It highlights the centrality of the concept of personhood in the capacity of the law to improve the lives of workers; that is, how the law

85 J. Nedelsky, *Law's Relations: A Relational Theory of Self, Autonomy and the Law* (Oxford: Oxford University Press 2011), 64.

86 Braudo-Bahat (n 75), 115.

87 M. Fineman, *The Autonomy Myth: A Theory of Dependency* (New York: The New Press 2005), 37.

88 Nedelsky (n 85), 123.

89 While there has been the suggestion that (narrow) AI can be 'autonomous' and 'rational', there has not (yet) been the suggestion that AI (at least in its narrow form) can be socialized in the same way as humans.

classifies the legal person determines the ability of the law to operate for the 'sake of humanity'.[90] This responds to the intuition among labour lawyers of the importance of the analysis of personhood in trying to understand the impact of AI in the workplace, while at the same time recognizing the inadequacy of our current legal tools to deal with that impact. It appears that our law holds within it a very narrow conceptualization of personhood which is hardly human at all. This makes it very difficult for the law to respond adequately to the threats posed by AI because those threats are not seen as existential. It comes down to a question of balance: if AI and workers and employers all hold 'rationality' and 'autonomy', the role of the law is to ensure that all these entities should be allowed to express their 'rationality' and 'autonomy' in a reasonable way. The classical/Kantian view of personhood also creates a downward pressure on intervention: AI, employers, and workers should be able to find an equilibrium with only a small steer from the law (through the expression of their respective autonomy and rationality). Finally, the asocial notion of personhood at the heart of law means that the law tends to undermine wider social justice aspirations. For example, there is no role for social partners in building or responding to worker 'autonomy'. This will be discussed further in the next section.

6. The 'human-centric' regulation of AI in the workplace

This section will consider two examples of institutional responses to AI (in the workplace): the EU-proposed AI Act[91] and the British government's 'pro innovation' response to AI regulation.[92] These approaches bear similarities, in that they view employment considerations in relation to AI as secondary to economic concerns. There are also differences: the EU approach is much more interventionist and detailed than in the UK. However, it is argued here that the most interesting elements of these proposals has been the response (and opposition) they have generated. In this response, there is a semblance of a more relational approach to the regulation of AI in the workplace. These responses and their implications will be discussed in this section.

The EU AI Act was drafted under the auspices of Article 114 of the Treaty on the Functioning of the European Union (TFEU) and so its main concern

90 H. Sinzheimer, 'Das Problem des Menschen im Recht' (1933) in H. Sinzheimer, *Arbeitsrecht und Rechtssoziologie: gesammelte Aufsätze und Reden* (Frankfurt: Europaische Verlagsanstalt 1976), 52.

91 Proposal for a Regulation Laying Down Harmonised Rules on Artificial Intelligence (AI Act) and Amending Certain Union Legislative Acts, COM (2021) 206 final.

92 UK Gov, 'A pro-innovation approach to AI regulation' (3 August 2023), available at: www.gov.uk/government/publications/ai-regulation-a-pro-innovation-approach/white-paper

was to 'improve the functioning of the internal market by laying down a uniform legal framework in particular for the development, marketing and use of artificial intelligence'.[93] As a secondary consideration, it recognized the need to maintain a 'high level of protection of health, safety and fundamental rights'[94] across the Union in the implementation of AI, and this included ensuring the appropriate operation of AI in the workplace. To this end, the AI Act designated the use of AI systems to carry out employment functions (such as recruitment, task allocation, or management) as 'high-risk'.[95] The designation of AI systems as 'high-risk' under the Act has several implications. First, AI 'providers' (including distributors, importers, users, or other third parties that can be considered as providers) are under a duty to establish, implement, document, and maintain a risk-management system in relation to those AI systems (Article 9 (1)). In implementing this risk assessment, due consideration should be given to the 'technical knowledge', experience, education, and training that is expected from the user (the employer), and the environment in which the AI system is intended to be used. Second, users must be informed about any risks which might result from the intended purpose and 'foreseeable' misuse of the AI system which 'may lead to risks to health and safety or fundamental rights'.[96] Those fundamental rights specifically include non-discrimination and gender equality, and the rights under the European Charter.

However, it has been argued that the definitions in the Act are likely to be under-inclusive and this will lead to weaknesses in any system of risk management created. For example, many of the AI systems used in employment are not included in the definition of high-risk AI in section 9 (1) and the problematic nature of data collection by AI is not adequately considered or regulated.[97] For example, the definition of high-risk AI does not include software which is not intended to be used to carry out recruitment or management functions but has this effect.[98] Furthermore, the duties on AI providers created by the Act are likely to be low in practice and the mechanisms for ensuring compliance are weak. One of the problems with the AI Act is that employers can be both producers and users of AI,

93 AI Act, Preamble, para 1.

94 AI Act, Preamble, para 1.

95 AI Act, reg 3 (5).

96 The Explanatory Memorandum specifically mentions non-discrimination and gender equality (along with the Charter of Fundamental Rights of the European Union and existing secondary EU law on data protection) as rights which must be complied with by employers.

97 A. Cefaliello and M. Kullman, 'Offering False Security: How the Draft Artificial Intelligence Act Undermines Fundamental Workers Rights' (2022) 13 (4) *European Labour Law Journal* 1.

98 Cefaliello and Kullman (n 97), 6.

and this reduces the level of systematic scrutiny in the system.[99] There is also the problem that the Act relies largely on self-regulation as the means of enforcement. Employers using high-risk AI have to ensure that it is safe and have to ensure that safety failures are adequately reported. Unfortunately, this means that employers are arbiters of their own fortune. They assess the risks of the software and also whether safety incidents should be reported without third-party scrutiny. This is likely to lead to overuse of AI and under-reporting of discriminatory activities.[100]

While the institutional feedback on the AI Act has often been positive, certain institutions have raised concerns that the AI Act does not go far enough to recognize the dangers posed to workers. For example, the European Trade Union Confederation (ETUC) has argued that the EU focus on 'risk management' in the regulation of AI is insufficiently ambitious and driven by a concern for economic growth over the promotion of fundamental rights.[101] The ETUC supports a 'human in command' approach which recognizes the potentially dehumanizing effects of AI and the need for greater control of workers over processes of AI integration in the workplace. Similarly, the European Parliament has attempted to strengthen the AI Act proposals through a series of amendments which emphasize the importance of human oversight of AI.[102] For example, the European Parliament introduced an amendment to Article 1 which states that the purpose of the AI Act is first and foremost to 'promote the uptake of human-centric and trustworthy artificial intelligence' and to ensure 'a high level of protection … from harmful effects' of AI systems. This is followed by a set of 'general principles' applicable to the development and use of all AI systems which includes 'human agency and oversight'. This implies that all AI should be used in a way that 'serves people respects human dignity and personal autonomy' and functions in a way that can be 'appropriately controlled and overseen by humans'.[103] In commenting on the Act, the European Economic and Social Committee (EESC) goes even further. It suggests that for a truly 'human in command' approach, some decisions should stay the preserve of humans and should not be delegated to AI at all.[104]

---

99 Cefaliello and Kullman (n 97), 6.

100 Cefaliello and Kullman (n 97), 7.

101 European Trade Union Institute (ETUI), 'AI – Humans must be in command' (17 February 2020), available at: www.etuc.org/en/document/ai-humans-must-be-command

102 Amendments adopted by the European Parliament on 14 June 2023 on the proposal for a regulation of the European Parliament and of the Council on laying down harmonised rules on artificial intelligence (Artificial Intelligence Act) and amending certain Union legislative acts (COM (2021)0206) – C90146/2021 (2021/0106/COD).

103 European Parliament (n 102), Amendment 213.

104 EESC, *Artificial Intelligence – The consequences of artificial intelligence on the (digital) single market, production, consumption, employment, and society* 2017 OJ C 288 1, para 1.6. See the comment

A further point of contention is the failure to integrate the social partners into the AI Act. The ETUC calls for trade unions to be given a higher degree of involvement in the development and implementation of AI in the workplace in order that safeguards for workers are properly upheld.[105] This approach is also adopted to a certain extent by the European Parliament which suggested amendments to certain provisions of the AI Act to include reference to the social partners. For example, the European Parliament inserted a provision in the AI Act to the effect that social partners should by consulted by the Commission on any decision as to whether an AI system is 'high-risk'.[106] Social partners should also be consulted on the possible impact on (worker) fundamental rights when AI is introduced into the workplace.[107] There has also been the suggestion that social partners should be empowered to intervene in the deployment of AI in the workplace; for example, in relation to the setting of appropriate targets for workers through AI or the type of data to be collected at work.[108] They should also be empowered to feedback on the use of AI to a third-party agency.[109]

The sentiment of these proposals is also reflected in the Trades Union Congress (TUC)'s response to the UK government's 'pro-innovation' approach to the regulation of AI at work. This pro-innovation approach has led the UK government to explicitly turn away from the introduction of new statutory regulation for AI in the workplace.[110] The government's view is that the current statutory employment law provisions are sufficiently flexible to deal with the challenge raised by AI. Instead, the government has introduced five cross-sectoral principles which are to be implemented by current regulators.[111] These cross-sectoral principles will be 'context-specific' and thereby avoid 'excessive regulation that could stifle innovation'.[112] These

at para 3.1.2 that 'it should be established which decision-making procedures can and cannot be transferred to AI systems and when human intervention is desirable or mandatory'.

105 ETUI, 'Press Release' (17 February 2020), available at: www.etuc.org/en/pressrelease/etuc-response-commission-strategies-digital-and-ai#:~:text=Commenting%20on%20the%20launch%20of%20the%20European%20Commission%E2%80%99s,surveillance%20or%20discriminatory%20treatment%20because%20of%20biased%20algorithms

106 European Parliament (n 102), Amendment 256.

107 European Parliament (n 102), Amendment 413.

108 Cefaliello and Kullman (n 97), 21.

109 Cefaliello and Kullman (n 97), 21.

110 UK Gov, 'Policy Paper: A Pro-innovation approach to AI regulation' (3 August 2023), available at: www.gov.uk/government/publications/ai-regulation-a-pro-innovation-approach/white-paper para 11.

111 These principles are (1) safety and security, (2) appropriate transparency and explainability, (3) fairness, (4) accountability and governance, and (5) contestability and redress.

112 P. Brione and S. Day, 'House of Commons Library: Artificial Intelligence and Employment Law' (11 August 2023), available at: https://researchbriefings.files.parliament.uk/documents/CBP-9817/CBP-9817.pdf

proposals run counter to the interventionist approach suggested by the TUC.[113] In its paper *Dignity at Work and the AI Revolution* the TUC set out a vision for AI regulation in which 'worker concerns and interests [are] always at the heart of the development and implementation of AI at work'.[114] This includes allowing everyone at work to have a say in deciding whether AI is introduced to make important decisions about people and 'genuine' and 'active' consultation with unions and workers before new technologies are introduced. The TUC suggests, in contrast to the government's position, that existing legislation does not go far enough to support the 'cross-sectoral principles' of the pro-innovation white paper. Rather, in order to ensure 'safety', 'fairness', and 'contestability' in the implementation of AI, there need to be new statutory duties established and amendments to existing employment legislation. It suggests the amendment of equality legislation to state that discriminatory data processing is always unlawful, and a reversal of the burden of proof in relation to discrimination claims that challenge high-risk AI.[115] There should also be a new right not be subject to detrimental treatment due to the processing of inaccurate data in the Employment Rights Act 1996.[116] The TUC suggests new rights to 'human review' and 'human contact' in relation to employer decision-making and amendments to legislation to ensure access to information about the use of AI in the workplace.[117] Finally, there should be a statutory duty to consult trade unions on the deployment of AI and trade unions should argue for a formal data-gathering role in relation to member data so that they can effectively monitor the use of high-risk AI in the workplace.[118]

7. Conclusion

The increasing incursion of AI into the workplace provides a real opportunity and need for reflection on how we theorize and experience the interaction between humanity, work, and regulation. Instinctively, we recognize that the incursion of AI into the workplace provides a challenge or threat to our 'autonomy' and that AI 'rationality' can act to undermine our experience of work in various ways. In this way, there has been a level of reflection on the human impact of AI in the workplace. However, it is the argument in this chapter that this level of reflection does not go far enough to meet the challenge to workers (and their humanity) posed by AI. Rather, the incursion

---

113 TUC, 'Dignity at Work and the AI Revolution' (March 2021), available at: www.tuc.org.uk/sites/default/files/2021-03/The_AI_Revolution_20121_Manifesto_AW.pdf
114 TUC (n 113), 4.
115 TUC (n 113), 8.
116 TUC (n 113), 8.
117 TUC (n 113), 9.
118 TUC (n 113), 7.

of AI into the workplace should make it clear to us that the 'rationality/autonomy' conceptualization of personhood itself is fundamentally flawed. It cannot be the case that 'rationality' or 'autonomy' in the Kantian sense truly captures what it means to be a human at work. How can this be the case when AI is more able to prove 'autonomy' and 'rationality' (for the purposes of the law) than workers are? Hence, we need to move beyond the 'autonomy/rationality' schematic and consider instead those elements which really set us as worker/humans apart and which (as yet) AI is not able to achieve; namely, corporeality and sociality.

Arguably there is some recognition of this alternative conceptualization of humanity at work in the 'human in command' or 'human-centric' approach to the regulation of AI discussed in this chapter. This approach promotes human control over AI in recognition of the distinctive nature of workers as humans. Under the human-in-command approach, the use and development of AI should be restricted, and workers should be able to ensure that decisions made about their work or performance are subject to human review. Furthermore, there should be deep and engaged consultation with workers over the deployment of AI in workplaces. This recognizes the importance of worker voice as a means of resistance. This also goes to the question of humanity: if the autonomy of the worker/person depends on relational experience, it must be the case that workers have the opportunity to develop and express their relationality and autonomy through consultation and the opportunity to reject pernicious changes posed upon them by employers.

The political capital generated by AI presents the impetus for a wide-ranging reconsideration of personhood at work and the re-regulation of labour law around the 'relational subject'.

8

Conclusions

The aim of this book has been to explore the possibility of generating a positive theory of social justice for labour law by changing the way in which 'personhood' is conceived. It aimed to incorporate feminist critique of personhood and the theorization of the 'relational' self into labour law to show the ways in which labour law is currently insufficiently 'human' despite purporting to have 'humanity at its core'. In order to achieve those aims, the book has been both inward- and outward-facing. It has been inward-facing in that it has reflected on the way in which personhood is incorporated into the law generally and labour law specifically. This has brought out the tensions which exist within the traditional labour law narrative when it comes to personhood. Labour law appears to hold within it different versions of personhood which are difficult to reconcile. It is argued that this analysis holds explanatory power and force when it comes to thinking about the limitations of labour law for workers. Individual labour law incorporates 'contractual' views of the person, to which labour (in its embodied materiality) can never match up. Collective labour law has the potential to incorporate a different view of the person, but the difficulties of reconciling this 'collective' view of personhood with the politically dominant individualized view of personhood means that it becomes compromised to the point of holding no value at all.

As well as looking inward, this book also aims to be outward-looking and future-facing. The hope is that changing the way in which we view personhood as a matter of labour law will lead to law and policies which are more effective in improving the lives of workers. In particular, embedding relationality will make us more able to respond to labour market changes and 'shocks'. This is demonstrated in the latter part of the book by an analysis of the challenges brought by the COVID-19 pandemic and the introduction of ever more sophisticated AI into the workplace.

The first part of these conclusions will focus on what might be called the inward-facing elements or theoretical reflections. During the course of writing the book, it has become clear that the process of reflection on the relationship between personhood and labour law and the promotion of the 'relational self' sheds new light on some of labour law's hardest problems and deepest set contradictions. The extent of these revelations has been surprising. First, it appears that the problem of personhood and the law was at the very heart of Sinzheimer's explanation of labour law's problematic and preoccupied Marx too. The application of feminist theory to this problematic thus *builds on* these concerns rather than representing a complete departure from what had gone before. Second, labour law's long-standing conviction of the importance of collective labour law alongside individual rights and the seeming contradictions which arise can be analysed in terms of the difficulties of personhood at the heart of labour law. Personhood drives an artificial schism through labour law as an individual and collective enterprise. Finally, the 'new' challenges posed by the pandemic and the incursion of AI into the workplace certainly do recast the relationship between humanity and work, and challenge the way in which labour law and personhood interact. However, this is not a new story. It turns out that the interaction between personhood and labour law has occupied theorists since its inception. These changes only cement the importance and centrality of the personhood preoccupation for labour law. The second part of these conclusions will focus on the implications for this analysis for the future of labour law.

1. An inclusive critical agenda

One of the deepest contradictions surrounding labour law theory concerns labour law's commitment to 'rights'. Of course, if labour law is going to allow for a mechanism for workers or employees to seek redress against their employers, then there must be a system of 'rights' which can be enforced in a court of law. Rights bring with them duties on employers, and these duties enable working individuals to be treated fairly and to seek redress if treated unfairly. For labour lawyers, however, rights are a problematic frame of reference. First, labour rights act to modify the 'rights' that individuals (employers) would rightly have as a matter of contract. This means that labour law has to accept the contractual system of rights at the same time as modifying/amending/rejecting it. Second, the problems faced by labour are not purely a problem of 'justice'; they are also a problem of 'social' justice. There are deep inequalities in labour markets and between individuals and employers as a result of their insertion into a capitalist mode of production. Rights, however 'market correcting', will never be able to correct those inequalities in practice. Furthermore, there is the problem of how to theorize the relationship between 'commodification' and 'rights'. On the one hand, the operation of the capitalist system of production treats workers as 'commodities' and this is problematic as it suggests that human workers are just 'things' to be traded and used on the market.[1] Giving workers rights forces employers to recognize individual workers as having (legal) value (and hence treat them better). On the other hand, giving individuals rights does not remove them from the economic system which treats workers as 'commodities'. Whether labour is ever 'decommodified' is thus open to debate. In any event, this does not deal with the problems of non-commodification; the exclusion of workers from legal rights because their work cannot be (adequately) 'commodified' and so does not count for the purposes of law. It appears that legal employment rights are a particularly poor mechanism for these workers to achieve (social) justice.

This scepticism has led certain authors to abandon rights as a mechanism for the achievement of social justice in the workplace. In some quarters, trade union organization and subversive social action are seen as a much more effective means of improving the lives of workers.[2] These mechanisms respect the social power differential between workers and employers and use social means to correct it. They are potentially more inclusive of different kinds and ideas of work. But it turns out that even subversive social action requires legal support to sustain it.[3] Trade union action relies on 'rights' (in the absence of widespread political and social change) so trade unions must at once reject the mechanism of rights while at the same time relying on rights to achieve their own ends.[4] Therefore the promotion of trade unions and subversive social action does not lead to an escape, in theoretical terms, from the problematic relationships between work and rights. Furthermore, this does not address the role of trade union organizations in processes of social exclusion. Trade unions have tended to focus on the 'core constituent' of workers at the expense of other social groups.[5] Workers who already face disadvantage in the labour law therefore risk exclusion both from rights and alternative mechanisms to improve their experience of work.

On the face of it, the critical theory that is applied to labour law is not very helpful in resolving these contradictions. Marxist theory suggests that law not only fails to correct inequalities in the labour market, but it

---

1 H. Sinzheimer, 'Grundzüge des Arbeitsrechts' (1927) in H. Sinzheimer, *Arbeitsrecht und Rechtssoziologie: gesammelte Aufsätze und Reden* (Band 1) (Frankfurt: Europaische Verlagsanstalt 1976), 8.

2 J. Choonara, A. Murgia, and R. Miguel Carmo, *Faces of Precarity: Critical Perspectives on Work, Subjectivities and Struggles* (Bristol: Bristol University Press 2022).

3 R. Dukes, 'Constitutionalizing Employment Relations: Sinzheimer, Kahn-Freund and the Role of Labour Law (2008) 35 (3) *Journal of Law and Society* 341, 342.

4 Z. Adams, 'Legal Mobilizations, Trade Unions and Radical Social Change: A Case Study of the IWGB' (2023) 52 (2) *Industrial Law Journal* 560, 564.

5 A. Bertolini and R. Dukes, 'Trade Unions and Platform Workers in the UK: Worker Representation in the Shadow of the Law' (2021) 50 (4) *Industrial Law Journal* 662, 677.

also reinforces those inequalities. Law is ultimately controlled by those powerful elements in society (coinciding with those who own the means of production) and serves to increase social equality so far as this furthers the aims of the ruling class. Where labour is able to gain rights, these function as concessions which only serve to legitimate the capitalist enterprise and continue the success of the capitalist regime of production.[6] Progress will only be made by widespread social and political change. Sinzheimer also asserted the necessity of social and political change if the lives of workers were to be improved in the longer term. For Sinzheimer this could be achieved through the creation of an 'economic constitution' under which the economy came under political control.[7] Although these may be worthy ambitions, they are disempowering for workers seeking an improvement in their terms and conditions of employment (in the short term). Furthermore, Marxist theorizations tend not to link well with broader (feminist) concerns around the relationship between work, regulation, and social exclusion. This is also true of early labour law theorizations which did not treat worker 'identity' as a central concern.

However, the research and analysis conducted as part of this book suggest that a focus on personhood has the potential to bring together Marxist, feminist, and labour law theory, and to suggest a more positive *legal* theory of rights for labour. In all three traditions there is the identification of the problematic nature of the concept of the 'person' at the heart of liberal legal rights. This conceptualization treats all humans as individuals, 'separated from other [persons] and from the community'.[8] According to Marx, the 'real man is recognized only in the shape of an egotistical individual', that is 'an individual withdrawn into himself, into the confines of his private interests and private caprice'.[9] This denies the essence of humanity in 'species-being' and leads to false aspirations for the law. The law's aspiration for 'emancipation' is a 'reduction of the human world and relationships to man himself'.[10] This cannot represent freedom in any meaningful sense:

> Only when the real, individual man re-absorbs in himself the abstract citizen, and as an individual human being has become a species-being in his everyday life, in his particular work, and in his particular situation

6 Z. Adams, 'Labour Law, Capitalism and the Juridical Form: Taking a Critical Approach to Questions of Labour Law Reform' (2021) 50 (3) *Industrial Law Journal* 434.

7 'Die Zukunft der Arbeiterräte' in H. Sinzheimer, *Arbeitsrecht und Rechtssoziologie: gesammelte Aufsätze und Reden* (Frankfurt: Europaische Verlagsanstalt 1976).

8 K. Marx, 'On the Jewish Question' in D. McLellan, *Karl Marx: Selected Writings* (Oxford: Oxford University Press 2000), 46.

9 Marx (n 8), 61.

10 Marx (n 8), 61.

> only when man has recognized and organized his 'own powers' as social powers, and consequently no longer separates social power from himself in the shape of political power, only then will human emancipation have been accomplished.[11]

Marx's views are reflected in Sinzheimer's work. Sinzheimer was convinced that law's conceptualization of personhood shapes its whole design and directs its outcomes: '[s]olving the problem of the existence of man is what the rules of law are destined to aim at'.[12] However, Sinzheimer saw in labour law the opportunity for a conceptualization of personhood which moves beyond that of 'civil law' or the 'rights of man' (as criticized by Marx). Labour law already recognized the 'species-nature' of human beings because its starting point is labour's dependent social position. Labour law moves from an 'abstract' view of the person, to an empirical view of labour's 'real existence'.[13] This allows labour law great potential. First, in accepting the person as an empirical being (determined by social condition), labour law necessarily adopts a dynamic notion of selfhood. Changing those social conditions can change the very 'essence' of a person. Labour law can therefore be doubly transformative. Labour law can achieve 'freedom' for workers by changing the social conditions which determine labour law's disadvantage as well as putting workers in charge of their own selves, and hence their own versions of freedom. Freedom then occurs not only through regulatory legal rights but also through auxiliary rights which allow participation in the process of social change.

Feminist scholars have also recognized the transformatory effects of addressing and reclaiming the concept of legal personhood (for labour law). They have recognized how the liberal legal subjectivity (of civil law) has served to reinforce existing power relations and maintained social exclusions. A static and uni-dimensional view of selfhood couched in the law is a way of making sure that 'justice' does not mean 'social' justice. For there is no social justice instinct in a law with an egotistical, 'autonomous', rational male at its heart.[14] In order to promote social justice, an alternative conceptualization of the person is required. This conceptualization must recapture the conceptualization of 'autonomy' and 'rationality', and restore them to humanity. These ideas must embed empirical experience, identity,

---

11 Marx (n 8), 64.

12 H. Sinzheimer, 'Das Problem des Menschen im Recht' (1933) in H. Sinzheimer *Arbeitsrecht und Rechtssoziologie: gesammelte Aufsätze und Reden* (Frankfurt: Europaische Verlagsanstalt 1976), 53.

13 Sinzheimer (n 12), 58.

14 R.L. West, 'Economic Man and Literary Woman: One Contrast' (1988) 39 *Mercer Law Review* 867, 871.

and relationality. In order to pursue social justice, we need a 'relational' subject of law.

2. Reconciling labour law's justificatory schemes

Labour law suffers from an age-old problem: how to reconcile the promotion of individual labour rights with the intuition that 'labour wants nothing more than to be left alone'.[15] This problematic is at the heart of the apparent set of divisions between 'individualist' scholars on the one hand and 'collectivist' scholars on the other. Individualist scholars uphold the value of individual rights for labour but have been accused of neglecting the importance of collectivism and collectivist action for worker experience.[16] Collectivist scholars are seen to promote the value of independent trade unions in improving the lives of workers, often as part of a set of political and social ambitions towards 'social' justice. On this view, if labour law is a social justice narrative, it should be concerned first and foremost with the equalization of social power and operate as a mechanism of private redress as between employers and employees only as a secondary concern. Tensions between individualist and collective scholars may be overstated but do remain. For example, collectivist scholars have been accused by individualists of neglecting the role of trade unions in undermining individual rights and promoting long-term (political) aims at the expense of short-term practical solutions for workers treated badly at work.[17]

The scepticism of collectivist scholars towards legal rights is no doubt an oversimplification, but it remains the case that the relationship between collective bargaining and the law is complex both historically and practically. Historically, collective bargaining has appeared to operate most effectively when it has not been dogged by (excessive) legal constraints. This has been rationalized theoretically on the basis that collective bargaining is a social response to structural disadvantage in which the law is complicit. It follows that if collective bargaining is to be an effective social justice response, it must operate outside of the law.[18] While the historical connection between collective laissez faire and the absence of law has now largely been discredited (even in the heady days of collective laissez faire, the law played an important role in helping collective bargaining to function)[19] the problematic of the

15 L. Wedderburn, *Worker and the Law* (Middlesex: Penguin 1986), 1.

16 B. Simpson, 'Freedom of Association and the Right to Organise: The Failure of an Individual Rights Strategy' (1995) 24 (3) *Industrial Law Journal* 235, 249.

17 S. White, 'Freedom of Association and the Right to Exclude' (1997) 5 *Journal of Political Philosophy* 373, 384.

18 O. Kahn-Freund, *Labour and the Law* (London: Stevens 1983), 18.

19 R. Dukes, 'Constitutionalizing Employment Relations: Sinzheimer, Kahn-Freund and the Role of Labour Law' (2008) 35 (3) *Journal of Law and Society* 341, 351.

effectiveness of the law in promoting collective bargaining remains. The ascendancy of collective rights, such as freedom of association, has only served to increase this tension. These collective rights have been criticized as promoting individual (contractual) freedoms over collective action and limiting trade union autonomy. It has been argued that freedom of association is now so couched in individualistic rights rhetoric that it has become more about the freedom to disassociate than the positive freedom to build a better life through collective enterprise.[20]

This book suggests that a reflection on personhood and labour law presents the opportunity to reconcile some of these contradictions. The argument proceeds that if we accept the centrality of relationality to both individual and collective experience then we can build a law which is a more genuine balance between the individual and the collective. The question becomes what kind of rights further 'autonomy' in a relational sense. This revives the collectivist instinct and makes it more relevant. Social justice can now be found through (collective) law rather than outside it, making all labour lawyers invested in the potential of legal rights. At the same time, a reflection on legal personhood can make individual labour rights a better force for social justice. One of the fundamental problems with qualification for employment rights at the current time is that this relies on employees or workers to prove 'subordination' or 'dependence'. This is problematic because the gold standard of the liberal contractual view of personhood is precisely the opposite: asocial independence, autonomy, and rationality. Workers have to prove that they are failing to meet the gold standard to qualify for legal rights. For many workers this 'subordination' is a chimera – they do not experience work primarily in terms of dependence. Other workers experience this dependence but cannot show this dependence as a matter of law because it is not reflected in the terms of the contract of employment.[21]

On the scheme of relationality, dependence is not a good proxy for the establishment of legal rights. First, dependency is part of the human condition and does not need to be 'proven'. It is already presumed.[22] Second, dependency is always partial, and changing and differentially experienced.[23] Proving 'dependency' of individuals on an employer simply undermines the multidimensional nature of the worker/human experience.

[20] B. Rogers, 'Three Concepts of Workplace Freedom of Association' (2016) 37 (2) *Berkeley Journal of Employment and Labor Law* 177.

[21] For a discussion of this problematic, see M. Freedland and N. Kountouris, *The Legal Construction of Personal Work Relations* (Oxford: Oxford University Press 2011), 370.

[22] J. Christman, 'Autonomy, Independence, and Poverty-Related Welfare Policies' (1998) 12 *Public Affairs Quarterly* 383.

[23] K. Abrams, 'From Autonomy to Agency: Feminist Perspectives on Self-Direction' (1999) 40 *Williams and Mary Law Review* 805, 810.

Ultimately, on the relationality scheme, the universality and ever-changing nature of dependency means that it does not work well as a criteria for the establishment of rights. What is much more important is the positive or negative contribution of employment relationships or engagements to relationality and the ability of workers to 'find their own law'.[24] Hence, embedding a different view of the person at the heart of labour law changes labour law's perspective from a damage limitation exercise to an opportunity creating one. It also removes the stigma of dependence which serves only to heighten the role of the law in promoting division and disadvantage.[25] In practical terms, adopting the relational subject at the heart of labour law expands the reach of labour law and breaks down age-old divisions between worker, employee, and self-employed status.[26] It also necessarily promotes a closer relationship between individual and collective rights in terms of qualification.[27] Furthermore, placing the relational subject at the heart of labour law breaks down divisions in the justificatory schemes between individual and collective rights. Both individual and collective rights have their role to play in promoting 'relational' autonomy and hence social justice.

3. Reacting to new labour market challenges

The ability of labour law to deal with labour market 'shocks' can be seen as an important measure of its efficiency and its effectiveness.[28] This book identifies two recent but seemingly unrelated and differentially constituted labour market shocks: the COVID-19 pandemic and the increasing incursion of AI and algorithmic management into workplaces. In some ways these can be seen as problems of a different order – the pandemic was a short-term labour market challenge which was impossible to predict in advance; the incursion of AI into the workplace has been in process for many years and represents a longer-term adjustment to the way in which labour markets operate and employers and workers interact.

However, it is argued that, theoretically speaking, these labour market shocks are raising similar questions and present similar dilemmas for labour

24 J. Nedelsky, *Law's Relations: A Relational Theory of Self, Autonomy and Law* (Oxford: Oxford University Press 2011), 123.

25 M. Fineman, *The Autonomy Myth: A Theory of Dependency* (New York: The New Press 2004), 19.

26 K. Ewing, J. Hendy, and C. Jones, *Manifesto for Labour Law* (Liverpool: Institute of Employment Rights 2016).

27 J. Atkinson and H. Dhorajiwala, '*IWGB v Roofoods*: Status, Rights and Substitution' (2019) 48 (2) *Industrial Law Journal* 278 and the discussion in Chapter 5 of this book.

28 N. Bruun, K. Lorcher, and I. Schomann, *The Economic and Financial Crisis and Labour Law in Europe* (Oxford: Hart 2014).

law. Both the pandemic and the AI incursion challenge and inform the way we think about the relationship between humanity and work. Fundamentally, they both expose labour law's flaws in failing to really get to grips with or promote labour's humanity. Labour law's vision of the person as it is incorporated in the law is both limited and outdated. For example, the pandemic really brought to the fore the corporeality of workers and the need for legal responses to engage with that corporeality. The increasing reliance of both employers and workers on health and safety law during the pandemic was evidence of that fact. The problem was that the health and safety regime's system of risk management worked counter to employee interests, and the experience of COVID did more to expose the lack of investment in health and safety systems than anything else.[29] Furthermore, the possibilities for legislative innovation or expansion to deal with the longer-term effects of COVID ('Long' COVID, working from home) have been left largely unexplored. Largely, the experience of COVID-19 has been compartmentalized and forgotten, and does not seem to have directed forward-thinking reflections on labour law.[30]

Likewise, the ever-increasing sophistication of AI and its incursion into management practice raises questions about how we view the humanity/work/management divide. It exposes the current bias in labour law regulation towards individualistic notions of autonomy and a reliance on 'rationality' as justifications for particular labour law outcomes. This both paralyses labour law regulation and reinforces or cements a bias towards management practice over worker experience. AI allows management to attain standards of 'rationality' and evidence the promotion of 'autonomy' and 'independence' among workers in ever more sophisticated ways. At the same time, the experience of these processes is that they undermine worker 'autonomy' and require standards which it is impossible for workers to meet. This suggests that we need a different way of thinking about the relationship between humanity, personhood, and work. It is the argument in this book that thinking in terms of relationality and relational autonomy is a useful and fruitful way of analysing the challenges raised and the responses required by labour law in the context of AI. Thinking in terms of relationality means that we can no longer accept the status quo, and we need to move to a much more joined-up legislative response. That legislative response needs to recognize the importance of the AI challenge to the humanity of

---

29 K. Ewing and Lord Hendy, 'Covid-19 and the Failure of Labour Law: Part 1' (2020) 49 (4) *Industrial Law Journal* 497, 498.

30 COVID is now treated as any other respiratory infection: see UK Gov, 'People with symptoms of a respiratory infection including COVID-19' (10 June 2022), available at: www.gov.uk/guidance/people-with-symptoms-of-a-respiratory-infection-including-covid-19

workers. For example, there should be amendments to discrimination law to recognize the discriminatory potential of AI and shift the burden of proof from workers to employers on this matter. There should be new rights to disconnect and to human reviews of decisions as well as greater transparency around the use of AI in the workplace. Trade unions should be given greater power to support workers by, for example, adopting a data-gathering role or seeking recognition as a data subject representative under the General Data Protection Regulation (GDPR).[31]

Workers should be able to ensure that AI is used only in ways which respect their relationality and agency. Otherwise, AI will be a force for division and disempowerment which labour law will find itself unable to challenge. The relationship between labour law and personhood is not just a theoretical issue; it is crucial to engage with personhood in order to move forward with a labour law agenda for social justice.

31 See Trades Union Congress, 'Dignity at Work and the AI Revolution' (March 2021), available at: www.tuc.org.uk/sites/default/files/2021-03/The_AI_Revolution_20121_Manifesto_AW.pdf and further discussion in Chapter 7.

References

Abrams, K. 'From Autonomy to Agency: Feminist Perspectives on Self-Direction' (1999) 40 *Williams and Mary Law Review* 805.

Adams, Z. 'Labour Law, Capitalism and the Juridical Form: Taking a Critical Approach to Questions of Labour Law Reform' (2021) 50 (3) *Industrial Law Journal* 434.

Adams, Z. 'One Step Forward for Employment Status, Still Some Way to Go: The Supreme Court's Decision in *Uber v Aslam* under Scrutiny' (2021) 80 *Cambridge Law Journal* 221.

Adams, Z. 'Legal Mobilizations, Trade Unions and Radical Social Change: A Case Study of the IWGB' (2023) 52 (2) *Industrial Law Journal* 560.

Adams, Z., Barnard, C., Deakin, S., and Fraser-Butlin, S. *Deakin and Morris' Labour Law* (Oxford: Hart 2021).

Adams-Prassl, J. 'What if Your Boss Was an Algorithm? Economic Incentives, Legal Challenges and the Rise of Artificial Intelligence' (2019) 41 *Comparative Labour Law and Policy Journal* 123.

Advisory, Conciliation and Arbitration Service 'Reasonable Adjustments at Work' (November 2022), available at: www.acas.org.uk/reasonable-adjustments

Aloisi, A. 'Automation, Augmentation, Autonomy: Labour Regulation and the Digital Transformation of Managerial Prerogatives' in T. Gyulavari and E. Menegatti (eds) *Decent Work in a Digital Age: European and Comparative Perspectives* Oxford: Hart 2022).

Aloisi, A. and Gramano, E. 'Artificial Intelligence Is Watching You at Work: Digital Surveillance, Employee Monitoring and Regulatory Issues in the EU Context' (2019) 41 *Comparative Labour Law and Policy Journal* 95.

Andersson, P. and Novitz, T. 'COVID-19 at Work: Exposing How Risk Is Assessed and its Consequences in England and Sweden' (2022) *Bristol University Research Papers* 31, available at: bristol.ac.uk/law/research/legal-research-papers.

Anthony, T. 'Marx and Anticolonialism' in F. Gordon (ed) *Leading Works in Law and Social Justice* (Oxford: Routledge 2020).

Arendt, H. *Totalitarianism: Part Three of the Origins of Totalitarianism* (FL: Harcourt 1968).

Arkwright, A. 'Can your employer force you back into the office' (September 2021), available at: www.tuc.org.uk/blogs/can-your-employer-force-you-back-office.

Ashiagabor, D. 'Race and Colonialism in the Construction of Labour Markets and Precarity' (2021) 50 (4) *Industrial Law Journal* 506.

Atkinson, J. 'Human Rights as Foundations for Labour Law' in H. Collins, G. Lester, and V. Mantouvalou (eds) *Philosophical Foundations of Labour Law* (Oxford: Oxford University Press 2018).

Atkinson, J. and Dhorajiwala, H. '*IWGB v Roofoods*: Status, Rights and Substitution' (2019) 48 (2) *Industrial Law Journal* 278.

Atkinson, J. and Dhorajiwala, H. 'The Future of Employment: Purposive Interpretation and the Role of Contract after Uber' (2022) 85 (3) *Modern Law Review* 787.

Autor, D. 'Why Are There Still So Many Jobs? The History and Future of Workplace Automation' (2015) 29 *Journal of Economic Perspectives* 3.

Bales, K., Bogg, A., and Novitz, T. 'Voice and Choice in Modern Working Practices: Problems with the Taylor Review' (2018) 47 (1) *Industrial Law Journal* 46.

Baker, A, 'The "Range of Reasonable Responses" Test: A Poor Substitution for the Statutory Language' (2021) 50 (2) *Industrial Law Journal* 226.

Baxi, U. *The Future of Human Rights* (Oxford: Oxford University Press 2002), 132.

Benson, M. 'The Political Economy of Women's Liberation' (1969) 21 (7) *Monthly Review* 13.

Benson, P. 'Oppressive Socialization' (1991) 17 *Social Theory and Practice* 385.

Berg, J. 'Protecting Workers in the Digital Age: Technology, Outsourcing and the Growing Precariousness of Work' (2019) 41 *Comparative Labour Law and Policy Journal* 96.

Bertolini, A. and Dukes, R. 'Trade Unions and Platform Workers in the UK: Worker Representation in the Shadow of the Law' (2021) 50 (4) *Industrial Law Journal* 662.

Bisom-Rapp, S. and Sargeant, M. 'Acknowledging but Transcending Gender at Work: Applying the Model of Lifetime Disadvantage and Vulnerability Theory to Women's Poverty in Retirement' in M.A. Fineman and J. Fineman (eds) *Vulnerability and the Legal Organisation of Work* (London: Routledge 2017).

Bodie, M.T. et al 'The Law and Policy of People Analytics' (2017) 88 *University of Colorado Law Review* 961, 971.

Bogg, A. 'The Hero's Journey: Lord Wedderburn and the "Political Constitution" of Labour Law' (2015) 44 (3) *Industrial Law Journal* 229.

Bogg, A. 'Individualism and Collectivism in Collective Labour Law' (2017) 46 (1) *Industrial Law Journal* 72.

Bogg, A. 'Status Update? Why Employment Status Is a Political Issue' (2019) *Futures of Work*, available at: https://futuresofwork.co.uk/2019/12/09/status-update-why-employment-status-is-a-political-issue/.

Bogg, A. and Ewing, K. 'Collective Bargaining and Individual Contracts in *Kostal UK Limited v Dunkley*: A *Wilson and Palmer* for the Twenty-First Century?' (2020) 49 (3) *Industrial Law Journal* 43.

Bogg, A. and Ford, M. 'The Death of Contract in Determining Employment Status' (2021) 137 *Law Quarterly Review* 392.

Boubil, E. 'The Ethics of Vulnerability and the Phenomenology of Interdependency' (2018) 49 (3) 183, 184.

Braudo-Bahat, Y. 'Towards a Relational Conceptualization of the Right to Personal Autonomy' (2017) 25 (2) *Journal of Gender, Social Policy and the Law* 111.

Breese, E. 'How does sick pay in the UK compare to the rest of the world', *Big Issue* (April 2023), available at: https://bigissue.com/news/employment/how-does-britains-sick-pay-compare-to-the-rest-of-the-world/.

Brione, P. and Day, S. 'House of Commons Library: Artificial Intelligence and Employment Law' (11 August 2023), available at: https://researchbriefings.files.parliament.uk/documents/CBP-9817/CBP-9817.pdf.

Brodie, D. 'Confronting the Gig Economy' (2021) 2 *Juridical Review* 102.

Brodie, D. 'Collectivism in Labour Law: Only by Exception' (2022) 5 (2) *Industrial Law Journal* 464.

Brodtkkorb, T. 'Employee Misconduct and UK Dismissal Law: Does the Range of Reasonable Responses Test Require Reform?' (2010) 52 (6) *International Journal of Law and Management* 429.

Brook, P. 'In Critical Defence of Emotional Labour: Refuting Bolton's Critique of Hochschild's Concept' (2009) 23 (3) *Work, Employment and Society* 531.

Bruun, N., Lorcher, K., and Schomann, I. *The Economic and Financial Crisis and Labour Law in Europe* (Oxford: Hart 2014).

Busby, N. and James, G. *A History of Regulating Working Families: Strains, Stereotypes, Strategies and Solutions* (Oxford: Hart 2020).

Byron, C. 'Marx's Theory of Human Nature' (2016) 80 (3) *Science and Society* 375.

Cabrelli, D. 'The Hierarchy of Differing Behavioural Standards of Review in Labour Law' (2011) 40 (2) *Industrial Law Journal* 146.

Cai, M. Moore, S., Ball, C., Flynn, M., and Mulkearn, K. 'The Role of Union Health and Safety Representatives During the COVID-19 Pandemic: A Case Study of the UK Food Processing, Distribution, and Retail Sectors' (2022) 53 *Industrial Relations Journal* 390.

Campbell, B. 'Social Justice and Sociological Theory' (2021) 58 *Society* 355.

Campbell, T. 'Human Rights: Moral or Legal' in D. Kinley, W. Sadurski, and K. Walton (eds) *Human Rights: Old Problems, New Possibilities* (Cheltenham: Edward Elgar 2014).

Cammack, P. 'Marx on Social Reproduction' (2020) 28 (2) *Historical Materialism* 1.

Carniol, B. *Social Services and Social Justice in Canada* (Toronto: Between the Lines 2010).

Carse, A. 'Vulnerability, Agency and Human Flourishing' in C. Taylor and R. Dell'Oro (eds) *Health and Human Flourishing* (Washington, DC: Georgetown University Press 2006).

Casalone, C. et al 'Human-centric AI: From Principles to Actionable and Shared Policies' (September 2021), available at: www.g20-insights.org/policy_briefs/human-centric-ai-from-principles-to-actionable-and-shared-policies/.

Cefaliello, A. and Kullman, M. 'Offering False Security: How the Draft Artificial Intelligence Act Undermines Fundamental Workers Rights' (2022) *European Labour Law Journal* 1–21.

Choonara, J. Murgia, A., and Miguel Carmo, R. *Faces of Precarity: Critical Perspectives on Work, Subjectivities and Struggles* (Bristol: Bristol University Press 2022).

Christman, J. 'Autonomy, Independence, and Poverty-Related Welfare Policies' (1998) 12 *Public Affairs Quarterly* 383.

Colling, T. 'Court in a Trap? Legal Mobilisation by Trade Unions in the United Kingdom' (2009) No 91 *Warwick Papers in Industrial Relations.*

Collins, H. 'Theories of Rights as Justifications for Labour Law' in G. Davidov and B. Langille (eds) *The Idea of Labour Law* (Oxford: Oxford University Press 2011), 137.

Conaghan, J. 'Work, Family and the Discipline of Labour Law' in J. Conaghan and K. Rittich (eds) *Labour Law, Work and Family* (Oxford: Oxford University Press 2005).

Conaghan, J. 'Labour Law and Feminist Method' (2017) (33) 1 *International Journal of Comparative Labour Law and Industrial Relations* 93.

Conway, E. 'Coronavirus: we are all in this together – but some more than others', *Sky News* (4 May 2020), available at: https://news.sky.com/story/coronavirus-were-all-in-this-together-but-some-more-than-others-11981917.

Coyle, S. 'Vulnerability and the Liberal Order' in M. Fineman and A. Greer (eds) *Vulnerability: Reflections on a New Ethical Foundation for Law and Politics* (London: Routledge 2013).

Crain, M. 'Sex Discrimination as Collective Harm' in D.S. Cobble (ed) *The Sex of Class: Women Transforming American Labor* (New York: Cornell University Press 2011).

Creighton, B. 'A Retreat from Individualism? The Fair Work Act 2009 and the Re-Collectivisation of Australian Labour Law' (2011) 40 *Industrial Law Journal* 116.

Cruz, K., Bales, K., and Sanders, T. 'False Self-Employment, Autonomy and Regulating for Decent Work: Improving Working Conditions in the UK Stripping Industry' (2016) 55 (2) *British Journal of Industrial Relations* 274.

Daguerre, A. 'The Unemployed and the Moral Case for Benefit Sanctions' (2015) 22 *Journal of Social Security Law* 130.

Dahlin, E. 'Are Robots Really Stealing our Jobs? Perception versus Experience' (2022) 8 *Socius* (online).

Daskova, V. 'Regulating the New Self-Employed in the Uber Economy: What Role for EU Competition Law? (2018) 19 *German Law Journal* 461.

Davidov, G. 'Three Axes of Employment Relationships: A Characterisation of Workers in Need of Protection' (2002) 52 *University of Toronto Law Journal* 357.

Davidov, G. 'Collective Bargaining: Purpose and Scope' (2004) 20 *International Journal of Comparative Labour Law and Industrial Relations* 81.

Davidov, G. *A Purposive Approach to Labour Law* (Oxford: Oxford University Press 2016).

Davidov, G. 'Subordination vs Domination: Exploring the Differences' (2017) 33 (3) *International Journal of Comparative Labour Law and Industrial Relations* 365.

De Stefano, V. 'The Rise of the Just-in-Time Workforce: On-Demand Work, Crowdwork and Labour Protection in the Gig Economy' 37 (2016) *Comparative Labour Law and Policy Journal* 471.

De Stefano, V. 'Negotiating the Algorithm: Automation, Artificial Intelligence and Labor Protection' (2019) 41 *Comparative Labour Law and Policy Journal* 15.

Deakin, S. 'Does the Personal Employment Contract Provide a Basis for the Reunification of Employment Law?' (2007) *Industrial Law Journal* 36 (1) 68.

Derham, D. 'Theories of Legal Personality' in L.C. Webb (ed) *Legal Personality and Political Pluralism* (New York: Cambridge University Press 1958).

Dews, P. *Logics of Disintegration: Poststructuralist Thought and the Claims of Critical Theory* (London: Verso 1987).

Dodh, P. 'Globalisation and Human Rights in India: A Communitarian and Multicultural Perspective' (2020) 20 (4) *World Affairs* 44.

Donnelly, J. 'Human Rights as Natural Rights' (1982) 4 (3) *Human Rights Quarterly* 391.

Donnelly, J. *Universal Human Rights in Theory and Practice* (2nd edn, London: Cornell University Press 2003).

Dukes, R. 'Constitutionalising Employment Relations: Sinzheimer, Kahn-Freund and the Role of Labour Law' (2005) 35 (3) *Journal of Law and Society* 341.

Dukes, R. *The Labour Constitution: The Enduring Idea of Labour Law* (Oxford: Oxford University Press 2014).

Dukes, R. and Streek, W. *Democracy at Work: Contract, Status and Industrial Justice* (Cambridge: Polity Press 2022).

Dworkin, R. *Law's Empire* (Cambridge, MA: Harvard University Press 1986).

Estlund, C. 'Book Review: For Labor to Build On: Wars, Depression, and Pandemic by William B. Gould IV (Cambridge: Cambridge University Press 2022)' (2023) 52 (3) *Industrial Law Journal* 834.

Eurofound *Automation, Digitalisation and Platforms: Implications for Work and Employment* (Luxembourg: Publications Office of the European Union 2018).

European Commission 'Communication from the Commission: Artificial Intelligence in Europe' (25 April 2018) COM (2018) 237 final, available at: https://eur-lex.europa.eu/legal-content/EN/TXT/HTML/?uri=CELEX:52018DC0237&from=EN.

European Economic and Social Committee *Artificial Intelligence – The consequences of artificial intelligence on the (digital) single market, production, consumption, employment and society* 2017 OJ C 288 1.

European Parliament *Amendments adopted by the European Parliament on 14 June 2023 on the proposal for a regulation of the European Parliament and of the Council on laying down harmonised rules on artificial intelligence (Artificial Intelligence Act) and amending certain Union legislative acts* (COM (2021)0206) – C90146/2021 (2021/0106/COD).

European Trade Union Institute 'AI – Humans must be in command' (17 February 2020), available at: www.etuc.org/en/document/ai-humans-must-be-command.

European Trade Union Institute 'Press Release' (17 February 2020), available at: www.etuc.org/en/pressrelease/etuc-response-commission-strategies-digital-and-ai#:~:text=Commenting%20on%20the%20launch%20of%20the%20European%20Commission%E2%80%99s,surveillance%20or%20discriminatory%20treatment%20because%20of%20biased%20algorithms.

Ewing, K. 'Tomlinson-Blake in the Supreme Court', *UK Labour Law Blog* (28 April 2021), available at: https://uklabourlawblog.com/.

Ewing, K. and Hendy, J. QC 'The Strasbourg Court Treats Trade Unionists with Contempt: *Svenska Transportarbetareförbundet and Seko v Sweden*' (2017) *Industrial Law Journal* 46 (3) 435.

Ewing, K. and Hendy, J. 'Covid-19 and the Failure of Labour Law: Part 1' (2020) 49 (4) *Industrial Law Journal* 497.

Ewing, K. Hendy, J., and Jones, C. *Manifesto for Labour Law* (Liverpool: Institute of Employment Rights 2016).

Ewing, K., Hendy, J., and Jones, C. *Rolling Out the Manifesto for Labour Law* (Liverpool: Institute of Employment Rights 2018), 36–7.

Fairwork 'The Gig Economy and Covid-19: Fairwork Report on Platform Policies' (April 2020), available at: https://fair.work/wp-content/uploads/sites/17/2020/11/COVID19-Report-Final.pdf.

Farquharson, C., Rasul, I., and Sibieta, L. *Differences Between Key Workers* (London: Institute for Fiscal Studies 2020).

Finegan, T. 'Conceptual Foundation of the Universal Declaration of Human Rights: Human Rights, Human Dignity and Personhood' (2012) 37 *Australian Journal of Legal Philosophy* 182.

Fineman, J. 'The Vulnerable Subject at Work: A New Perspective on the Employment-at-will Debate' (2013) 43 *Southwestern Law Review* 275.

Fineman, M. 'Challenging Law, Establishing Difference: The Future of Feminist Legal Scholarship' (1990) 42 *Florida Law Review* 25.

Fineman, M. *The Autonomy Myth: A Theory of Dependency* (New York: The New Press 2004).

Fineman, M. 'The Vulnerable Subject: Anchoring Equality in the Human Condition' (2008) 20 (1) *Yale Journal of Law and Feminism* 1.

Fineman, M. 'Beyond Identities: The Limits of an Antidiscrimination Approach to Equality' (2012) 92 *Boston University Law Review* 1713.

Fineman, M. '"Elderly" as Vulnerable: Rethinking the Nature of Individual and Societal Responsibility' (2012) 20 *Elder Law Journal* 101.

Fineman, M. 'Introducing Vulnerability' in M.A. Fineman and J.W. Fineman (eds) *Vulnerability and the Legal Organisation of Work* (London: Routledge 2018).

Fineman, M. 'Vulnerability and Social Justice' (2019) 53 *Valparaiso University Law Review* 341–70, 368.

Friedman, M. 'Relational Autonomy and Individuality' (2013) 63 *University of Toronto Law Journal* 327.

Foucault, M. 'The Subject and Power' (1982) 8 *Critical Enquiry* 777.

Fox Piven, F. and Cloward, R. *Poor People's Movements, Why They Succeed, How They Fail* (New York: Vintage 2012).

Fraser, N. *Fortunes of Feminism* (London: Verso 2013).

Fraser, N. 'Behind Marx's Hidden Abode: For an Expanded Conception of Capitalism' in P. Deutscher and C. Lafont (eds) *Critical Theory in Critical Times: Transforming the Global Political and Social Order* (New York: Columbia University Press 2017).

Fredman, S. 'Labour Law in Flux: The Changing Composition of the Workforce' (1997) 26 (4) *Industrial Law Journal* 337.

Fredman, S. 'Substantive Equality Revisited' (2016) 14 *International Journal of Constitutional Law* 712.

Freedland, M. *The Personal Employment Contract* (Oxford: Oxford University Press 2003).

Freedland, M. 'Otto Kahn-Freund, the Contract of Employment and the Autonomy of Labour Law' in A. Bogg, C. Costello, A.C.L. Davies, and J. Prassl (eds) *The Autonomy of Labour Law* (Oxford: Hart 2015).

Freedland, M. and Kountouris, N. *The Legal Construction of Personal Work Relations* (Oxford: Oxford University Press 2011).

Fudge, J. 'From Women and Labour Law to Putting Gender and Law to Work' in M. Davies and V. Munro (eds) *The Ashgate Research Companion to Feminist Legal Theory* (London: Ashgate 2013).

Fudge, J. 'Feminist Reflections on the Scope of Labour Law: Domestic Work, Social Reproduction, and Jurisdiction' (2014) 22 *Feminist Legal Studies* 1.

Garben, S. 'The Constitutional Imbalance Between the "Market" and the "Social" in the European Union' (2017) 13 (1) *European Journal of Constitutional Law* 23.

Giddens, A. *Capitalism and Modern Social Theory: An Analysis of the Writings of Marx, Durkheim and Weber* (Cambridge: Cambridge University Press 1971).

Gilabert, P. 'Dignity at Work' in H. Collins, G. Lester, and V. Mantouvalou (eds) *Philosophies of Labour Law* (Oxford: Oxford University Press 2018).

Gilson, E. 'Vulnerability, Ignorance and Oppression' (2011) 26 (2) *Hypatia* 308.

Glasbeek, H. 'Coerced and Unfree in the Private Sector' (2018) 26 (2) *Critical Criminology* 579.

Goldin, A. 'Labour Subordination and the Subjective Weakening of Labour Law' in G. Davidov and B. Langille (eds) *Boundaries and Frontiers of Labour Law* (Oxford: Oxford University Press 2011).

Grear, A. 'Challenging Corporate Legal Humanity: Legal Disembodiment, Embodiment and Human Rights' (2007) 7 (3) *Human Rights Law Review* 511.

Grear, A. *Redirecting Human Rights: Facing the Challenge of Corporate Humanity* (London: Palgrave Macmillan 2010).

Grear, A. 'Deconstructing Anthropos: A Critical Legal Reflection on "Anthropocentric" Law and Anthropocene Humanity' (2015) 26 *Law and Critique* 52.

Grear, A. 'Embracing Vulnerability: Notes Towards Human Rights for a More-Than-Human World' in D. Bedford and J. Herring (eds) *Embracing Vulnerability: The Challenges and Implications for Law* (London: Routledge 2020).

Griffin, J. *On Human Rights* (Oxford: Oxford University Press 2008).

Haipeter, T. and Hoose, F. 'Don't Gig Up: Never!: Country Case Study Report Germany' (May 2023), available at: www.dontgigup.eu/wp-content/uploads/2023/06/Dontgigupnever_case-studies_GERMANY_ENG.pdf.

Hart, H.L.A. 'Are There any Natural Rights' in A. Quinton (eds) *Political Philosophy* (Oxford: Oxford University Press 1967).

Hayek, F.A. *Law, Legislation and Liberty* (London: Taylor and Francis 1982).

Hayek, F.A. *The Constitution of Liberty* (London: Routledge 2006).
Hendrickx, F. 'Foundations and Functions of Contemporary Labour Law' (2012) 3 (2) *European Labour Law Journal* 108.
Hendy, J. and Ewing, K. *Reconstruction after the Crisis: A Manifesto for Collective Bargaining* (Liverpool: Institute of Employment Rights 2013).
Hepple, B. 'Factors Influencing the Making and Transformation of Labour Law in Europe' in G. Davidov and B. Langille (eds) *The Idea of Labour Law* (Oxford: Oxford University Press 2011).
Herring, J. 'Defining Vulnerability' in J. Herring (ed) *Vulnerable Adults and the Law* (Oxford: Oxford University Press 2016), 10.
Hochschild, A. *The Managed Heart: Commercialization of Human Feeling* (3rd edn, Berkeley, CA: California University Press 2012).
Horton, R. 'Independent Science Advice for C-19 – At Last' (9 May 2020), *The Lancet*.
HSE 'HSE's enforcement of guidelines on coronavirus (COVID-19) in workplaces' available at: www.hse.gov.uk/coronavirus/regulating-health-and-safety/enforcement-coronavirus.htm.
HSE 'Protect vulnerable workers during the coronavirus (COVID-19) pandemic', available at: www.hse.gov.uk/coronavirus/working-safely/protect-people.htm.
HSE *Reducing Risks, Protecting People: HSE's Decision-Making Process* (Norwich: HSE 2001).
HSE 'Risk assessment: Steps needed to manage risk' – HSE, available at: https://www.hse.gov.uk/simple-health-safety/risk/steps-needed-to-manage-risk.htm
Industrial Disablement Benefits Scheme 'Industrial Disablement Scheme: Technical guidance (updated 11 July 2023)', available at: www.gov.uk/government/publications/industrial-injuries-disablement-benefits-technical-guidance/industrial-injuries-disablement-benefits-technical-guidance#appendix-1-list-of-diseases-covered-by-industrial-injuries-disablement-benefit.
Industrial Injuries Advisory Council 'COVID-19 and occupational impacts', available at: www.gov.uk/government/publications/covid-19-and-occupational-impacts/covid-19-and-occupational-impacts#recommendations.
Ingram, J.K. 'Work and the Workman: An Address to the Trades Union Congress' (1880–1) *Journal of the Statistical and Social Inquiry Society of Ireland* 106.
International Labour Organization 'ILO Centenary Declaration for the Future of Work' (21 June 2019), available at: www.ilo.org/wcmsp5/groups/public/@ed_norm/@relconf/documents/meetingdocument/wcms_711674.pdf.

International Labour Organization 'ILO Monitor: COVID 19 and the World of Work', 7th edn, 25 January 2021, 20, available at: www.ilo.org/wcmsp5/groups/public/-dgreports/-dcomm/documents/briefingnote/wcms_767028.pdf.

IOSH Magazine 'The Robens Report: 50 years on' (May/June 2022), available at: www.ioshmagazine.com/2022/04/26/robens-report-50-years.

James, P. 'HSE and Covid at work: A case of regulatory failure' (Liverpool: Institute of Employment Rights 2021), available at: www.ier.org.uk/product/hse-and-covid-at-work-a-case-ofregulatory-failure/.

Johnson, D. *A Brief History of Justice* (Chichester: Wiley-Blackwell 2011).

Jones, P. *Rights: Issues in Political Theory* (Basingstoke: Palgrave 1994).

Jydebjerg, C.S. 'Vulnerability, Workfare Law and Resilient Social Justice' in M.A. Fineman and J. Fineman (eds) *Vulnerability and the Legal Organisation of Work* (London: Routledge 2017).

Kahn-Freund, O. 'Intergroup Conflicts and Their Settlement' (1954) *The British Journal of Sociology* 193.

Kahn-Freund, O. 'Legal Framework' in A. Flanders and H. Clegg (eds) *The System of Industrial Relations in Great Britain* (Oxford: Basil Blackwell 1954).

Kahn-Freund, O. 'Labour Law' reprinted in O. Kahn-Freund, *Selected Writings* (London: Stevens 1978).

Kahn-Freund, O. *Selected Writings* (London: Stevens 1978).

Kahn-Freund, O. 'Hugo Sinzheimer 1875–1945' in R. Lewis and J. Clark (eds) *Labour Law and Politics in the Weimar Republic* (Oxford: Basil Blackwell 1981).

Kahn-Freund, O. *Labour and the Law* (London: Stevens 1983).

Kairys, D. (ed) *The Politics of Law: A Progressive Critique* (New York: Pantheon 1982).

Kairys, D. 'Law and Politics' (1984) 52 *George Washington Law Review* 243.

Kant, I. *Grounding for the Metaphysics of Morals* (tr J.W. Ellington, Indianapolis, IN: Hackett 1981).

Kant, I. 'Foundations of the Metaphysics of Morals' in L.W. Beck (ed) *Kant Selections* (New York: Macmillan 1988).

Kant, I. *Metaphysics of Morals* (tr M. Gregor, Cambridge: Cambridge University Press 1996).

Katsaroumpas, I. 'Crossing the Rubicon: The Strikes (Minimum Service Levels) Act 2023 as an Authoritarian Crucible' (2023) *Industrial Law Journal* forthcoming (available advanced access).

Knox, R. 'Law, Neoliberalism and the Constitution of Political Subjectivity: The Case of Organised Labour' *Neoliberal Legality* (Oxford: Routledge 2016).

Knox, R. 'A Marxist Approach to *RMT v The United Kingdom*' in D. Gonzalez-Salzberg and L. Hodson (eds) *Research Methods in Human Rights Law: Beyond the Traditional Paradigm* (Oxford: Routledge 2019).

Kolben, K. 'Labor Rights as Human Rights' (2009) 50 *Virginia Journal of International Law* 449.

Kountouris, N. 'The Concept of "Worker" in European Labour Law' (2018) 47 (2) *Industrial Law Journal* 192.

Kritzman, A. (ed) *Politics, Philosophy, Culture: Interviews and Other Writings 1977–1984* (London: Routledge 1988).

Kurki, V.A.J. *A Theory of Legal Personhood* (Oxford: Oxford University Press 2019).

Langille, B. 'The Freedom of Association Mess and How We Got into it and How We Can Get out of it' (2009) 54 *McGill Law Journal* 177.

Langille, B. 'Labour Law's Theory of Justice' in G. Davidov and B. Langille (eds) *The Idea of Labour Law* (Oxford: Oxford University Press 2011).

Langille, B. and Trebilcock, A. 'Introduction: A Framework for Thinking about the Future of Social Justice' in B. Langille and A Trebilcock (eds) *Social Justice and the World of Work: Possible Global Futures* (Oxford: Hart 2023).

Legge, K. 'Ethics and Work' in M. Korczynski et al (eds) *Social Theory at Work* (Oxford: Oxford University Press 2006).

Leighton, P, and Wynn, M. 'Classifying Employment Relationships – More Sliding Doors or a Better Regulatory Framework? (2011) 40 (1) *Industrial Law Journal* 5.

Lukes, S. *Individualism* (Oxford: Blackwell 1973).

Lupton, D. *The Quantified Self: A Sociology of Self-Tracking* (Cambridge: Polity 2016).

MacKenzie, C. 'Feminist Innovation in Philosophy: Relational Autonomy and Social Justice' (2019) 72 *Women's Studies International Forum* 144.

MacKinnon, C. 'Francis Biddle's Sister: Pornography, Civil Rights, and Speech' and 'The Sexual Politics of the First Amendment' in *Feminism Unmodified* (Cambridge, MA: Harvard University Press 1987).

MacKinnon, C. 'Substantive Equality Revisited: A Reply to Sandra Fredman' (2016) 14 *International Journal of Constitutional Law* 739.

Manning, C. 'Artificial Intelligence Definitions' (September 2020), available at: https://hai.stanford.edu/sites/default/files/2020-09/AI-Definitions-HAI.pdf.

Mantouvalou, V. 'Are Labour Rights Human Rights' (2012) 3 (2) *European Labour Law Journal* 151–72.

Mantouvalou, V. 'Labour Rights in the European Convention on Human Rights: An Intellectual Justification for an Integrated Approach to Interpretation (2013) 13 (3) *Human Rights Law Review* 529.

Mantouvalou, V. 'Welfare to Work, Structural Injustice and Human Rights' (2020) 83 (5) *Modern Law Review* 929.

Mantouvalou, V. *Structural Injustice and Labour Rights* (Oxford: Oxford University Press 2023).

Marx, K. 'Fragment on Machines' in K. Marx (ed) *Grundrisse: Foundations of the Critique of Political Economy* translated with a forward by M. Nicolau (London: Penguin 1858/1993).

Marx, K. 'Economic and Philosophic Manuscripts of 1844' in D. McLellan (ed) *Karl Marx: Selected Writings* (Oxford: Oxford University Press 2000).

Marx, K. 'On the Jewish Question' in D. McLellan (ed) *Karl Marx: Selected Writings* (Oxford: Oxford University Press 2000).

Marx, K. *Das Kapital: A Critique of Political Economy* (Seattle: Pacifica Publishing Studio 2010).

McCann, D. 'Temporal Casualisation and "Availability Time": Mencap, Uber and the Framed Flexibility Model', *SSRN* (27 April 2020), available at: https://ssrn.com/abstract=3789540 or http://dx.doi.org/10.2139/ssrn.3789540.

McClain, L.C. 'Formative Projects, Formative Influences: Of Martha Albertson Fineman and Feminist, Liberal and Vulnerable Subject' (2018) 67 *Emory Law Journal* 1175.

McColgan, A. *Discrimination Law: Text, Cases and Materials* (Oxford: Hart 2005).

McDowell, L. 'Thinking Through Work: Complex Inequalities, Constructions of Difference and Trans-National Migrants' (2008) 32 *Progress in Human Geography* 491.

McNay, L. *Foucault and Feminism: Power, Gender, and the Self* (Cambridge: Polity Press 1992).

Meyers, D.T. 'Decentralising Autonomy: Five Faces of Selfhood in J. Christman and J. Anderson (eds) *Autonomy and the Challenges to Liberalism* (Cambridge: Cambridge University Press 2005).

Moore, M. 'Liberalism, Communitarianism and the Politics of Identity' in T. Christiano and J. Christman, *Contemporary Debates in Political Philosophy* (Oxford: Wiley-Blackwell 2009).

Moore, P. *The Quantified Self in Precarity: Work Technology and What Counts* (New York: Routledge 2018), 6.

Moore, P. 'AI Trainers: Who Is the Smart Worker Today' in P. Moore and J. Woodcock (eds) *Augmented Exploitation: Artificial Intelligence and Work* (London: Pluto Press 2021).

Moseley, J. *Coronavirus (COVID-19) Employment Cases* (London: LexisNexis 2023).

Naffine, N. *Law's Meaning of Life: Philosophy, Religion, Darwin and the Legal Person* (Oxford: Hart 2009).

Nedelsky, J. 'Reconceiving Autonomy' (1989) 1 (1) *Yale Journal of Law and Feminism* 7.

Nedelsky, J. *Law's Relations: A Relational Theory of Self, Autonomy and the Law* (Oxford: Oxford University Press 2011).

NeJaime, D. 'Winning Through Losing' (2011) 96 *Iowa Law Review Bulletin* 61.

Neocleous, M. 'Staging Power: Marx, Hobbes and the Personification of Capital' (2004) 14 *Law and Critique* 147.

NHS 'Guidelines for Supporting our NHS People affected by Long Covid' (7 July 2022), available at: www.england.nhs.uk/wp-content/uploads/2022/02/C1672_Guidelines-for-supporting-our-NHS-people-affected-by-Long-COVID_July-2022.pdf.

Nickel, J. *Making Sense of Human Rights* (2nd edn, Oxford: Blackwell 2009).

O'Donovan, K. *Sexual Divisions in Law* (London: Weidenfeld and Nicolson 1985).

Office for National Statistics 'Prevalence of ongoing symptoms following coronavirus (COVID 19) infection in the UK' (2 February 2023), available at: www.ons.gov.uk/peoplepopulationandcommunity/healthandsocialcare/conditionsanddiseases/bulletins/prevalenceofongoingsymptomsfollowingcoronaviruscovid19infectionintheuk/2february2023.

Office for National Statistics 'Which occupations have the highest potential exposure to the coronavirus (COVID-19)' (11 May 2020), available at: www.ons.gov.uk/employmentandlabourmarket/peopleinwork/employmentandemployeetypes/articles/whichoccupationshavethehighestpotentialexposuretothecoronaviruscovid19/2020-05-11.

Oliver, D. 'Lack of PPE Betrays NHS Clinical Staff' (2021) *British Medical Journal* 372.

Organisation for Economic Co-operation and Development 'Recommendation of the Council on Artificial Intelligence' (2019), paragraph I, available at: https://legalinstruments.oecd.org/en/instruments/OECD-LEGAL-0449.

Organisation for Economic Co-operation and Development 'Tools for trustworthy AI: a framework to compare implementation tools for trustworthy AI systems' (2021), OECD Digital Economy Papers, No. 312, OECD Publishing, Paris, available at: https://dx.doi.org/10.1787/008232ec-en.

Otto, D. (ed) *Queering International Law* (Abingdon: Routledge 2018).

Page-Tickell, R. and Ritchie, J. 'Presence and Pretence: Trade Unions and the Gig Economy' in R. Page Tickell and E. Yerby (eds) *Conflict and Shifting Boundaries in the Gig Economy: An Interdisciplinary Analysis* (Bingley: Emerald 2020).

Pashukanis, E. *Law and Marxism: A General Theory* (London: Pluto Press 1987).

Pateman, C. *The Sexual Contract* (Cambridge: Polity Press 1997).

Phoenix, A. and Pattynama, P. 'Intersectionality' (2006) 13 *European Journal of Women's Studies* 187.

Public Accounts Committee 'Oral evidence: Covid-19: Government procurement and supply of personal protective equipment' HC 928 Thursday 10 December 2020 Ordered by the House of Commons to be published on 10 December 2020, available at: https://committees.parliament.uk/oralevidence/1373/default#page=9.

Public Health England 'Beyond the data: understanding the impact of Covid 19 on BAME groups' (June 2020).

Ravid, D.M., Tomczak, D.L., White, J.C., and Behrend, T.S. 'EPM 20/20: A Review, Framework, and Research Agenda for Electronic Performance Monitoring' (2019) 46 (1) *Journal of Management* 100–26.

Rawls, J. *A Theory of Justice* (Oxford: Oxford University Press 1971).

Raz, J. *The Morality of Freedom* (Oxford: Clarendon Press 1986).

Reitsch, M. *The Routledge International Handbook of Social Justice* (Oxford: Routledge 2014).

Riley, S. and Pele, A. 'For a Right to Health Beyond Biopolitics: The Politics of Pandemic and the Politics of Life' (2021) *Law Culture and the Humanities* 1.

Robinson, B. 'Remote Work is Here to Stay and will increase in 2023', available at: www.forbes.com/sites/bryanrobinson/2022/02/01/remote-work-is-here-to-stay-and-will-increase-into-2023-experts-say/.

Rodgers, L. 'The Potential and Limitations of a Vulnerability Approach for Labour Law' in D. Bedford and J. Herring (eds) *Embracing Vulnerability: The Challenges and Implications for Law* (London: Routledge 2020).

Rodgers, L. 'Going Backwards: Statutory Sick Pay after the pandemic', *UK Labour Law Blog* (12 April 2022), available at: https://uklabourlawblog.com/2022/04/12/going-backwards-statutory-sick-pay-after-the-pandemic-by-dr-lisa-rodgers/

Rodgers, L. and Davies, A. 'Towards a More Effective Health and Safety Regime for UK Workplaces post Covid-19' (2023) 52 (3) *Industrial Law Journal* 665.

Rogers, B. 'Passion and Reason in Labor Law' (2012) 47 *Harvard Civil Rights – Civil Liberties Law Review* 47.

Rogers, B. 'Employment Rights in the Platform Economy: Getting Back to Basics' (2016) 10 *Harvard Law and Policy Review* 479.

Rogers, B. 'Three Concepts of Workplace Freedom of Association' (2016) 37 (2) *Berkeley Journal of Employment and Labor Law* 177.

Roosevelt, E. 'Making Human Rights Come Alive' in A. Black (ed) *What I Hope to Leave Behind: The Essential Essays of Eleanor Roosevelt* (Brooklyn, NY: Carlson 1995).

Rose, E. 'Reinterpreting Law's Silence: Examining the Interactions between Legal Doctrine and the Rise of Immaterial Labour' (2020) 47 (2) *Journal of Law and Society* 588.

Rosenstock, E. May, E., and Grünberg, M. 'Werkstattaussiedlung: Untersuchungen über den Lebensraum des Industriearbeiters' (Berlin: Springer Verlag 2013).

Rosin, A. 'The Right of a Platform Worker to Decide Whether and When to Work: An Obstacle to Their Employee Status' (2022) 13 (4) *European Labour Law Journal* 530.

Royal College of Nursing 'Long Covid: how the RCN can help you' (10 January 2023), available at: www.rcn.org.uk/magazines/Advice/2023/Jan/Long-COVID-benefits-support.

Salvi del Pero, A., Wycoff, P., and Vourch, A. 'Using Artificial Intelligence in the Workplace: What Are the Main Ethical Risks?' (2022) OECD Social, Employment and Migration Working Papers No 273.

Sandel, M. 'The Procedural Republic and the Unencumbered Self' in S. Avineri and A. de Shalit (eds) *Communitarianism and Individualism* (Oxford: Oxford University Press 1992).

Sandel, M. *Liberalism and the Limits of Justice* (2nd edn, Cambridge: Cambridge University Press 1998).

Sanders, A. 'Fairness in the Contract of Employment' (2017) 46 (4) *Industrial Law Journal* 508.

Savell, K. 'The Mother of the Legal Person' in S. James and S. Palmer (eds) *Visible Women: Essays on Feminist Legal Theory and Political Philosophy* (Oxford: Hart 2002).

Schultz, V. 'Telling Stories About Women and Work: Judicial Interpretations of Sex Segregation in the Workplace in Title V11 Cases Raising the Lack of Interest Argument' (1990) 103 *Harvard Law Review* 1749.

Schultze Buschoff, K. and Schmidt, C. 'Adapting Labour Law and Social Security to the Needs of the "New Self-Employed" – Comparing the UK, Germany, and the Netherlands' (2009) 19 (2) *Journal of European Social Policy* 14.

Scruton, R.A. *A Short History of Modern Philosophy: From Descartes to Wittgenstein* (London: Routledge 1989).

Selnick, P. *Law Society, and Industrial Justice* (New York: Russell Sage Foundation 1969).

Sensoy, O. and DiAngelo, R. *Is Everyone Really Equal? An Introduction to Key Concepts in Social Justice Education* (New York: Teachers College Press 2017).

Siegel, R., König, C., and Lazar, V. 'The Impact of Electronic Monitoring on Employees' Job Satisfaction, Stress, Performance, and Counterproductive Work Behaviour: A Meta-Analysis' (2022) 8 *Computers in Human Behaviour Reports* 1.

Simpson, B. 'Individualism versus Collectivism: An Evaluation of Section 14 of the Trade Union Reform and Employment Rights Act 1993' (1993) 22 *Industrial Law Journal* 181.

Simpson, B. 'Freedom of Association and the Right to Organize: The Failure of an Individual Rights Strategy' (1995) 24 (3) *Industrial Law Journal* 235.

Sinzheimer, H. 'Grundzüge des Arbeitsrechts' (1927) in H. Sinzheimer, *Arbeitsrecht und Rechtssoziologie: gesammelte Aufsätze und Reden* (Band 1) (Frankfurt: Europaische Verlagsanstalt 1976).

Sinzheimer, H. 'Demokratisierung des Arbeitsverhältnisses' (1928) in H. Sinzheimer, *Arbeitsrecht und Rechtssoziologie: gesammelte Aufsätze und Reden* (Frankfurt: Europaische Verlagsanstalt 1976).

Sinzheimer, H. 'Der Mensch im Arbeitsrecht' (1930) in H. Sinzheimer, *Arbeitsrecht und Rechtssoziologie: gesammelte Aufsätze und Reden* (Frankfurt: Europaische Verlagsanstalt 1976).

Sinzheimer, H. 'Das Problem des Menschen im Recht' (1933) in H. Sinzheimer, *Arbeitsrecht und Rechtssoziologie: gesammelte Aufsätze und Reden* (Frankfurt: Europaische Verlagsanstalt 1976).

Sinzheimer, H. 'Das Wesen des Arbeitsrechts' in H. Sinzheimer, *Arbeitsrecht und Rechtssoziologie: gesammelte Aufsätze und Reden* (Band 1) (Frankfurt: Europaische Verlagsanstalt 1976).

Sinzheimer, H. 'Die Zukunft der Arbeiterräte' in H. Sinzheimer, *Arbeitsrecht und Rechtssoziologie: gesammelte Aufsätze und Reden* (Frankfurt: Europaische Verlagsanstalt 1976).

Sirrs, C. 'Risk, Responsibility and Robens: The Transformation of the British System of Occupational Health and Safety 1961–74' in T. Crook and M. Esbester (eds) *Governing Risks in Modern Britain* (Basingstoke: Palgrave Macmillan 2016).

Slaughter, J. 'Hijacking Human Rights: Neo-Liberalism, the New Historiography and the End of the Third World' (2018) 40 *Human Rights Quarterly* 735.

Smith, S. 'How Bogus Self-Employment is Harming Workers', available at: How bogus self-employment is harming workers (huckmag.com).

Spector, H. 'Philosophical Foundations of Labor Law' (2005–6) 33 *Florida State University Law Review* 1119.

Stammers, N. *Human Rights and Social Change* (London: Pluto Press 2009).

Standing, G. *The Precariat: The New Dangerous Class* (New York: Bloomsbury 2011).

Stoljar, N. 'Autonomy and the Feminist Intuition' in C. MacKenzie and N. Stoljar (eds) *Relational Autonomy: Feminist Perspectives on Autonomy, Agency and the Social Self* (New York: Oxford University Press 2000).

Stone, K.V.W. 'Green Shoots in the Labour Market: A Cornucopia of Social Experiments' in M.A. Fineman and J.W. Fineman (eds) *Vulnerability and the Legal Organisation of Work* (London: Routledge 2017).

Struhl, K. 'Marx and Human Nature: The Historical, the Trans-Historical, and Human Flourishing' (2016) 80 (1) *Science and Society* 78.

Sunder, S. and Siibak, A. 'Employers as Nightmare Readers: An Analysis of Ethical and Legal Concerns regarding Employer-Employee Practice on Social Networking Sites' (2017) 10 *Baltic Journal of Law and Politics* 76.

Supiot, A. *Beyond Employment: Changes in Work and the Future of Labour Law in Europe* (Oxford: Oxford University Press 2001).

Tasioulas, J. 'On the Nature of Human Rights' in G. Ernst and J.-C. Heilinger (eds) *The Philosophy of Human Rights: Contemporary Controversies* (Berlin, Boston: De Gruyter 2011).

Tasioulas, J. 'On the Foundations of Human Rights' in R. Cruft, S. Liao, and M. Renzo (eds) *Philosophical Foundations of Human Rights* (Oxford: Oxford University Press 2015), 51.

Taylor, C. 'Atomism' in *Philosophical Papers* (Cambridge: Cambridge University Press 1985).

Thrift, N. *Knowing Capitalism* (London: Sage 2005).

Todoli-Signes, A. 'The End of the Subordinate Worker? The On-Demand Economy, the Gig Economy, and the Need for Protection for Crowdworkers' (2017) 33 (2) *International Journal of Comparative Labour Law and Industrial Relations* 241.

Tombs, S. and Whyte, D. 'A Deadly Consensus: Worker Safety and Regulatory Degradation under New Labour' (2010) 50 (1) *British Journal of Criminology* 46.

Trades Union Congress 'Union Health and Safety Reps Survey' (2020–1), available at: www.tuc.org.uk/sites/default/files/2021-03/Safety%20reps%20survey%202021.pdf.

Trades Union Congress 'Dignity at Work and the AI Revolution' (March 2021), available at: www.tuc.org.uk/sites/default/files/2021-03/The_AI_Revolution_20121_Manifesto_AW.pdf.

Trades Union Congress 'Coronavirus (COVID-19) Guidance to Unions (Updated January 2021) Activist Template', available at: tuc.org.uk.

Tuana, N. 'Viscous Porosity: Witnessing Katrina' in S. Alaimo and S. Hekman (eds) *Material Feminisms* (Bloomington, IN: Indiana University Press 2008).

Tushnet, M. 'Marxism as Metaphor' (1983) 68 *Cornell Law Review* 281.

UK Gov 'Explanatory Memorandum to the Deregulation Act (Health and Safety at Work) (General Duties of Self-Employed Persons) (Consequential Amendments Order)' 2015, available at: www.legislation.gov.uk/uksi/2015/1637/memorandum/contents.

UK Gov 'People with symptoms of a respiratory infection including COVID-19' (10 June 2022), available at: www.gov.uk/guidance/people-with-symptoms-of-a-respiratory-infection-including-covid-19.

UK Gov 'A pro-innovation approach to AI regulation' (3 August 2023), available at: www.gov.uk/government/publications/ai-regulation-a-pro-innovation-approach/white-paper.

UK Gov 'Industrial Injuries Disablement Benefits: technical guidance', available at: www.gov.uk/government/publications/industrial-injuries-disablement-benefits-technical-guidance/industrial-injuries-disablement-benefits-technical-guidance

UK Gov NIHR 'The effectiveness of PPE in reducing the transmission of COVID-19 in health and social care settings: December 2021 update' (12 December 2021), available at: www.gov.uk/government/publications/nihr-the-effectiveness-of-ppe-in-reducing-the-transmission-of-covid-19-in-health-and-social-care-settings-december-2021-update-12-december-2021/nihr-the-effectiveness-of-ppe-in-reducing-the-transmission-of-covid-19-in-health-and-social-care-settings-december-2021-update-12-december-2021.

United Nations Educational, Scientific and Cultural Organization, COMEST 'Preliminary Study on the Ethics of Artificial Intelligence', 26 February 2019.

United Nations Educational, Scientific and Cultural Organization 'Recommendation on the ethics of artificial intelligence' (23 November 2021), available at: https://unesdoc.unesco.org/ark:/48223/pf0000381137.

Ventegodt Liisberg, M. *Disability and Employment: A Contemporary Disability Human Rights Approach Applied to Danish, Swedish and EU Law and Policy* (Mortsel: Intersentia 2011).

Vickers, L. 'Promoting Equality or Fostering Resentment? The Public Sector Equality Duty and Religion and Belief' (2011) 31 (1) *Legal Studies* 135.

Vickers, L. *Religious Freedom, Religious Discrimination and the Workplace* (Oxford: Hart 2016).

Vincent, J. 'Giving Robots Personhood Is Actually about Making Corporations Accountable', *The Verge* (19 January 2017), available at: www.theverge.com/2017/1/19/14322334/robot-electronic-persons-eu-report-liability-civil-suits.

Vogel, L. 'Forward' in T. Bhattachary (ed) *Social Reproduction Theory: Remapping Class, Recentering Oppression* (London: Pluto Press 2017).

Vyas, L. 'New Normal at Work in a Post-COVID World: Work–Life Balance and Labor Markets' 41 (1) (2022) *Policy and Society* 155.

Waltzer, M. 'Communitarian Critique of Liberalism' (1990) 18 *Political Theory* 6.

Webb, B. 'Women and the Factory Acts' (Fabian Tract No. 67).

Wedderburn, Lord K. 'Industrial Relations and the Courts' (1980) 9 *Industrial Law Journal* 65.

Wedderburn, Lord K. 'Otto Kahn-Freund and British Labour Law' in Lord Wedderburn, R. Lewis, and J. Clark (eds) *Labour Law and Industrial Relations: Building on Kahn-Freund* (Oxford: Clarendon Press 1983).

Wedderburn, Lord K. 'Freedom of Association and Philosophies of Labour Law' (1986) *Industrial Law Journal* 1.

Wedderburn, Lord K. 'Freedom of Association or Right to Organise' (1986) *Industrial Relations Journal* 244.

Wedderburn, Lord K. *The Worker and the Law* (Middlesex: Penguin 1986).

Weinrib, E. *The Idea of Private Law* (Oxford: Oxford University Press 1995).

Weiss, M. 'Digitalisation and Basic Principles of Labour Law' (2022) in T. Gyulavari and E. Menegatti (eds) *Decent Work in the Digital Age: European and Comparative Perspectives* (Oxford: Hart 2022).

West, R.L. 'Economic Man and Literary Woman: One Contrast' 39 *Mercer Law Review* 39.

White, S. 'Freedom of Association and the Right to Exclude' (1997) 5 *Journal of Political Philosophy* 373.

Wiblen, S. and Marler, J.H. 'Digitalised Talent Management and Automated Talent Decisions: The Implications for HR Professionals (2021) 32 (12) *International Journal of Human Resource Management* 2592.

World Health Organization, 'Post-Covid-19 Condition (Long Covid)' (7 December 2022), available at: www.who.int/europe/news-room/fact-sheets/item/post-covid-19-condition.

Zbyszewska, A. and Routh, S. 'Challenging Labour Law's "Productivity" Bias Through a Feminist Lens: A Conversation' in A. Blackham, M. Kullmann, and A. Zbyszewska (eds) *Theorising Labour Law in a Changing World: Towards Inclusive Labour Law* (Oxford: Hart 2019).

Zietlow, R.E. 'The Constitutional Right to Organise' in M.A. Fineman and J.W. Fineman (eds) *Vulnerability and the Legal Organisation of Work* (London: Routledge 2017).

Index

References to footnotes show both the page number and the note number (89n65).

D

Printed and bound by CPI Group (UK) Ltd, Croydon, CR0 4YY

17/09/2026

14964141-0004